APPRECIATIVE INQUIRY AND ORGANIZATIONAL TRANSFORMATION

APPRECIATIVE INQUIRY AND ORGANIZATIONAL TRANSFORMATION

Reports from the Field

Edited by Ronald Fry, Frank Barrett,
Jane Seiling, and Diana Whitney
Foreword by David L. Cooperrider

Q

QUORUM BOOKS
Westport, Connecticut · London

Library of Congress Cataloging-in-Publication Data

Appreciative inquiry and organizational transformation : reports from the field / edited
   by Ronald Fry . . . [et al.] ; foreword by David L. Cooperrider.
      p.   cm.
   Includes bibliographical references and index.
   ISBN 1–56720–458–9 (alk. paper)
   1. Organizational behavior. 2. Organizational change. I. Fry, Ronald E. (Ronald
Eugene)
   HD58.7.A664   2002
   658.4′06—dc21   2001019589

British Library Cataloguing in Publication Data is available.

Library of Congress Catalog Card Number: 2001019589
ISBN: 1–56720–458–9

First published in 2002

Quorum Books, 88 Post Road West, Westport, CT 06881
An imprint of Greenwood Publishing Group, Inc.
www.quorumbooks.com

Printed in the United States of America

The paper used in this book complies with the
Permanent Paper Standard issued by the National
Information Standards Organization (Z39.48–1984).

10 9 8 7 6 5 4 3 2 1

Contents

Foreword: The Coming Epidemic of Positive Change

David L. Cooperrider

Jonas Salk M.D. would ask people three simple but powerful questions. None were about illness. In Salk's view, "health" was not simply the absence of disease. It was qualitatively different and vastly more. He wanted people to discover, through systematic study and positive awareness, those things that they do that *make them healthy*. He was amazed with the wisdom people possessed, and varieties of techniques, behaviors, and lessons identified in these interactions. He would conclude each conversation with a request: Please share your insights with as many people as possible. Salk's great hope was to discover the means and methods "to create an epidemic of health."

These creative conversations would be anchored in people's own life experiences, reflecting on moments in their lives when they felt most alive and healthy, including times when they were in the midst of healing or when they were taking valuable steps toward visions of better health. Three questions always followed:

What keeps you healthy?

What do you want to teach your–our grandchildren?

What would keep the world healthy for those children?

These questions are especially remarkable when contrasted with the disease-oriented ones asked by most physicians in the deficit-based medical industry, a sector where there are now over 440,000 professional terms for illness!

A leading advocate of Salk's vision, Tom Munneke, recently engaged me in an interview using these exact questions. It was a powerful experience; there were times in fact when my eyes filled with tears. I had never even thought about or identified some of my experiences as health-changing moments. One excerpt from my responses in the interview provides good illustration:

The last thing I remembered about the game was that the Chicago Bears (the '84 Bears) had just taken the lead over the Cleveland Browns. It was Sunday afternoon. The kind of free time you really cherish. I was in the sunroom, lying on the soft couch; at home it was one of my favorite spots.

I had just fallen into a deep, relaxed slumber—so contented, oblivious to just about everything. The only thing I didn't lose touch of was the small heartbeat of the infant lying fully stretched out (all 21 inches) on my chest. It was Daniel, our first child. He was just 3 days old. And somewhere between wakefulness and sleep I felt him radiating; call it energy, health, the miracle of life. I was mesmerized. When he took a little breath, I too inhaled; when he made a small movement, I shifted effortlessly in the same rhythm. All my senses reverberated: sounds, smells, feelings, sights were all intensified. I noticed a ray of sunlight, as it seemed to bend itself between the leaves of the large oak tree and our window. It made Daniel's face sparkle. Time stopped. Then I slept.

When I awoke I felt different. Not only was the idea of "fatherhood" beginning to really take root, perhaps for the first time, but also I felt an inner joy. Absorbed in the stillness, I noticed Daniel's healthy and precious presence. I hardly saw anything of the game's fourth quarter. I think our Browns lost.

The next Monday at work, things felt easy. Nothing major happened that I can remember. But as I look back now—when you ask what keeps me healthy—something special might have taken place. In the next weeks and months I brought a new energy to my lifework; I related differently with colleagues, seeing qualities in them I had not appreciated before; and physically I lost almost ten pounds without having a plan or a diet. There was no effort. But it in fact happened. Maybe I started eating better or exercising more. I don't recall. I do know, however, that the impulse to "something greater" grew unmistakably. My doctoral dissertation was written that year. I dedicated it to Daniel.

This book is an attempt to understand, through real-life stories in organizational life, precisely this kind of "managing change." It is about a nondeficit type of change that has yet to be named. And it is about the exciting, rapidly emerging methodology called Appreciative Inquiry (AI) that sets "it"—this phenomenon of positive change—in motion.

As the authors of this volume propose, AI is reshaping the way we conceptualize organizational analysis and development. For those of us raised in the era of problem management, it is literally a 180-degree revolution in the way "change" is enacted, conceived, and embedded in our institutional operations. Think about AI as a "life-centric" kind of inquiry that creates an ever-expanding context of discovery for the connection or fusion of relational capacity: health connected to another's health, strength connected to another's strength, trust connected to another's trust, agility connected to another's agility, and innovation connected to another's innovation. And its premise is this: *Human systems construct their "worlds" in the direction of what they persistently ask questions about, and this propensity is strongest and most sustainable when the means and ends of inquiry are positively correlated. The single most prolific thing a group can do, if it aims to liberate the human spirit and consciously construct a better future, is to make the "positive change core" of any system the common and explicit property of all.*

Let us make it more concrete. People in an organization, for example, are concerned about morale and want to be part of a system that nurtures passion, excitement, and engagement. Where might they start? Do they administer yet another low-morale survey—to document the "problem" and diagnose root causes—and feed back the data as catalyst to gap analysis and intervention? Or would it be possible to mobilize an organization-wide analysis into moments when people felt most engaged, alive, and passionate in their work, and then bring the whole system together, in full voice, not just to make sense of the "data," but to use the new insights to articulate images of the future organization they most want to create?

Yes, the shift is exciting and it is opening wide a myriad of new ways to approach not only surveys but strategic business planning, mergers, culture change, e-commerce partnerships, diversity initiatives, self-organizing designs, union–management relations, quality management, and organization learning. Appreciative approaches are, in essence, rewriting all the rules of deficit-based change and bypassing, in simple ways, many complexities. Conspicuously absent in the stories in this volume are the vocabularies of "gap analysis," "root causes of failure," "unfreezing," "defensive routines," "variances," "organizational diagnosis," "resistance," "flaming platforms," "problem solving," "fixing the organization," and the like. Yet there is change—vital change—like GTE's award-winning union–management negotiations using AI, Hunter Douglas's empowering work leading to breakthroughs in product strategies, or the historic creation of the global charter for a U.N.-like organization among all the world's religions, the United Religions Initiative. None of these stories are unlike the one we shared right at the outset about Jonas Salk's idea of creating an "epidemic of health": my story of nondeficit change, of suddenly becoming healthier by noticing and touching health itself.

Through powerful case presentations like these, Ronald Fry, Frank Barrett, Jane Seiling, Diana Whitney, and their contributing colleagues have created a "gallery exhibition" of key concepts, practices, and insights illuminating the path of positive change. What I like most is the rigor in this work: compelling cases coupled with soul-searching reflection and scholarship in ideas. In all of it the editors and authors are both humble and honest when they say we are in our infancy when it comes to our understanding of appreciative processes of knowing and social construction of reality. They are also clear, in an invitational way, that AI does not demand belief but invites experiment.

To be sure, we are in the very earliest, even tentative, moments when it comes to understanding the positive core of change. But something else is also clear: deficit-based modalities are increasingly falling short and cynicism about the very idea of planned change is rampant. So in the spirit of a work in progress, not a finished product, this book leaves all of us with several important questions:

- How can we inquire into organization existence in ways that are simultaneously economically, humanly, and ecologically significant; in ways that increasingly help people discover, dream, design, and transform toward the greatest good?

- Could it be, for example, that we as a field have reached "the end of problem solving" as a mode of inquiry capable of inspiring, mobilizing, and sustaining significant human-system change?

- What would happen to our change practices if we began all of our work with the positive presumption that organizations, as centers of human relatedness, are "alive" with infinite constructive capacity? If so, how would we know?

- Is it possible that appreciative modes of knowing may be to the Web-based, Internet-worked enterprises of the future what problem-oriented ways of knowing have been to the twentieth-century corporation rooted in machine metaphors, command-control cultures, and "scientific management"?

We are on the eve of revolutionary changes—the World Wide Web; the new economy of knowledge and an economics of abundance; the ability to share the inexhaustible resource of "what works" at near zero cost, with just a click; and new organizational forms as vast global networks of collaboration—all calling for methods that require an appreciative eye capable of shaping, as Peter Drucker might say, an alignment of strengths in ways that make weaknesses irrelevant. But what's next?

How about an epidemic of positive change?

NOTE

I am grateful to Heather Wood Ior, a friend and colleague of Jonas Salk—and keeper of the flame—for sharing these ideas with me in June 2000. Heather's contributions sparked the concept for a think tank at the Fetzer Institute where we would explore the possibility of using AI and questions like these to create a cascade of thousands of interviews across the nation into people's visions of health and care for our future.

1

Appreciative Inquiry in Action: The Unfolding of a Provocative Invitation

Frank Barrett and Ronald Fry

It has been only twelve years since the publication of Cooperrider and Srivastva's (1987) article, "Appreciative Inquiry in Organizational Life." The subsequent impact of this publication on scholars and practitioners in the applied behavioral sciences has been of a magnitude perhaps not seen since that of Kurt Lewin's classic article outlining an "action" research. The general thrust of the article was highly provocative and yet immediately applicable: It boldly suggested that those who specialize in leading and planning change have been straddled by deeply held implicit assumptions that construct the social–organizational world as a problem to be solved. The role of the consultant or change agent in this paradigm logically becomes one of problem finder, solution designer, and (often) prescription giver. Further, the implications of holding onto a problem-centered approach to inquiry are far reaching for the system under investigation as well as for the inquirer: Problem finding and problem solving beget more problems. To the contrary, Cooperrider and Srivastva invited us to consider the proposition that adopting an appreciative stance to organizational dynamics leads to more innovative and long-lasting transformation.

The expansive interest and excitement that this appreciative inquiry (AI) stance has generated suggests that it is uniquely calibrated to our postmodern era. The chapters in this volume show us why: They evidence that AI unleashes a will to do good and enhances our collective wisdom. We can say with confidence that appreciation is an idea whose time has come.

The original proposal for an appreciative rather than a problem-oriented search into organizational life was indeed a passionate invitation. Yet there was necessarily a tentative, even if hopeful, tone to the proposal. How could one stand in an appreciative space amidst a messy, anxiety-filled world (Pagès, 1999)? There were many ideas to consider and challenges to be worked out. What steps should one take? Since this invitation was first articulated there have been numerous proposals, experiments, and attempts to apply appreciative methodologies. Faculty and doctoral students at Case Western Reserve University, party to many conversations and consulting projects that linked them with Srivastva and Cooperrider, began experimenting with and expanding the ideas. Two of the editors of this volume were part of this circle. In 1990 the Taos Institute adopted appreciative inquiry along with social constructionism as cornerstones of its mission and purpose. Two of the editors of the present volume were part of this group from its inception. In addition,

- Since 1993, U.S. AID (Agency for International Development) has partnered with Case Western Reserve University to support an international leadership and organizational development (OD) effort based on appreciative inquiry methods. Twice a year, leaders and members of global social change organizations have attended workshops to learn the principles of AI. To date, over 200 such change agents from over thirty countries have applied AI to enhance organizational capacity, establish enduring partnerships, and create new social change initiatives at regional and global levels.

- Academic disciplines and programs have incorporated appreciative inquiry as an important innovation to social change theory. Organizational development and educational change curricula have begun to introduce appreciative inquiry as part of their core training. At least two Ph.D. programs have made AI a cornerstone of their social change paradigm. There is a growing number of master's theses and Ph.D. dissertations devoted to appreciative methodologies and applications (see the bibliography at the end of this volume). Scholarly papers on AI have received award recognition from the International Management Association (Cooperrider, Sorenson, Whitney, & Yaeger, 2000).

- Since 1992 the Taos Institute and National Training Laboratories have offered workshops in the method of appreciative inquiry to consultants and change agents worldwide. Over 1,000 academics and consultants have attended these workshops and are using some form of appreciative inquiry in their practices.

- In 1998 the Academy of Management cosponsored with Case Western Reserve University a conference on Global Social Change Organizations using appreciative inquiry as the primary lens for scholarly contributions to theory and practice (Cooperrider & Dutton, 1999).
- In 1997 the American Society of Training and Development bestowed its prestigious Culture Change Project Award on the GTE corporation for their diverse and systemwide applications of AI to aid in the transformation of that culture. The story of this large system transformation is included in this volume.
- In 1997 the Catalyst Award for "best place to work in the country for women" was given to Avon Mexico for their innovative use of appreciative inquiry to develop healthy cross-gender relationships in the workplace, ending a disturbing history of gender discrimination and harassment. One consultant's story of this amazing transformation is reported in this volume.

We have learned much about AI over the past decade. As members of these growing communities began to share stories and cases, it was felt that it was time to gather some of these cases in a collection. It is in this spirit that this book was imagined. This book affirms what Cooperrider and Srivastva hoped for: Appreciative premises certainly make a difference.

As this volume attests, appreciative ideas have been applied in a wide range of settings, including corporate boardrooms, strategic-planning task forces, work teams, schools, decaying urban neighborhoods, community development projects, and global change organizations. Further, the methods and approaches vary widely, from small, intuitive interventions to full-scale planned change projects. Consequences vary as well, from team and organization improvement to transformation of workplace cultures to creation of new social systems, alliances, and partnerships. Yet there is one theme we would like to play in the background throughout this volume: an appreciative approach, by definition, is linked to inclusion and participation that makes a positive difference. In each of these stories we are witnessing attempts to include diverse voices in creating future scenarios. All the appreciative methods described in this volume are intentionally designed to democratize conversations: Participants are encouraged to share various parts of their own voices, to give voice to hopes, dreams, wishes, visions, intuitions, beliefs, ideals. And they are encouraged to create and expand these imaginings through conversations, narratives, metaphors, and imagery, consistent with the social-constructionist foundations of the theory. At the heart of the stories and experiences that emerge from this book is the call or invitation to be in question, to stand with others in front of appreciative and affirmative questions: How do we include a wider and wider variety of voices from the social system? How do we legitimize various modes of participation? How do we make room for dreams, visions, and other utterances and constructs that so often are overlooked or marginalized in the name of pragmatism and effectiveness? How do we preserve and nurture our strengths and what we do well in the face of complex, uncertain, and virtual adaptation? What is the positive core to our shared existence thus far and how can we exploit it to actually become the future we most hope for?

In the rest of this chapter we will provide a brief introduction to the principles and process of appreciative inquiry—the state of the theory—as it has evolved in the last ten years, and then overview the ten case-study illustrations, divided into the following themes:

- Building Relational Resources: fostering human cooperation.
- Renewing Organizational Vitality: transforming systems in decline.
- Building Enduring Collaboration: transforming organizational cultures.
- Building Community: transforming for the global good.

We will include an introduction to each of these themes, a brief description of each case study, and a few words about how this study adds to the emerging theory and practice of AI. Finally, we conclude with our highest hopes for the emerging practice of AI; lessons and suggestions for an epidemic of positive change.

A SHORT INTRODUCTION AND HISTORY OF APPRECIATIVE INQUIRY

AI emerged through the work of David Cooperrider and his colleagues from Case Western Reserve University in the mid-1980s as an alternative to traditional action research.[1] The impetus for this was the insight that action research had not lived up to its potential as an innovative change method, largely because of its reliance on a problem-centered approach to social dynamics. The appreciative paradigm or mind-set is based on the following principles:

- Constructionist Principle: Knowledge and organizational destiny are interwoven. To be effective—as members, managers, change agents, or leaders—all of us must be adept in the art of understanding, reading, and analyzing organizations as living human constructions. Successful leaders "read the world" of their organizations (or departments, sections, etc.) in ways that attract constituencies to want to engage in cooperative effort. These "readings" come from continuous sense-making about the people and world around us. Knowing the organization stands at the center of any and virtually every attempt at change. Thus, *the way we know is fateful*.

- Simultaneity Principle: Here it is recognized that inquiry and change are not separate moments or agendas, but are simultaneous. Inquiry is intervention. The seeds of organizational change—the things people think and talk about, the things people discover and learn, and the things that inform dialogue and inspire images of the future—are implicit in the very first questions we ask. The questions we ask (e.g., who versus what versus why) set the stage for what we find, and what we discover (the data) become the material out of which the future is conceived and made. If we accept the proposition that patterns of social–organizational action are not fixed by nature in any direct biological or physical way, that human systems are made and imagined in relational settings by human beings (socially constructed, as in the constructionist principle), then attention turns to the source of our ideas, our discourses, our studies; that is, our questions. Alterations in linguistic practices—including the linguistic practice of crafting questions—hold profound implications for changes in social practice. Hence, *change begins at the moment we ask a question*.

- Poetic Principle: Like a good piece of poetry that is open to endless interpretive possibilities, human systems are also open books. Any organization's story is constantly being coauthored or co-created by those living in it. As such, we can study virtually any topic related to the human experience in any human system. We can inquire into the nature of alienation or joy, sabotage or excellence, bureaucratic stress or creativity, efficiency or excess in any human organization. With this principle, AI invites us to reconsider the aims and focus of any inquiry in the domain of organizational life. For it is becoming clearer that our topics, like windsocks, continue to blow steadily onward in the direction of our conventional gaze. Hence, *in choosing the topic for interpretation, we help write the next story of the organization*.

- Anticipatory Principle: The most important resource we have for changing organizations is our unlimited imagination and our capacity to unleash the imaginations and minds of groups. Appreciative inquiry is a way to reclaim this imaginative competence. One of the basic theorems of the anticipatory view of organizational life is that it is the image of the future that in fact guides what might be called the current behavior of an organism or system. Much like a movie projector on a screen, human systems are forever projecting ahead of themselves a horizon of expectation (in their talk, in the hallways, in the metaphors and language they use) that brings the future powerfully into the present as a mobilizing agent. To refashion anticipatory reality—especially the artful creation of positive imagery on a collective basis—may be the most prolific thing any inquiry can do. Hence, *deep change comes from first changing our images of the future*.

- Positive Principle: This last principle is not so abstract. Put most simply, it has been our experience with AI that building and sustaining momentum for change requires large amounts of positive affect and social bonding; things like hope, excitement, inspiration, caring, camaraderie, sense of urgent purpose, and sheer joy in creating something meaningful together are all essential to peak moments in organizational effectiveness. We have found that the more positive the question we ask in our work, the more long-lasting and successful the change effort. It does not help to begin our inquiries from the standpoint of the world as a problem to be solved. The exact opposite is true in our experience: Organizations as human constructions are largely affirmative in nature and therefore responsive to positive thought, language, and knowledge. People and organizations are thus heliotropic. They grow toward the "light" of a positive anticipatory image. The major thing we accomplish through AI—indeed, the "art" of it—is to craft and seed, in better and more catalytic ways, the unconditional positive question. Hence, *positive images lead to positive actions*.

In its most practical form, AI has evolved as a type of study that selectively seeks to locate, highlight, and illuminate what are referred to as the life-giving properties of any organization or human system. In this sense, there are two basic questions behind any appreciative inquiry:

1. What, in this particular setting and context, makes (some aspect of) organizing possible?
2. What are the possibilities, expressed and latent, that provide opportunities for more effective, or value-congruent, forms of (this aspect of) organizing in the future?

The pursuit of these questions has revealed much about the "art of appreciation." This is the art of discovering and valuing those factors that give life to an organization or group. Primarily through interviewing and storytelling, the best of the past is revealed to set the stage for effective visualization of what could be. AI searches for the best of what is (one's experience up to now) to provide the basis for imagining what might be. The aim is to generate new knowledge that expands the "realm of the possible" and helps members of an organization to envision together a desired future. Such "futures," based on hope and a positive anticipatory image, and linked to actual experience of being at one's best, are naturally compelling and attractive. They attract energy and mobilize intention. Groups and organizations cannot help but behave in ways to achieve these visions.

This method of organization analysis—or way of being in the world around us—obviously differs from conventional managerial problem solving. The basic assumption of problem solving seems to be that organization is a problem to be solved. The subsequent task of improvement involves removing deficits, obstacles, or root causes. This process typically includes (1) identifying the key problems or deficiencies, (2) analyzing the causes, (3) analyzing solutions, and (4) developing a treatment or action plan.

By contrast, the underlying assumption of AI is not that organizing is a problem to be solved, but rather that it is a solution to be embraced. Standing in wonder, full of curiosity, about the miracle of organizing when it is at its best calls forth a radically different process and language. That process—often referred to as the "4Ds" in the chapters that follow—approximates key activities and discourses that have become central to many AI efforts to date. The key elements of the 4D process are (1) discovery and valuing the best of what has been, (2) dreaming and envisioning what might be, (3) dialoguing about what can be, and (4) coconstructing what will be.

- Discovery: You discover and value those factors that give life to an organization when it is at its best. The challenge of valuing is to discover, for example, the "commitment" of the organization and to find out when that commitment was at its highest. Regardless of how few the moments of high commitment were, the task is to focus in on those "peak moments" and to discuss the factors or forces that created the possibility for them. The list of positive or affirmative topics for discovery are endless: high quality, integrity, teamwork, customer responsiveness, self-confidence, partnering, technological excellence, sense of ownership, and so on.
- Dream: You envision what might be. When the best of what is has been discovered, the mind naturally begins to search beyond this; it begins to dream new possibilities. Dreaming involves passionate thinking about a positive image of a desired and preferred future state.
- Design: You engage in dialogue to foster open sharing of exciting discoveries and possibilities. This builds consensus, whereby members say, "Yes, this is an ideal or vision that we value and should aspire to." Individual will—based upon a positive, anticipatory image—gives way to a collective will. AI helps create a deliberately supportive context for conversation. It is through this sharing of ideals that social bonding and shared vision occurs. A blueprint of an attractive, compelling future state emerges.
- Destiny (or Delivery): You construct the future through innovation and action. AI establishes a momentum of its own. Because the ideals are grounded in past realities, there is confidence to try to make things happen. Members naturally find new ways to move the organization closer to the shared ideal image, many times without any of the traditional change-management techniques of action planning, task forces, project timetables, and deliverables.

It is important to note that the practice of AI is really in its infancy. Like the curious child that stands in wonder at the surrounding world, a widening net of scholars and practitioners are experimenting with appreciative principles, discovering new "fateful questions," and documenting their stories (Hammond & Royal, 1998; Elliott, 1999). Emerging from all this pioneering is a thesis or provocative proposition that goes something like this: *We have reached the limits of problem solving as a mode of inquiry capable of inspiring, mobilizing, and sustaining human system change; the future of organizational development belongs to methods that affirm, compel, and accelerate anticipatory learning involving larger and larger levels of collectivity.* These new methods promise to view "reality" as more radically relational, widening the circles of dialogue to groups of hundreds, thousands, and more, with cyberspace relationships into the millions. The arduous task of changing organizations will give way to the speed of imagination and innovation. Instead of negation, criticism, cynicism, and spiraling notions of deficit, there will be discovery, dream, design, and destiny: We are truly poised to enter this new millennium with no limits to cooperation. The stories in the chapters that follow attest to this powerful idea.

THE UNFOLDING OF A PROVOCATIVE THEORY: PRACTITIONERS REFLECT ON THEIR EXPERIENCES

In the spirit of John Dewey, the cases that follow are social experiments, attempts to extend innovative ideas into new arenas and reflect on outcomes and consequences that in turn modify emerging theories. In each case, the author(s) discusses the background of the system(s), the motivating factors that initiated the intervention, the process of inquiry (including experimentation with methods), and the unfolding of client awareness (including innovative actions and strategic developments). We have encouraged our authors to share their personal lessons in these cases, how they will apply their learning in future settings, and what, if any, new questions they will carry with them. While not all the cases give equal attention to each of these dimensions, they each provide a glimpse into a unique social change journey and the learning that emerges when people are open to experimentation and collective reflection.

Part I—Building Relational Resources: Fostering Human Cooperation

Sociologists and economists agree that with the advent of the postindustrial society, knowledge and learning have become the new forms of capital. It has become increasingly clear that the postindustrial revolution is a revolution in relating. Command and control systems, once heralded as creative achievements, are now seen as barriers to innovation, efficiency, and responsiveness precisely because they restrict relational access, diminish shared sensemaking, and truncate collective action. Traditional boundaries of hierarchy and functional specialties that divide work and separate stakeholders are being dismantled as managers seek to coordinate diverse skills and multiple knowledge specialties and integrate streams of technologies.

While many agree that transforming relationships at work into learning conversations is a high priority, we are still in our infancy in understanding how. The antedote of "shared vision" is in danger of becoming a cliché if we forget about the "organic humus" that supports and nurtures any shared vision: conversations and sensemaking about values and ideals. What the cases in this part illustrate is how an appreciative mind-set cultivates exploration of values, ideals, and vision in the service of creating, maintaining, and transforming generative relationships. This is a core foundation that separates appreciative inquiry from the populist school of "positive thinking." Significant change involves transforming relationships, and does not begin with individual thought per se. Clearly, we have much in common with many of these movements and we support their flourishing. But our stance is that creating appreciative learning cultures involves transforming relationships into vital and life-enhancing forces that support innovative actions, strategies, designs. As these cases demonstrate, some of the core implicit questions that AI poses are these: What kind of conversations are our relationships sustaining? Toward what purpose and in what direction are parties directing their attention? What are people expected to talk about? How does this talk further an expansive, life-enhancing version of organizational–social activity (versus a deficit, problem-centered view)? How can conversations be expanded to include a focus on past strengths, present potential, and future ideals?

There are also design issues to consider, as these cases demonstrate. How can we facilitate the creation of new avenues of access between multiple parties? How can we help participants see that the organizational world is open ended, evolving, and adaptable so that stereotypes and repetitive cycles can be transcended? These interventions often involve creating new relationships between parties that have been separated by conventional boundaries, transforming participants into shared partnership and discovering the future that their relating co-creates.

George and McLean—Putting the Client before the Horse: Working with Appreciative Inquiry in a Small Business

George and McLean discuss a very simple but potent application of appreciative principles and demonstrate how small actions can have profound consequences on a social system. They discuss their work in the hospitality industry, a business that requires intense and specifically attuned customer service. Briefly, a small business that provides uniquely designed horse riding secured the sole-provider contract with an upscale resort service that enjoys a high profile throughout Europe. Along with this reputation, of course, came high expectations of guest service standards. The client staff at the resort had no relationship with the staff of the riding stables; they were not aware of the need to probe customers for skill levels and desired level of service so that when guests complained about service, the client staff encouraged the guest to write up an "incident report." What unfolded is a classic story of deterioration in relationships, full of negative attributions. These incident reports had to be redressed. As stories circulated that the service providers had been rude and abrupt, this led to "ill-tempered monthly inquests" between managers of the two systems. When some of the customers' unique needs were not met, their complaints received a sympathetic hearing from those booking the service, who passed on incidents to the service providers. The regular telling and reporting of such stories led to strained relationships, defensiveness, and blaming: The two staffs became deeply suspicious of one another. Worse, the service providers became suspicious of the guests, who they feared would report. Staff felt their efforts were not acknowledged. The negative cycle of problem focus and blaming was encapsulated when the client system told the service provider, "We wouldn't be getting these reports if you weren't doing something wrong."

It is here that the consultants devised a simple and powerful intervention: Alter the topic of discourse. Intuitively sensing that the customer complaints received far more attention than what was warranted, they devised a way to widen the focus: Spend energy talking about what the guests enjoy in the service instead of only talking about what (they intuit) the minority is complaining about. Convinced that many of the guests had successful experiences that went unnoticed, they began to initiate small changes in affirmative directions. They began their weekly staff meetings by discussing what was going well. They introduced feedback forms that specifically asked for appreciations for any moments of "exceptional service." They began to publish a newsletter (appropriately named, "Above and Beyond") that highlighted stories of exceptional moments of guest service. The outcomes of these basic shifts in relational attention had immediate and decisive consequences: There was a decrease in incident reports, the relationships between the two staffs improved, and morale of the service providers improved. There was a clear lesson in a simple principle that can be applied to every human system: Since you will find what you look for, ask more about what you want to have happen.

Bushe—Meaning Making in Teams: Appreciative Inquiry in Preidentity and Postidentity Groups

Perhaps the key feature of postbureaucratic organizing is the focus on teams as a means to organize work and as the primary context for relationships at work. If we have learned anything from these experiments it is a greater appreciation for the complexity of life in teams. Simply removing middle managers and forming teams is not a panacea. "Real teams" (Katzenbach & Smith, 1993) are truly closer to miracles to behold than the lucky assembly of personalities and skill sets. While the normative literature sings the glory of teams, in practice we have reluctantly come to realize that the creation and maintenance of effective teams is only the first step toward organizational transformation. As Bushe points out in his chapter, we can assist in the formation and development of a group by thinking of them as working through issues of identity. Bushe highlights two important stages or periods of a team's life: preidentity and postidentity. He depicts the myriad dilemmas and paradoxes that groups face as members grapple with their identities and roles. Groups are subject to dysfunctional and irrational actions unless individual members are able to experience a sense of identity that is both consistent with their ideal self-image and appreciated by other members. Bushe introduces an adaptation of appreciative storytelling he calls the "Best Team Inquiry" (BTI) as an intervention that helps a group work through individual and collective boundary issues. When individuals can talk about their peak experiences, those memorable moments in prior groups or the present one, it transforms the capacity of the group to make meaning together. The process helps to transcend the "dilemma" in which healthy groups depend upon individuals achieving a sense of identity, yet individuals depend upon other group members in achieving that identity. The resulting "stuckness" is often experienced as lack of trust, hidden agendas, superficial harmony, or careless fighting. Bushe reminds us that in such moments of stuckness or uncertainty, appreciative storytelling and appreciative listening are luminous. Through personal reflections on instances where his Best

Team Inquiry was applied, Bushe demonstrates convincingly that such AI applications are timely and indispensable in transcending previous boundaries and creating new horizons for members to journey toward.

Part II—Renewing Organizational Vitality: Transforming Systems in Decline

One of the more insidious and dominant social constructions that shape our approach to organizations and management is that concerning the ineptness and hopelessness in the public sector. As this "story" goes, organizations in this sector are full of well-meaning but less able (than corporate) folks. They are mired in political wrangling and infected with chronic lack of resources. Among the worst off in this milieu are, arguably, urban school systems and social-services organizations. The weight of such assertions in our current discourse about these institutions is the very reason we have grouped the next two chapters under this section. AI is poised to alter this metanarrative about the state of decay—or health—of such systems. As the cases suggest, any social system is capable of renewing its vibrancy, rediscovering its positive, healthy core, and changing its own story of decline or need. They have the inherent ability to reinvent themselves via conversations aimed at surfacing the best of the past in order to imagine the possible future and honest inquiry into themes and impressions that emerge from the substance—the data—of these conversations.

The chapter by William Van Buskirk shows how AI interviews are themed and used as data to feedback to urban schools in order to foster new dialogue and affect about their states of health. As stakeholders in each school setting engage around the feedback reports, they collectively make new meaning out of "old" problems. Discipline, parent involvement, and faculty governance, for example, are seen in more positive and opportunistic ways; their historical value to the school and surrounding communities is used to ignite new initiatives to sustain and grow each school. A sense of urgency related to impending doom is transformed into a sense of urgency to create and engage in new relationships within and across various stakeholder groups.

As AI practitioners continue to engage with such social systems as these, where the dominant conversation is one of decline or dismay, they have come under criticism for being too "Pollyannaish," for simply denying the "reality" of serious problems facing these systems. Indeed, walking the talk of the Positive Principle is not always a stroll in the park! The chapter by Charlyse Pratt takes the reader inside the deep self-questioning of an AI practitioner as she tries to honor her belief in the AI principles described earlier and the deeply felt human emotions of grief, anger, hostility, and mistrust she encountered in two social-service agencies being forced to merge against their will. Out of her struggle to value the positive experiences of the participants in the face of their expressed wishes to express and confront the futility and inhumaneness of their situation, Pratt discovered powerful insights about relational integrity in using AI. As she began to feel herself "under siege," much as the participants did, she found what needed to be appreciated most in order for a new story of hope, possibility, and unity to be authored by the members of the two agencies.

The third contribution to this section could also be included in the next section on transforming organization cultures. It is placed here simply because the context is one of total despair, refusal to cooperate, hopelessness, and incivility. Being appreciative, using appreciative language, or genuinely relating from a positive stance is unquestionably difficult under these circumstances. The fact that AI worked in this instance, as in the two other cases, is not the only story here. Why AI succeeded is explored by Barrett and Cooperrider, leading them to the notion of the "generative metaphor." In this award-winning case analysis, the authors encountered a hotel management team within a large, tertiary health care institution. They found a group stuck in a downward spiral of negative attribution and defensive reaction at the same time that the owners were demanding that the hotel operation transform to a world-class level of service and productivity. Unable to alter the group's dynamics through conventional, issue-based team building, Barrett and Cooperrider invited the team to appreciatively inquire into the best practices of an entirely independent, dissimilar, and unfamiliar world-class hotel. This discovery learning process not only led to eventual changes in the team's hotel, but also to fundamental transformation of the working relationships among the team members. The use of the other organization as a metaphor truly became generative, as it caused the group to learn, share, create, and perform as never before.

Van Buskirk—Appreciating Appreciative Inquiry in the Urban Catholic School

This is a compelling report of an appreciative inquiry research project into two Catholic schools in Philadelphia, Pennsylvania. Each school faced the challenge of educating multiethnic "at risk" urban youth. But they faced a bigger dilemma as well: the threat of closure due to declining enrollments. This is a story of how these schools used appreciative inquiry to reconnect with their core values and, in the process, rediscovered their tradition. Each school embarked on a journey of collaborative interviewing, with faculty, alumnae, and students telling one another stories about important "life giving" experiences that bound them to one another as well as to the institution. The schools each experienced a welling up of support and a renewed sense of generative identity. Through detailed quotes from appreciative interviews, we witness communities rediscovering their core identities at a crucial moment in their lives. As members were inspired to imagine expansive possibilities, they formed a new appreciation of such core values as the transformational power of discipline, the valuing of diversity, and the strengthening power of conflict. Even though each school had just survived a near closure and considerable loss of morale, the rediscovery of their history and core identity gave them the strength to transform and renew themselves. Everyday practices were transformed: endowment campaigns, faculty meetings, and recruiting efforts took on a new revitalized energy that renewed and recreated core values of the institution. The appreciative process seems to have reminded these institutions what they themselves had been practicing with extraordinary success: Individual transformation becomes possible when communities hold out a vision of human possibility and goodness.

Pratt—Creating Unity from Competing Integrities: A Case Study in Appreciative Inquiry Methodology

With the occurrence of mergers increasing in both the public and private sectors, Pratt's chapter is particularly timely. She describes the application of AI to a healing and reforming process where two nonprofit social-service agencies had essentially been forced to merge in order to retain funding. The traditions and cultures of the two agencies varied, as did their perceptions of one another. As she began to collect stories that celebrated the best of each agency, Pratt quickly discovered that not only did they have competing views and antagonistic feelings toward each other, but that she was also competing with them by trying to model and apply an appreciative stance in a situation filled with deficit talk and mistrust. Her choices and experiments with AI principles in the face of these multilevel battles of integrity were noteworthy. She reflects on her personal dilemma regarding "walking her talk" while also honoring the negativism she experienced with members of the merged agency. The healing possibilities of AI are vividly demonstrated in a retreat setting where she applied AI to foster healthy dialogue between the newly merged staffs. In a poignant interchange during this session, she discovered how we can appreciate "apologies with invitation to make the future better" as life-giving acts in the reformation of multiple units or cultures into one. Pratt's reflections remind us of the importance of inviting the "whole" person into an appreciative process and how this becomes a microcosm of the larger situation; that of creating unity from the parts.

Barrett and Cooperrider—Generative Metaphor Intervention: A New Approach for Working with Systems Divided by Conflict and Caught in Defensive Perception

This chapter proposes that one way to help a group liberate itself from dysfunctional conflict and defensive routine is through the introduction of generative metaphor. By intervening at a tacit, indirect level of awareness, group members are able to generate fresh perceptions of one another, thereby allowing for the revitalization of the social bond and a heightened collective will to act. Combining a benchmarking effort with AI, the authors report a case in which generative metaphor was successfully used to help a hotel management team achieve (1) liberated aspiration and renewed hope, (2) decreased interpersonal conflict, (3) strategic consensus around a positive vision for the future, (4) renewed collective will to act, and (5) egalitarian language reflecting a new sense of unity and mutuality in the joint creation of the group's future. In appreciatively and collectively inquiring into the best practices of a nationally renowned "five-star" hotel, the team was able to discover, learn, share, and create together like never before. The experience with AI in a foreign, independent, unfamiliar, but slightly similar setting generated a new sense of capacity and will to act as a unit in their once dismal and impossible organizational setting. The original version of this report earned the National Academy of Management OD Division's award for best paper of the year in 1988.

Part III—Building Enduring Collaboration: Transforming Organizational Culture

Since the 1980s the notion of organizational cultures has been a focal point of interest for scholars, change agents, and managers. Organizational cultures emerge from the lasting patterns of assumptions regarding how members interpret and shape the environment, the nature of reality, the nature of time and space, and the nature of human nature, relationships, activity, and so on. Much organizational change literature in recent years emphasized the role of top leadership in managing and changing organizational culture. Management literature has offered prescriptions for how to "manage" culture, suggesting symbols, rites, and rituals leaders can employ to shape the direction of values and assumptions. However, as recent studies of major organizational change have shown, most major cultural change efforts do not always achieve the intended results.

Practitioners of appreciative inquiry are developing change models that offer innovative and hopeful guidelines for intervening in large systems. These guidelines are very loosely structured and emergent, but as the next three cases demonstrate, they hold considerable promise for creating large-scale cultural change. In these stories, appreciative processes have been utilized to empower, challenge, and develop leaders and teams in the context of entire system transformation. These interventions involve deliberately searching for and documenting highly valued experiences, and exploring and maximizing understanding of those moments in organizational life when members experience a meaningful contribution to the organizations' vital purpose. These cases involve experimenting with including diverse voices, shaping information technologies to create new relationships, and forging new visions, revitalizing current systems and processes. These cases involve a collective storytelling that is at once spontaneous and planned.

An appreciative approach to change begins with a deceptively simple if elusive assumption: To maximize organizational effectiveness, one should begin by noticing and valuing the strengths, the enduring elements of the current culture. On the surface it seems paradoxical: To transform the future direction of a human system, one should honor the past, the continuity and enduring history. These cases experiment with ways to surface the unique historical life of large organizations. As these cases demonstrate, this transformation does not have to be exclusively driven from the top. These interventions offer a variety of techniques for creating a collective inquiry, involving multiple voices in collecting and disseminating inspirational stories.

Schiller—Imagining Inclusion: Men and Women in Organizations

One of the most contested and problematic areas of social relations is the division between the genders. Organizations are scrambling to create diversity management programs and sexual harassment training to offset the shocking escalation of legal scandals surrounding the relations between the genders. Clearly this is an issue that will not go away.

Gender, however, is also an ongoing social "accomplishment," a human construct, that organizes social life and marks groups as similar and different, each with unique contributions to offer. In this sense, sex is a biological dichotomy; gender is a cultural marker. People learn to draw upon masculine or feminine norms and discourses to describe themselves, to construct identities, to define their activities. Clearly, we are still in our infancy as we devise programs to change the norms that constrain and discriminate along gender lines. As Marjorie Schiller illustrates in her case chapter, most of these sexual harassment training programs begin from the assumption that there is something wrong with members of one or both sexes that needs to be fixed. Typical diversity change methods have been problem centered, with role-playing, simulations, lectures, and so forth designed to correct erroneous behavior. Such "fire fighting" that works at noticing and labeling unacceptable behavior has created some unintended consequences. Not only do such programs create fear and defensiveness, they contribute little in the way of defining valued and desirable behavior.

Schiller describes two case studies using an appreciative approach to creating cross-gender collaboration in the workplace. In these interventions, members were invited in cross-gender pairs to explore the dynamics of their relationships, and how they had created and maintained successful cross-gender relations. Members conducted interviews into successful relationships. The analyses of these discoveries resulted in additional insights into how diversity is framed in organizational cultures. The resulting model of varying forms of male–female working relationships not only helped to appreciate and affirm all that organization members were experiencing, but helped to frame possibilities for the future ideal organization in one instance. She describes how at Avon Mexico this exploration led to the articulation of a new vision regarding what policies and procedures facilitated gender equality and successful cross-gender relations. Avon Mexico subsequently initiated a number of new programs and policies to support this vision.

Whitney, Cooperrider, Garrison, and Moore— Appreciative Inquiry and Culture Change at GTE: Launching a Positive Revolution

This chapter chronicles the continuing application and expansion of AI principles and methods to help transform a huge, diverse, global corporate culture. Of particular interest is the "grassroots" adoption and adaptation of AI to seed culture change on multiple fronts simultaneously. The authors' lessons from the ongoing work at GTE included observations on how to sustain AI over time, and what constitutes appropriate top-down versus bottom-up influence in facilitating positive change. This story received national recognition by the American Society of Training and Development and is published in detail here for the first time.

It will strike the reader that GTE's story is much more emergent, nonlinear, and opportunistic than any model or cycle of 4D phases. Indeed, it is as if the authors helped people at GTE to approach change, not as something to be forcefully managed, but rather as something to be unleashed—as if it were waiting to be let loose—or to be tapped into like an underground stream. There was significant support and understanding from very senior managers, to be sure. Yet the powerful image we get from this story is one wherein everyone who is touched by a "peak moment" interview is helped to get in touch with the change in themselves waiting to happen. Numerous interventions emerged from varying levels and in different functional areas. Supervisors, once introduced to the concepts and basic aspects of AI, decided themselves how and where to use it. An employee group of "zealots" formed and self-organized appreciative initiatives throughout the system. As union members began to participate in AI, their leadership took notice and asked serious and potentially energy-killing questions. A union–management summit resulted, where AI was applied to redirect that relationship toward more mutually positive and hopeful images of the future. As the importance and power of positive stories was experienced, those responsible for corporate communications began to find ways to share more positive imagery through their media and create initiatives to alter the everyday language people used to talk about GTE. As the momentum grew for change and for engaging in intentionally positive conversations about the past and future, one senses that the culture was in transformation.

Also emerging here is a profound lesson about individual change. As the authors posit, what they discovered was the Positive Principle in action. Where GTE employees had often balked at changing their individual behavior, they were now actively engaged in changing. What was different? The authors cite the positive anticipatory image of the future GTE, built from best past experiences, as the difference. Rather than being told to change themselves (as if they were doing wrong), GTE employees were invited to dream and be the future they wanted. Lesson: If you want to change the system, focus on the positive image of that future system, not on the need for individual change in behavior. The positive image, once owned by the members, will compel the change.

Trosten-Bloom—Creative Applications of Appreciative Inquiry in an Organization-Wide Culture Change Effort: The Hunter Douglas Experience

Like the GTE case, the experience described by Amanda Trosten-Bloom at Hunter Douglas helps to reduce some of the mystique surrounding, "How does AI seem to just catch on, ignite like a fire, to enthuse people and propel action?" Through very detailed reflections about how and why internal change agents decided what to do next, Trosten-Bloom unveils a story of organizational development. We are reminded often that the path taken in a systemwide AI effort is truly like a journey with numerous twists, turns, and unexpected challenges along the way. From a traditional organization development project to feedback employee survey data to launch change initiatives, AI was applied to frame and guide a whole system transformation entitled "Focus 2000." As in the GTE case, internal, catalytic groups were key to building momentum and including more and more participants. In this case, a RAT (Rapid Action Team) committed to using AI to engage the system in reflecting on its positive core and historical strengths in order to imagine the future Hunter Douglas for the new millennium. Trosten-Bloom shows convincingly how the AI process can quickly and powerfully create relationships dedicated to improvement. As part of an introductory session on AI, a group was "suddenly" bussed after lunch to a plant location where they immediately conducted peak experience interviews with employees they had never met. The power of this quick and direct experience of appreciation was profound. Barriers were temporarily suspended in order to reveal strengths and common knowledge. Another barrier was suspended in a subsequent decision to allow employees to interview stakeholders outside the company. This outsider group became a symbol of the system's willingness to be flexible and to trust in the process. The results were "worth-y," as Trosten-Bloom poignantly describes the transforming experiences reported by employees in this group as they engaged with customers and suppliers. In addition to sharing numerous ideas and suggestions for change agents using AI, the author boldly addresses issues concerning "hard" versus "soft" results from AI. Her reflections about when and how the AI efforts taken might have been oriented even more toward "bottom-line" topics and outcomes can only advance the practice of AI. Finally, the Hunter Douglas experience demonstrates how positive changes derive from rediscovery of core success factors imbedded in an organization's history: in this case, speed, boundarylessness, and the creative values of the founders.

Part IV—Building Community:
Transforming for the Global Good

Organizational development and community development have shared many theories, designs, and lessons across their naturally related practices. Kurt Lewin's early work involved working with racial groups in conflict. Ron Lippit's work with community development inspired the development of the Search Conference methodology. Clay Alderfer's work on racial relations in the 1960s provided important experiments in action research and made contributions to the OD theory and practice. Appreciative inquiry is also making entries into the great social divides: religion, race, class, and gender (see Chapter 7). These divisions have such a long history and appear so commonplace that renowned scientists have devoted their research careers to demonstrating that differences in race, gender, and class are innate and are expressions of natural differences in abilities, personality styles, and intelligence itself. Hence, the challenge of organizing and managing "differences" to accomplish a common goal.

AI began with a commitment to the generative potential of theory and research to transform the very world under study. The two chapters in this section boldly theorize—based on direct experiences in large social systems—that people of varying economic, religious, ethnic, and cultural backgrounds are innately also capable of discovering shared values, creating hope amidst dire conditions, self-organizing where formal systems have failed, spanning social and political boundaries that have existed over lifetimes, and fundamentally changing the world around them, be it a megalopolis or a new, global organization to unite all religions for peace on earth. In both instances, appreciative storytelling becomes the core activity to generate new understanding, relationships, and possibilities for human cooperation. The concept that organizations and networks of organizations are stories in the telling (or making) and, as such, immanently changeable based on our collective hopes and aspirations is a powerful theoretical contribution emerging from these chapters. In addition, the authors show convincingly the utility of AI in creating the opportunity and process for such shared ideals to emerge across traditional social divides.

Khalsa—The Appreciative Summit:
The Birth of the United Religions Initiative

According to Karl Weick, the purpose of organizing is to reduce equivocality through processes of sense-making. But what about organizations that are designed to value and honor experiences that are by nature equivocal, mysterious, and ineffable? To add another complication, what if our task was to bring together multiple organizations, each with a committed, historically embedded perspective on the nature, rituals, and practices that embody the ineffable? Is it possible to create a conversation, let alone an organizational network between such communities? Is it possible to create a common ground among peoples who have been socialized through different traditions to make sense of spirituality in different ways? This chapter describes an effort to create a United Religions Initiative through appreciative modes of learning.

Khalsa reports on an inspiring effort of William Swing, Archbishop of Episcopal Church of California, to create a network of world religions that parallels U.N. efforts to form a collaborative network of nations. This case study describes an experimental five-day "summit" conference design that combined two innovative change methods: the future search method and an appreciative method, investigating high points from the past and the best of present forces as groundwork for imagining a future organization to unite all communities of faith for the purpose of peace. The summit included representatives of Native Americans, Buddhists, Hindus, Jews, and Christian traditions including people from Africa, South America, Europe, and Asia in hopes of creating a dialogue. The conference was designed within the context of the 4D cycle. The participants discovered common ground by inquiring into one another's essential spiritual experiences; building on this ground to dream what a collaborative network of world religions would look like, they designed and mobilized collective action toward the creation of global networks and a United Religions charter. Participants inquired into one another's past, the prior one-hundred years of organized religion, and the important events and forces that impacted and shaped each of these major institutions. This case describes how an appreciative method facilitates learning between individuals and between institutions with a long history of differences. Khalsa helps us feel like we are at the summit as he details the design flow and key choices made, and shares actual outputs during the process. The reader cannot help but get a sense of the nobleness and truth underlying this social innovation. One of the core outcomes of this story was the decision from this initial summit to expand the process of appreciative inquiry. They agreed to begin a series of regional conferences throughout the world, each designed with AI dialogues as their foundation; to build strategic alliances; to create a "spiritual bill of rights"; and to move toward the writing of a United Religions charter.

Ludema—Appreciative Storytelling: A Narrative Approach to Organization Development and Change

The storyline of urban decay is one of the most widely read in today's society. One can hardly open a newspaper or turn on the TV news without being reminded of the seemingly irreversible drift toward more crime, more pollution, more unemployment, more truancy, more decay of families, and more vacancy in our major metropolitan settings. As with gender relationships, it seems more and more difficult or unrealistic to see today's cities as wonderous social accomplishments. Yet the possibility that these social institutions are, literally, the product of the narratives we choose to describe them by is shown in convincing fashion by Ludema. Building upon the constructionist and poetic principles cited earlier in this chapter, he demonstrates the power of storytelling in shaping people's intentions and willingness to work "against all odds" to create the city of their dreams. He relates the application of AI to a formative program evaluation of Vision Chicago, now a world-class benchmark for urban community development. Vision Chicago was the merger of formerly fragmented, competitive initiatives to aid and assist the transformation of a decaying civic infrastructure. From histories of hopelessness and skepticism, AI was used to surface alternative his and her stories of hope, pride, and cooperation that enabled members of multiple community constituencies and generations to imagine and enact collaborative initiatives. A new history or metanarrative about a hopeful and possible Chicago for future generations emerged from the sharing of appreciative stories of the past and using these to imagine the future ideal city. Revisiting the current conversations of the past enabled thousands of citizens to discover richer, more promising, and more attractive possibilities for community development where the same people had been ready to give up. Ludema convincingly shows us that organizations and social systems are truly stories, if not poetry, in motion. AI can serve to direct and energize that motion.

Fry and Barrett—Conclusion: Rethinking What Gives Life to Positive Change

In the final chapter, Fry and Barrett draw from the previous reports and their own field experiences with AI to revisit Cooperrider's call for an "epidemic of positive change" in the Foreword. They boldly assert the appeal of looking at organizational change and transformation from a truly different, appreciative perspective. They compare the implications for changing social systems inherent in these reports from the field with the predominant, century-old notions of managing change. Specifically, they offer four "life giving" properties of positive organizational change: (1) an appreciative dislodgment of certainty, (2) the elaboration of the system's "cooperative core," (3) synchronous experiences of positive affect, and (4) centrifugal processes of "attunement." Each of these factors is explained and evidenced using experiences with AI methodology from the field. Woven through these four properties of positive change is the overarching theme Fry and Barrett conclude from the reports in this volume: that positive change is fostered, first and foremost, through an appreciative declaration of faith in the universal goodness of human groups and organizations.

CONCLUSION

The reports from the field in this book are each experiments in collective courage, attempts to systematically create shared visions for a future of hope. The ongoing storytelling and guided conversations that project these visions embolden the participants to attempt new action, which, in turn, inspires hope. In this way the editors hold these cases up as exemplars for systems that are committed to learning and innovation. These cases are testimony to the transformational power of stories. It is in this spirit that we have decided to share these particular ten stories. Our hope is that other leaders and change agents can see lessons for themselves here; to imagine opportunities to take on old problems in new ways. Kurt Lewin's famous dictum that there is nothing so practical as a good theory has new meaning in this regard. Perhaps we can augment this insight: *There is nothing quite so practical as an inspiring story.* As applied social scientists and consultants, perhaps our most potent tool is the capacity to facilitate the collection and dissemination of inspiring stories that in turn become occasion for theoretical musings. It is the editors' dream that the following chapters inspire readers to embrace the power of theory construction and narrative imaginings as ways to create the future in a positive, life-affirming direction.

NOTE

1. This section is adapted from workshop material and handouts created by a number of colleagues including Frank Barrett, David L. Cooperrider, Ronald Fry, Charlyse Pratt, and Diana Whitney.

PART I

Building Relational Resources: Fostering Human Cooperation

2

Putting the Client before the Horse: Working with Appreciative Inquiry in a Small Business

Marsha George and Adrian McLean

As appreciative inquiry (AI) develops, much debate and interest surrounds the protocols and methodologies for its use in organizations: the 4D cycle, provocative propositions, topic choice, the framing of the inquiry questions, and so on. This chapter describes an example of working with appreciative inquiry, with an affirmative paradigm, but in a way that follows the spirit of the ideas more than the letter of its protocols. It is an account of the consequences of bringing an "appreciative eye" to a riding stables business where high standards of customer care are a commercial imperative.

As OD practitioners, we have been supporting organizations through periods of change for more than twenty years, working primarily through the metaphor of organizations as cultures. Our serious acquaintance with AI began in 1994 and we have found that it complements our cultural approach to consulting in a natural and powerful way. This is not a story about our consulting lives, however. It is about our experience of using AI in our other business, a riding stable based in Wiltshire, England, and the consequences of choosing an AI frame for intervening into a pattern of relations that was becoming a matter of some concern.

We will begin with a brief description of our riding business and its background, and will then portray how a settled but unsatisfactory ecology of relations evolved with respect to customer care, staff morale, and relationships with the our major client, an up-market holiday village. We will discuss how we introduced an AI approach into this system and the consequences for each of the parties and for the system as a whole. Our story is essentially a very simple one in a very small organization, where applying the spirit of AI has made a big difference.

LONGHORN WESTERN RIDING: BACKGROUND

Longhorn Western Riding Ltd. began operating in August 1994 with fifteen horses and three full-time employees. It was set up on a twenty-acre farm on the boundaries of a large estate known as Longleat, home of the Marquess of Bath. As a business, its primary purpose was, and still is, to provide riding experiences to guests of an up-market holiday village that we will refer to here as Forest Adventures. The holiday village opened that same summer on another boundary of the estate.

Longhorn Western Riding, as its name implies, specializes in American-style riding using American breeds of horses such as Appaloosas and quarter horses. It offers guests of Forest Adventures, and private customers as well, the somewhat unique experience of riding American style through the English countryside while watching African animals graze at the estate's safari park. We pride ourselves on our friendly, informal approach to riding and are delighted when we receive occasional feedback that affirms this perception.

Initially the provision of riding services to Forest Adventures was by two stables. We provided Western riding and another stable offered English-style riding. In the winter of 1996 Longhorn secured the sole-provider contract with Forest Adventures. This meant that Longhorn had to add to its riding capability. Accordingly, the company grew from its original fifteen horses and three staff to twenty-four horses and five full-time and two part-time staff.

Securing the sole-provider contract assured the future of Longhorn. It also brought with it the responsibility of being seen as part of the Forest Adventures way of doing things. Guests who book their riding activity at a Forest Adventures booking point often do not distinguish it as a separate company from our stables business. Expectations of guest care standards by Forest Adventures employees also apply to Longhorn employees. We were delighted to have won the contract and excited at the prospect of a long and mutually beneficial relationship.

It is in this context that we set out here some of the patterns that evolved between these two organizations and an intervention that has produced a fundamental change.

ATTENDING TO THE DEFICIENCIES

Forest Adventures enjoys a high profile throughout Northern Europe and is well known for the quality of its environment as well as its guest care. Thus, when complaints began to come in about the guest care at Longhorn, Forest Adventures was quick to bring it to the attention of the stables. While we shared their aspirations for high-quality customer service, we soon came to feel that their sensitivity toward negative feedback amounted to a preoccupation and that this represented their dominant perceptual frame toward Longhorn. Forest Adventures's manner of addressing customer service and our corresponding reactions led to a deteriorating pattern of interaction between us and them, a dynamic that ultimately resulted in more complaints. To our dismay, we came to discover the validity of the assertion that social systems move in the direction of that which they inquire into.

The parties involved, ourselves included, comprised a system that exhibited a characteristic pattern of relating. It was defined by an approach to improvement that was predicated on the principle of fault or complaint eradication. The idea that a riding experience could be controlled or managed to avoid the unexpected seemed antithetical to our experience. Horse riding can be unpredictable, as all experienced riders recognize. It is easy to conjure a romantic image of riding through beautiful leafy woodlands, and this clearly is compelling for many of the guests at Forest Adventures, as approximately 65 percent of our guests are novices. When confronted with the reality of a living, breathing, moving animal, some guests become apprehensive and anxious. Others exhibit a certain level of bravado, overestimating their ability to control a horse in open countryside and endangering themselves, their horses, and other riders. In circumstances of heightened anxiety guests can become difficult to reassure and require high levels of skill and patience on the part of staff. In addition, working with horses often attracts people who prefer the company of animals and finding staff who show a combination of horse skills and people skills is quite a challenge. Inevitably, this combination of factors creates an environment in which incidents occur from time to time.

We began to receive feedback in the form of customer complaints. Invariably guests would complain to staff at Forest Adventures after completion of a ride and would be invited to complete an "incident report" form. Often Forest Adventures would telephone us to discuss the complaint and we would jointly agree on an appropriate form of redress. At the end of each month an envelope would arrive containing copies of these incident reports and some letters of complaint written after guests had returned home. The most common complaints were of rude, abrupt staff, the allocation of inappropriate horses, and feeling rushed or inadequately prepared. These reports would form the basis of an ill-tempered monthly "inquest" between us and the manager at Forest Adventures's sports center. The subtext of these meetings was defensive, recriminatory, and blaming. The main point of contact and tension was between the booking staff at the holiday village and Longhorn's yard manager.

When incident reports were received, we would review them with the yard manager and discuss who else on the staff, if anyone, needed to see them. Typically, it was felt that all staff should have access to the reports. They usually felt resentful that their hard work and genuine efforts to give guests an enjoyable ride were not being acknowledged, and also that many of the complaints had their origin at the point of booking, where "inexperienced" booking staff, who had little if any knowledge of riding, would book guests onto rides that were unsuitable to their level of skill and experience. Our staff began to feel betrayed by guests who would not complain directly but would then make "exaggerated and unrealistic complaints" once back in the holiday village. They gradually acquired a negative and critical attitude to guests, and a harsh, judgmental rhetoric evolved in their conversations with us about them. Coincidentally, we were experiencing a fairly high turnover of staff, losing about one every three months. This, of course, didn't help matters, as it takes time to train staff to acceptable standards and finding staff with a suitable temperament was proving difficult.

NEW YEAR'S REVOLUTION

This pattern of receiving complaints monthly, reading and discussing them, and replying to Forest Adventures in writing with "our side of the story" continued for six months. January 1, 1997, proved to be a watershed for relations between Longhorn and Forest Adventures. A series of particularly boisterous guests in a festive mood had pushed our staff beyond the limits of their patience. Our yard manager and her first assistant resigned. They'd had enough, feeling taken for granted and unappreciated. This shocked us into thinking about how we might be able to influence our client system into a more positive way of interacting with us.

What was becoming increasingly clear was that Forest Adventures's way of bringing customer complaints to our attention was not resulting in the improvements to customer service that we all desired. In fact, the pattern of interaction that developed was creating just the opposite. The solution had become the problem (Watzlawick, Weakland, & Fisch, 1974). In order to break this downward spiral, we needed to find a different way of framing the needs of both systems.

AN EVENING OUT

For Forest Adventures, Longhorn had become a problem to be solved and the solution, it was felt, lay in customer-care training. Forest Adventures offered to run a tailored version of their customer-care course especially for Longhorn staff. We welcomed this offer and saw it as a major opportunity to interrupt the deteriorating pattern of relations between the two companies. In addition to some standard inputs on customer care, the idea of the program was to involve some of the booking staff from Forest Adventures in order to encourage a constructive dialogue and to build relations. As the first evening session began, we spent time discussing some of the most frequent complaints made by guests and useful suggestions were made regarding how these might be minimized. The style of the evening was heavily didactic, however, with lengthy presentations by the seminar leader and with Longhorn staff, the authors included, participating in the manner of pupils in a classroom. We felt that the tacit message was unmistakable: "You, Longhorn, are the problem and this is how you need to behave differently to satisfy our customers." Only one member of their booking staff attended the evening. We were disappointed by this and took it as a further expression of the mind-set that saw the problem as being located in Longhorn. We also saw the low turnout as symptomatic of (in our view) the root cause of many of the complaints; namely, the booking staff's lack of interest in and knowledge about Longhorn's service.

The presence of the leisure manager at the event sitting among us as a participant in the session, however, mitigated the impact of these "hidden" messages, particularly as he was sympathetic toward the dilemmas regularly experienced by Longhorn staff. He openly acknowledged the stress they felt when having to deal with the consequences of booking errors. He was also manifestly embarrassed at the poor turnout by his own staff. After the seminar he hosted all of us for a meal in one of the village's many restaurants. This, together with his thoughtful and friendly listening style, was

much appreciated and expressed a positive and supportive attitude toward the relationship that was instrumental in reversing
the downward spiral of relations. It also represented a small glint
of hope in an otherwise gloomy situation.

INTRODUCING CHANGES, AN EARLY WIN, AND . . . MORE OF THE SAME!

A number of specific changes occurred as a result of this session:

- A standardized briefing for all riders at the beginning of the ride.
- A concerted effort by Longhorn staff to give more eye contact during one-on-one instructions once guests are on their horses.
- The introduction of a short assessment to verify guests' riding ability for more advanced rides.
- Some amendments to the information shown to guests when they are selecting their ride at the booking point.

In addition, our staff felt that they had acquired some useful tips
for communicating with guests, especially when things became
particularly difficult.

The overwhelming feeling on the part of our staff, however, was
that Forest Adventures had learned at least as much as we had. In
particular, we felt that those staff from the holiday village who had
been present were struck by our concern for guest safety and the
real stress that careless or uninformed bookings caused our staff.
The 100-percent attendance by Longhorn staff on their own time
and without pay also carried its own message.

Longhorn staff worked hard putting the new ideas into practice.
An early opportunity presented itself the morning after the customer-
care evening, when a rider fell off her horse. The feedback from her
companion was that they received outstanding customer care, and
she should know since her profession was customer relations. The
new safety procedures were also introduced and everyone was making a conspicuous effort.

At the end of the month an envelope arrived from Forest Adventures containing copies of seven incident reports. Everyone felt dev-
astated. A phone call from the acting sports manager at Forest
Adventures booking center swiftly followed. Her tone was serious
and concerned. We discussed each incident in turn and, as we did,
a mood of despair, resentment, and resignation settled like fog on a
calm night. We had made a big effort to ensure customer satisfaction and gone out of our way on many occasions to delight customers. Had they heard anything from those customers? No. At the

root of our despair was a comment from the sports manager: "We wouldn't be getting these reports if you weren't doing something wrong."

SHIFTING OUR ATTENTION TO THE POSITIVE

This marked a nadir in our customer-care journey and as such represented a turning point. In retrospect, we realize that it was a gift. With one brief sentence she had encapsulated the problem-focused deficit orientation characteristic of our client's attitude. What had been figural up to this point in time was customers' complaints and the consequent assertion on the part of Forest Adventures that Longhorn must be doing "something wrong." We began to speculate what might happen if, instead, we started to pay attention to what our staff were getting right, not only in terms of customer care but in the totality of their duties. It was our belief that the "ground" or essence of our customers' experiences was overwhelmingly positive and we realized that we had done nothing to test this belief or to make any overt acknowledgment of it. We knew of countless times when the staff had gone to exceptional lengths to take care of guests, often at their own discomfiture. But shared knowledge of such client-centered effort was clearly limited to the stables.

We considered the situation from the perspective of AI and determined to formulate a strategy that gave attention to the positive, life-giving aspects of Longhorn Western Riding in general and customer care in particular. The threads of this strategy were as follows:

- Weekly review meetings with senior staff that were inquiries into what was going well.
- The introduction of customer feedback forms.
- The monthly publication of stories of exceptional customer care called, "Above and Beyond."

Weekly Meetings

We set up two meetings per week, one between the director and the yard manager (who had by this time withdrawn her resignation) and another that also included the "head girl." These meetings ostensibly were to review the week and to plan for the next week in terms of anticipating any unusual events, to monitor use of horses and their specific and general health, and to review staffing needs for the foreseeable future. The director decided to begin the meetings by asking, "What went really well this week?" "What do you feel proud about having done or accomplished?"

The meetings themselves were fun, informative, and highly participative. In the aftermath of each meeting, we observed subtle but significant differences in the behavior of the yard manager. Her attitude shifted from one of feeling hostile and dismissive toward Forest Adventures to a more constructive stance summed up by, "What can we collectively do this week so that we can report it back in the next meeting?"

Another shift was that the relationship between the director and the yard manager improved. This relationship became more stable and harmonious. The yard manager became noticeably more relaxed and began to offer innovative suggestions. The staff began to be playful with each other and with the customers. The yard manager started looking for new ways to develop and recognize the efforts of staff on a daily basis.

The introduction of the meetings had signaled two things. Most important, that we cared about and believed in our staff's ability to do an excellent job, and that Longhorn was no longer focused on Forest Adventures's preoccupation with what we were getting wrong.

Customer Feedback

Based on our initial success, we decided to persevere. If Forest Adventures offered their guests the opportunity to complain, then we would offer guests the opportunity to praise. We developed a simple customer comment form that could be given at random to guests after their riding experience with us.

This simple, and in retrospect, obvious device proved to have a dramatic effect. We thought carefully about the wording of the request for feedback on the form. How could we orientate it toward affirmative, constructive language without totally discouraging guests from giving their honest perspectives on their experiences. In the United Kingdom, such forms are commonly used for customers' complaints, and hence most people who take the time to fill them in do so with complaining in mind. In the end, we settled on the following: "While we make every effort to offer high standards of service to our guests we are always looking for ways in which we can improve. We also like to hear appreciations from guests when you feel that our service has been exceptional in some way." The feedback was overwhelmingly positive. A short sample gives the overall flavor:

"Simply great! Fantastic ride, thank you Justina."

"Very enjoyable Emma! Nicest horses I have ever ridden."

"The ride was absolutely brilliant, very comfortable, everything was explained very, very well—Katherine was brilliant!"

"You all have lots of patience under difficult circumstances. Sam was brilliant to us."

"Many thanks for the first class tutorial, Jo."

The effect of this feedback was immediate and powerful. The staff glowed with pride, eagerly reading feedback forms as soon as they were returned, and made sure that their colleagues saw the comments for rides they had escorted. The sense of feeling appreciated and valued was palpable and with it came relief from the tacit assumption that Longhorn staff didn't care about the quality of the riding experience they provided. They cared deeply and here at last was the affirmative feedback they yearned for. We also were delighted, with the feedback itself but much more significantly because of its effect on the staff. The change in their demeanor was comprehensive. They laughed more, smiled more, and were more relaxed and friendly with customers. In conversation with them we realized that the fear of receiving negative incident reports had led to a cautious and defensive mind-set toward guests. They had begun to mistrust guests and this mistrust was a key connector in the negative spiral. Suddenly the incident reports could be seen in the context of a very positive ground of appreciation, and the effect was truly transformational.

Above and Beyond

This is the title of a monthly one-page bulletin modeled on a newspaper format. It comprises short accounts of what we consider to be examples of exceptional service by Longhorn staff, together with quotes from customer feedback forms. The following two stories are typical:

When the bough breaks

On a recent City Slicker ride a large bough broke off a tree next to the trail just as the ride was passing and came crashing down from 30 feet. Just in front were four guests on a Hackney ride, yards from the start of a descent down a tricky section of Bridle Way. The unexpected crash startled the City Slicker horses and they set off the Hackney horses. The escort at the front of the Hackney ride heard the sound of galloping hooves behind her and quickly spun her horse sideways to block their path. She held her ground, stopping the horses at the point where they would have headed down the slope. Her quick thinking and brave action most probably prevented a frightening incident from resulting in serious injuries to horses and riders. Well done!

What a shower!

Caught in a sudden downpour, a pair of toddlers on a Pony ride at Forest Adventures were saved from a drenching when the escorts loaned them their own waterproof jackets. Our escorts returned to the stables soaking wet and cold but the children stayed warm and dry. This has happened often on our regular trail rides especially with small children. Coats and gloves are frequently loaned to ensure their well-being.

"Above and Beyond" has been well received by Longhorn staff. They are especially keen that copies be sent to Forest Adventures, and anxious that any positive feedback they receive is included. They have taped past copies to the office wall in full view of all guests and visitors.

In addition to these high-profile efforts used to create an apprecia-tive mind-set, we also made a conscious effort to acknowledge positive examples of customer service on a more routine basis, not just with Longhorn staff but also with booking staff at Forest Adventures.

The flow of incident reports was reducing, and for the two busi-est months of the summer there were none at all. We even received phone calls from booking staff at Forest Adventures informing us that customers had been singing our praises and they wanted to let us know. Other staff at Forest Adventures were also beginning to comment on the scarcity of incident reports.

REFLECTIONS AND EMERGING PATTERNS

At a follow-up customer-care evening that we organized and fa-cilitated, there was equal representation from both organizations and very constructive discussions of the weekly dilemmas experienced by both sets of staff. What felt like a much more egalitarian relation-ship was emerging and Longhorn staff no longer felt "one down."

The benefits arising from this pattern change are far more than a positive, nonadversarial relationship with our client, Forest Ad-ventures. We no longer felt submissive and powerless, but rather that we were a genuinely respected partner and a valued contribu-tor to the overall image of the holiday village. The greatest satis-faction for us, however, has been to witness the dramatic shift in the morale of Longhorn staff. The entire team has remained intact for more than a year, and it is by far the most caring and profes-sional team in the short history of this business.

None of this is to suggest that customer complaints have dried up completely. What has markedly changed, however, is the way in which they are processed and discussed between Longhorn and Forest Adventures. We no longer feel blamed and made to feel guilty by them. Now we are part of a system that is inquiring into ways of continuously improving service.

While none of the steps and stages normally associated with AI are clearly evident in this simple story, we believe that it demonstrates the power of the underlying premise of social constructionist thinking; namely, that the choices we make in terms of how we construct reality are of consequence. It also demonstrates that the domain of our inquiry, that which we choose as the deliberate focus of attention and curiosity, is of enormous import and consequence.

We also conclude that our experience affirms a central principle of appreciative inquiry; namely, that organizations and social systems move in the direction they inquire into. The more attention Forest Adventures gave to complaints about Longhorn, the more complaints they received. In terms of social construction theory, the effect of the complaints procedure was to lead to a construction of guests as irresponsible, unappreciative, and mendacious. As staff enacted these constructions, relations deteriorated and complaints increased. Imperceptibly, we developed a discourse that was increasingly critical of guests. Without realizing it we had created an habitual inner dialogue regarding guests that was overwhelmingly deficit oriented. This dialogue, in turn, affected our behavior in dysfunctional ways.

In this process we rediscovered the power of asking positive questions: moving from asking what went wrong to what went right, shifting a simple customer complaint form to a customer-care form that asked for appreciation for a hard-working staff, and moving into meaningful dialogue with booking staff instead of feeling like we were a "problem to be solved." This experience has also highlighted the importance of searching for the positive amidst a sea of negative. The behavior of the leisure manager on the first evening of the customer-care course represented a seed of hope for us in an otherwise fallow field, and noticing this helped us to persevere through a difficult time.

Cooperrider (1999) writes, "While negative affectivity is notably linked to the phenomenon of learned helplessness, positive affect is intimately connected with *social helpfulness*" (p. 106). This was certainly our experience and is of particular interest in the field of customer relations. Feelings of powerlessness, resignation, and resentment pervaded our response to the critical feedback from customers. Only when we created opportunities for the expression of positive affect in the form of customer appreciations as well as the publication of "Above and Beyond" did we see a change in behavior in the direction of what Cooperrider terms "social helpfulness." And it was an almost instantaneous shift. The sense of self-worth and esteem among our staff escalated overnight.

Last, we directly experienced the positive effect of shifting the balance between deficit and positive language. Our weekly meetings were intended to create more positive imagery and language while the problem-centered talk was still rife. While negative discourse did not and has not disappeared altogether, we have created a new mix or ratio of positive to negative talk that has, in turn, stimulated new attitudes and behavior in staff, Forest Adventures management, and guests. The "Above and Beyond" newsletter serves to maintain this new ratio.

ONE YEAR ON

There is a postscript to this story. Almost one year on, we are still experiencing the benefits of bringing an "appreciative eye" to Longhorn as a business. The stability amongst the staff team continues and increases. We have lost only one member of staff in a year. This was unimaginable during our low-morale days.

We no longer hear about incident reports from Forest Adventures. Yes, guests still complain from time to time, but reports of problems at Longhorn are no longer an agenda item at the holiday village. Our yard manager goes from strength to strength. One example of this was her desire to hold a meeting at the beginning of our busy summer season so that all staff—us and the management of Forest Adventures—could together create a positive scenario for the busy summer period and engage in dialogue about how we could best serve guests. The success of that meeting set the business up for its most profitable and trouble-free summer season to date.

3

Meaning Making in Teams: Appreciative Inquiry with Preidentity and Postidentity Groups

Gervase Bushe

In this chapter I am going to reflect upon a series of cases where I and others have used appreciative inquiry (AI) for team building. My interest in this began when, inspired by AI, I began using a more incidental, less systematic form of what I came to call an "appreciative process" in my change practice (Bushe & Pitman, 1991). The success I had when I reoriented my clinical research from a problem-focused to a solution-focused one led me to even more interest in systematic applications to groups and teams. A series of experiments convinced me of the value of AI for team building and emboldened me to experiment further with it. I have found that an appreciative inquiry can have useful, even transformational effects on teams (Bushe & Coetzer, 1995). I wish to focus on a specific application of AI that I call the "Best Team Inquiry," discussing where it is and isn't useful and why. I will make the point that there are two very different kinds of groups and they construct the meaning of events very differently. As such, AI has different impacts, and must be used in different ways, in each type of group.

My use of AI with teams has led me to think differently about teams, team development, and, most important, how meanings get constructed in teams that support a team's ability to survive and prosper in its environment. This chapter is therefore a description of my work "in progress." I hope to add some new perspectives in understanding how an appreciative inquiry can be developmental for groups.

SOME INITIAL OBSERVATIONS ABOUT GROUPS

To begin, I wish to explain the perspective on human groups in organizations that has come out of my use of AI so that what comes later will be clearer to the reader. A group is as much of a socially constructed reality as any other social system, and the constructionist principle of AI (see Chapter 1) applies as much to groups as to organizations. Groups go in the direction of what they most talk and ask questions about. The "meanings" they share become their reality. The meanings that get socially constructed, particularly in the formation and functioning of the team, are there to support at least two sometimes complementary and sometimes contradictory ends: (1) the ability of the group to survive and prosper in its environment, and (2) the ability of each individual to survive and prosper in his or her environment. The relevant environment of a team consists of other individuals and teams in the organization, and sometimes suppliers, customers, and other stakeholders outside of the organization. It is interesting to note that the relevant environment of each individual is far more complex, as it includes individuals and groups, both past and present, that impinge on the person from outside as well as inside the work environment. Forces outside the work environment, like the family and personal history, can have much more influence on a person's meaning making than anything going on in the work environment. I find that the meanings that individuals construct are a function of their perceived self-interest and the meaning web of groups they identify with, but it is not as simple as it sounds. The groups an individual identifies with are many and varied, past as well as present, and each can influence meaning making at any moment in unexpected ways.

Before a person identifies with a group, the group itself is seen as a potential source of threat and/or opportunity for furthering that person's self-interests. It is outside, rather than inside, the meaning-making nexus of the individual. From a social construction of reality perspective, the dynamics of group formation are best seen as a complex interaction of sometimes complementary, often competing attempts to socially construct a shared reality that will support each individual's aims. A group exists only when the group has been constructed in such a way that a person comes to identify with it and the group resides inside the person's meaning-making nexus.

Now the group's needs to survive and prosper become forces in shaping the ongoing process of creating, maintaining, and changing social reality going on inside the individual's mind. For ease of exposition, I will refer to these as "preidentity" and "postidentity" groups:

1. A preidentity group is one in which most individuals are not identified with the group and so the aims of individuals are far more salient than the aims of the group in the meaning making taking place.
2. A postidentity group is one where most individuals identify with the group. By this I mean that they see their personal and social identities as including their membership in this group, and that what affects the group affects them. Here, individuals are willing to take the needs of the group into account, sometimes even willing to sacrifice their personal needs in the ongoing processes of action and meaning making.

Both kinds exist in organizations. While length of tenure probably has a small correlation with postidentity grouping, I have found that groups can exist for a long time in an organization and remain preidentity. It is also true that well-formed groups can develop into a strong postidentity state fairly rapidly. A key lesson from my experience thus far is that the consequence of any inquiry that seeks to influence the process of social reality (meaning making) will be very different in preidentity and postidentity groups.

One more point is important before I delve into experiences using AI with pre- and postidentity groups. Because this is a chapter on team building, the bias is clearly that postidentity is what we are aiming for. From a larger perspective, there is certainly room to debate whose interests are being served by identification with organizational groups, and I am sidestepping that completely. Rather, I will take the organization's and team's points of view that postidentity groups are more functional for organizational well being. This too can be challenged by those that worry about "groupthink" (Janis, 1972) and the "Abilene paradox" (Harvey, 1988). I think it is safe to say that organizations are more likely to be undermined by preidentification processes than postidentification ones. Furthermore, postidentification with organizational groups does not have to be at the expense of individual identity. It would take us too far afield to explore in depth the path through which a team comes to have "differentiated relationships," a state where people are both separate from yet connected to each other and so go beyond the self-versus-group paradox of human association. Let me just note in passing my belief that postidentity groups are the required platform for the most effective teams of all, "differentiated teams," those where people are willing to tell each other the truth of their experience, and neither groupthink nor going on unwanted journeys to Abilene are possible (Bushe, 2001).

APPRECIATIVE INQUIRY IN PREIDENTITY GROUPS

In this section I will look at two different kinds of preidentity groups in this order: those that are newly formed and those that are created out of a merger of two or more past groups. The appreciative inquiry process that I'll be discussing throughout most of this chapter is one I call the Best Team Inquiry (BTI) and, used with newly formed teams, it goes like this:

- Group members are asked to recall the best team experience they have ever been a part of. Even for those who have had few experiences of working with others in groups, there is a "best" experience.
- Each group member is asked, in turn, to describe the experience while the rest of the group is encouraged to be curious and engage in dialogue with the focal person.
- The facilitator encourages members to set aside their clichés and preconceptions, get firmly grounded in their memory of the actual experience, and fully explore what about themselves, the situation, the task, and others made this a "peak" experience.
- Once all members have exhausted their exploration, the facilitator asks the group, on the basis of what they have just discussed, to list and develop a consensus on the attributes of highly effective groups.
- The intervention concludes with the facilitator inviting members to publicly acknowledge anything they have seen others in the group do that has helped the group be more like any of the listed attributes.

In my experience, the BTI process can help a team to work through many of the preidentification group processes normally associated with the "storming phase" in groups to the point where they, in effect, skip the phase. While I still believe that a successful experience of managing conflict is useful for strengthening trust and cohesiveness in a group, I have also found that it is not necessary for developing into a postidentification group. Part of this impact can come from the content of the BTI (the stories and the vision) and part of it from the process (talking to each other appreciatively). Note a couple of important points about this process:

1. Public Sharing: Each member tells his or her story in front of all the other team members.
2. Dialogue: Other team members are encouraged to not just listen attentively, but to engage in dialogue with the member telling the story.

The facilitator models appropriate levels of depth and breadth in the questions he or she asks.

3. Meaning Making: The group summarizes what it has heard in the stories by developing a common vision of itself at its best.

4. Affirmation: There is an invitation to appreciate each other as a way to bring the process to closure.

I have used this intervention with about a dozen teams, early in their lives. Each of these teams was a project team created to accomplish some objective. Sometimes there was a designated leader in the group and sometimes the group's leader was not a team member. Experimental testing of this intervention with preidentity teams showed that they significantly outperformed teams that did not receive team-building interventions (Bushe & Coetzer, 1995).

Perhaps the most important effect of the Best Team Inquiry is that members get to describe their ideal social identities without naming them as such. As they talk about "what about themselves made this a peak team experience," they are, in effect, describing the roles and role complements they most value. When they discuss "what about other" and "what about the team," they get to describe the character and process of a team that supports their ideal social identities. In the space of a couple of hours the underlying needs and issues that might take months to work through are surfaced, not as problems, conflicts, or highly emotional reactions, but simply as good memories, punctuated with deep emotion.

The questions that other members ask are, for the most part, coming from their personal agendas, and therefore they have an opportunity to clear up misperceptions and uncertainties about the other's motivations and character that impinge on the questioner's ability to get his or her interests met. The opportunities for successful interrole complements are revealed as each person, in turn, gets to tell their story.

It is important to recognize the meaning that is being invested in each story. It is different for the tellers and the listeners. For the teller, a couple of things seem to consistently happen. First, people's "peak" team experiences are almost always couched in terms of highly successful teams. It is as though, in displaying the quality of the person's past experience, implicit claims are being made about the kind of resource this person can be for the new group. This is most noticeable in the discomfort shown by people who don't have a story of a wildly successful team to share. They often need to qualify and discount their stories, as if to say, "I know this wasn't a terribly successful team and I really am capable of more success than this story shows." Second, the teller is generally attending to the impact he or she is having on group members as the story is being told, looking to see if the impact is consistent with the ideal social identity he or she is trying to establish in the group. If the story veers away from that, the teller is usually quick to qualify how that part of the story might be less than "peak."

For the listeners, however, the nexus of meaning is in each of their own ideal social identities. They seem to be listening mainly for how the teller's story matches or conflicts with the kind of group they want to create for themselves. This is most apparent, of course, in the questions they ask. One real advantage of appreciative inquiry is that it allows people to ask each other questions about their values, motivations, and interests without appearing to be confrontational. A question like, "What are your real motivations?" is difficult to ask without the receiver feeling confronted and defensive. A question like, "Why was this detail in your story important to you?" is much less likely to evoke negative affect. When they ask each other questions about their peak experiences, on the surface they are simply asking questions about a concrete event that can be answered by reference to that concrete event. This is at least a benign experience and can even have a bonding effect. Talking to each other about happy memories that are meaningful provides a place where friendship can grow. Underlying that, however, much less benign meanings are being construed. Even if they are not fully aware of it, the questioners are asking questions that have big stakes. They are questions that allow them to gauge the extent to which this other person will support the ideal social identity the questioner is trying to construct in the group.

A Digression into Group Development Theory

I have come to see much of the drama of early group life as a journey to establish one's social identity in a way that matches the beliefs and perceptions about survival and prosperity in that individual's unique environment. Let us call this an ideal social identity. Establishment of this identity requires that other individuals take on complementary identities and that the group take on consonant characteristics and processes. This rarely falls into place neatly (though occasionally does), because of the many possibilities for conflict among the differing ideal social identities of the different members. In unstructured, leaderless groups these issues are most visible. In structured, task-oriented groups with an externally imposed authority hierarchy, these issues are much more submerged, but just as present. Early group life, and the sociopolitical constraints of corporate realities, result in a period of time when these conflicts do not get aired. Adults are willing to forgo immediate need satisfaction when groups first form in order to develop the credibility and alliances that will allow them to get their needs satisfied later. The first stage of group development is a "wait-and-see" time, when people put their "best face forward" and look for opportunities to establish their ideal social identities in a harmonious and peaceful way. It is only after they have concluded that things are not going their way, and probably won't without aggressive action, that the next stage of group development may surface.

I have found that the main underlying issues in what we call the storming stage, a stage described in numerous theories of group development, comes from the "role complements" that people get put into when others assert their ideal social identities (Srivastva, Obert, & Neilsen, 1977). Roles are the basic building blocks of social reality. It is here where the press of group norms and expectations meets the individual's will to act. A role is a set of expectations held by the collective about the behavior of the incumbent. It contains the product of the meaning-making process the group has engaged in, and is a mechanism by which meaning is made within a group, but is not fully determinant or static. The individual occupying a role will bring his or her unique set of abilities and motivations to the role and, in so doing, shape the ongoing meaning of the role within the group. All roles, by definition, are intersubjective. They cannot exist in isolation because they are an expression of the individual's place within the collective. As such, for any person to enact a role, others must be willing to take on the compliementary roles. In practice, this means for me to take on the "boss" role you have to be willing to take on the "subordinate" role. Conversely, I cannot act like a subordinate without someone willing to play the boss role for me. For me to be the "wise one" you have to be willing to be the "respectful listener," and so on. Of course, roles are not always mutually exclusive or singularly inclusive, nor do all require well-defined complements, but all do require the consent of the group within which the role is enacted. Without this consent the behavior of those trying to assert a role will be ignored or undermined. Within teams, the group's character and processes also have to complement the individual's role. For example, someone whose ideal social identity entails "being creative" will not feel at ease in a group that eschews creativity. A person with a strong ideal social identity of "rebel" is only going to identify with a group that is itself identified as rebellious.

When a group is first forming, the social reality of the group is vague and ambiguous. Part of how it is constructed is through finding roles for the various members. The more ambiguous and indeterminate the existing social structure in which the group is embedded (its environment), the more latitude individuals have to attempt to construct their own role identities, thus building the social order from the "bottom up." Of course, the obverse is true as well. The more structured the preexisting social reality, the more social reality is built from the "top down," with individuals slotted into preexisting roles.

To make this more concrete, a new team that is formed by a reshuffling in a company that has a manager and a number of direct reports who each head up their own departments has a great deal of its role definitions predetermined. In contrast, a task force consisting of peers drawn from various functions is much less determined. If the prevailing role structure of the first team is well suited to the tasks and individuals, then there is little reason to expect a storming phase of much intensity. In such a case, the larger social structure has embedded within it an appropriate and harmonious network of role complements.

The more social reality has to be created from the bottom up, however, the more likely conflict over role complements will need to take place for members to identify with the team. More often than not, the conflict is not of the "I don't want you to have that role" variety, but of the "I don't want to have that role complement" sort. One irony is that the meaning given to this kind of role conflict is most often "personality clash." The process of constructing a social reality is not generally visible to members, and being so self-oriented rarely enters the meaning-making nexus. Rather, one member will notice how upset she gets when another member talks in a certain way. Others will notice her upsetness (if they notice anything at all). What they do not notice is that the other person's "way of talking" is putting her into a role complement at odds with her ideal social identity.

Until enough people feel that there is a good fit between their ideal social identities and the social identities granted them through membership in the group, the team remains in a preidentity state. In such a state, all interactions are primarily concerned with meeting the needs of individuals. Talk of group goals and tasks simply masks individual agendas. The meaning-making process at play in the group is entirely at the service of individual survival and prosperity, and is therefore highly fragmented. It is probably more appropriate to talk about competing and contrasting realities than any kind of coherent group reality. If the group lasts awhile (because, for example, it is embedded in an environment that forces it to last), a social reality develops that covers for the lack of identification with the group, generally leaving such groups in a state of repressed tension and mediocrity.

The team moves out of the preidentity state and enters the postidentity state only when a sufficient number of members believe that membership in the team aids them in surviving and prospering in their individual environments. I don't know what a sufficient number is, but it is certainly more than half.

Back to the Appreciative Intervention in Newly Formed Teams

So what the BTI does with a preidentity group is allow people to declare what kind of group and what kind of role matches their ideal social identity. As each person gets to tell his or her peak experience story it is not unusual for it to become apparent that there is a fair degree of convergence in the processes and character of the team that all members identify with. This becomes explicit in the next stage of the inquiry, when the group is asked to list the qualities of highly effective teams. Regardless of the question, of course, they are listing the qualities of teams that support their ideal social identity. A list will get constructed and people will agree that is what they want from the team, but the listing and agreement by itself will have little impact on the team. People still have to wait and see if others' behavior matches their good intentions.

I believe, however, that this activity does aid development of the group beyond the preidentity stage because the meaning-making process has been positively altered. What does it mean when John says so and so or Sally does such and such? Actions are given meanings by the perceivers. In a vacuum of information there is a clear tendency for people to perceive the worst. Even when there is information, caution and cynicism are common tendencies of corporate life. The BTI changes the filter by which group members perceive each others actions. Now that I understand more about the positive intentions behind John's behavior and see how they can further my own needs and interests, I make a different kind of meaning out of his future actions, one that is more consonant with my own ideal social identity and one that makes me more willing to identify with the team. This is how I think the best team appreciative inquiry helps a group develop into a postidentity state.

It can happen, of course, that someone's peak team story is quite at odds with the ideal social identities of other members.

I recall one team in which a young man described in some detail his peak team experience where everyone else did whatever he told them and how grateful they were for his expertise and leadership. It was clear that others in the team did not think much of that. Interestingly, this allowed members to bond together even more quickly through an identified "negative other" who was repeatedly "put in his place" in following meetings. This person did not have the personal or political clout to block the rest of the group from forming into a team they could identify with and, after "being put in his place," he was able to find a role for himself that he and others could value.

More often, however, people discover that they share similar beliefs and values about what great teams are all about.

In one team each of the stories people told were about teams that overcame great odds and obstacles in order to be successful, where members were under a lot of stress and were willing to put in long hours. As members explored each other's stories they noticed that as a group they did not want to just meet expectations; they wanted to exceed expectations and everyone liked pushing themselves to the limit. "No slackers here" was one person's excited comment, and it seemed to me that people left the session having already bonded through their stories almost as if they had lived through them together.

The last step of the inquiry—giving each other appreciation for what has been done already to help the new team be like the list of attributes—is only possible if the team has some history. If the group has had less than ten hours of meeting or work time together, the last part of the intervention may need to be altered. In this instance, members typically find it hard to think of anything to appreciate in others, especially right after the question is first asked. This is to be expected, because in preidentity groups members have been focusing mainly on themselves, not each other. If after the invitation to appreciation there is a silence that lasts too long, I alter the request. I point out that I am not asking them to describe actions that made the group like the listed attributes, just things that helped the group move in those directions. I then ask them to spend a few minutes alone and think of anything they have personally done to help the group be more like the listed attributes and, if anything comes to mind, to note things others have done as well. Another alternative I have not tried, but could imagine following the 4D model, would be to guide the group into dreaming together at this point, to talk about how they could do more to become the kind of team they have just described.

This last step of declaring the positive intention behind previous acts is an important intervention into a preidentity group. It allows for further differentiation of the members. In describing what they have done for the group, they are also making claims to roles that fit with their ideal social identities. It gives people a chance to describe the intentions behind their past behaviors, increasing the level of disclosure and giving each other more insight into each person on the team. In doing this, people often remember things others have done as well and this recognition is important in building group cohesion.

One final point about newly formed, preidentity teams in organizations. It is common for some members of new teams to know each other or know of each other. This, of course, will have an effect on the meaning making going on. People may begin with negative views of each other based on stories they have heard, and this will, of course, skew how they interpret each other's actions. The Best Team Inquiry can be extremely useful in overcoming this kind of problem.

In one team that used this process, one of the members had a reputation for being cold, uncaring, and rigid. At first she refused to take part in telling stories of good teams. After others had completed their stories, however, she said she was now willing to do so and told an extremely touching story of a wonderful team experience early in her career at this organization. By the end of it she (and others) were in tears. The story also described how her peak experience team was poorly treated by the organization and helped to explain her fear of getting close to others at work. This event radically altered members' perceptions of this woman, the quality of relationships that developed, and the whole developmental trajectory of this group toward much more positive ends.

AI with Newly Merged Teams

A newly merged team is a special case of a newly formed, preidentity team where two groups that were previously separate teams are now merged into one. This is a common phenomena in business where companies are merging and putting together new teams from parts of their old organizations. This also applies to internal restructurings that have the same effect. I have come to the conclusion that AI may be one of the most effective ways to begin the process of integrating two old teams into one new one. Let me note my debt of gratitude to Randy Evans, vice president of North American human relations and quality at Compaq Computers who first got me thinking about the potential of AI in merger situations. During the merger of Compaq with Tandem Computers he contacted me about using AI and decided to apply the Best Team Inquiry process. Here is my account of that story:

In August 1997, two teams of operating executives from Compaq and Tandem met in Denver, Colorado, to begin a business integration management process in anticipation of the merger of Tandem Computers and Compaq Computer Corporation. The twenty-five executives supported the North American sales, marketing, and customer service functions within their respective organizations, although at the time the Tandem team also had responsibility for Latin America. Thirteen managers represented Compaq and twelve were from Tandem.

The two-day meeting commenced with each person presenting his or her personal history. The areas covered were recommended in advance of the meeting, and included "peak career experiences," management style, and personal/family background. During the sharing process that lasted until 2 P.M., "stories" emerged that informed everyone about what had been happening personally, in the company, the computer industry, and society in the collective experience of the participants. For example, there was a common experience of career choices driven by rapid changes in technology, involvement with small entrepreneurial ventures, personal and business failures from company bankruptcies to divorces. The process was accomplished with a great deal of openness, humor, and goodwill, and this grounding seemed to have a positive impact on the rest of the meeting.

Next, representatives of each company presented the mission, values, culture, organization structure, products, and current operating priorities of their respective organizations. These information-sharing presentations brought each company group closer together in recognizing common challenges. The presentations evoked numerous questions and open dialogue about business integration issues.

The first day closed with a "Prouds and Sorries" exercise, whereby each company, meeting separately, listed and prioritized organizational strengths and weaknesses and then presented the lists to each other. The total group discovered even more areas of common ground.

Before the scheduled start time on the second day, a group of volunteers from both organizations met to draft team operating norms to govern the postacquisition integration process. Each member of the group was invited to sit back and recall images of integration practices in their experience that met or exceeded their highest expectations. The group shared their "best practices" stories, and based on this input, drafted the norms. The norms were then presented to the larger group later in the day, and were endorsed and referred to over the subsequent months. (The norms were not always followed, but when there were deviations, there was dialogue and reference to the preestablished ground rules. As a result, the North American organization appeared to resolve conflicts expeditiously, based on the norms and the overall team-building effect of the meeting.)

The balance of the second day served to develop top-level action plans with begin–end dates, clear assignment of responsibilities, and agreement on the next steps for the total integration team.

The meeting ended with a critique. There was general agreement that the meeting was productive. Over the following months, the North America integration team continued to work their action plans, and established a number of processes that were adopted by the rest of the Compaq organization.

I believe that the same preidentity dynamics operate in a newly merged team as in a newly formed one. In addition, however, there are "ending" dynamics that are also playing out (Tannenbaum & Hanna, 1985). In a merger situation there is the loss and letting go of the past that must be managed in addition to the issues of ideal social identity that precede movement to a postidentity state. A good deal of attention has been given to the psychological dynamics of transition in the past two decades, and we have come to understand that part of the letting-go process is appreciation for what is being left behind. Appreciative inquiry, therefore, fits very snugly into the needs individuals have for appreciating and affirming the past before they step into a new future.

Some managers, in an attempt to move on with building a new team identity, try to forget or ignore the past too quickly. They fear that by constantly differentiating the newly merged team by referencing the two old teams, the divisions that exist continue to be reinforced. There is a time to stop referring to the two old teams, but it is not when they are first brought together, especially if either or both have been strongly postidentification. The fact that people identify with the old teams means that they are losing part of themselves in the loss of the old team. To let go requires that they first get to "eulogize" the old team, and then see that their ideal social identity might be found in the new team. Without proper endings, people have difficulty letting go of the past and this can account for a substantial portion of "resistance to change."

The exact design of bringing together a merged team needs to be customized to each particular situation, but let me offer a basic template. I do not think the basic BTI is appropriate. I suggest that newly merged teams begin by having members tell stories to each other about the best of their previous team or organization. This, in effect, allows them to do all the same things that happen in the Best Team Inquiry in newly formed teams, and has the additional effect of allowing for an affirmative look to the past, a prerequisite for letting go. At this point, the structure of the intervention implicitly recognizes that this is not one team but two teams. After hearing the stories, each of the old teams goes off separately and compiles a list of the positive attributes of the old team or organization that it wants to bring into the new team, and then shares this with the other team. This works with the psychological ending process by affirming the past and, in a sense, eulogizing it. Then, together, the two teams dream and design, together, the new team's character and processes. At this point the team is now implicitly operating as one. Some ritual demarcation, a symbolic transition point, is useful to bring closure to the identification people feel with their old teams. From this point on, further work should focus on helping people identify with the new team.

In the newly merged team, the preidentity dynamics ensure that whatever is done, the meaning nexus of individuals constructs meaning in the context of threats and opportunities for regaining the positive social identity one had in the old team, and perhaps developing an even better one in the new team. At the same time, there is a postidentity meaning nexus that exists for the members of old teams, especially if they were strongly cohesive, that construes events from the perspective of the dignity and respect the old team deserves. Appreciative inquiry has clear advantages for beginning the process of forming a new team by working with, not against, the meaning-making processes typically found in such situations.

The following is a summary of the steps for using AI with preidentity teams:

- Each person describes the best team they have been a part of, and all other team members probe and ask any questions they have about that experience.
- Once everyone has had a turn, the team dreams together its list of the attributes of a great team.
- People's sense making is primarily aimed at their personal safety and success, not the team's, even though their language will be primarily group centered.
- The focus of the intervention is on increasing personal identification with the team.
- People's stories will implicitly describe the kind of team and roles they want in order to fully commit to belonging to the team.
- Questions from other teammates will often be attempts to figure out the likely role complement they would have with this member.
- People will welcome opportunities to clarify the positive intent behind their previous actions.
- In merger situations, begin by appreciating the best of the two founding teams.
- Ritualize the demarcation between appreciating the past and dreaming a new future.

APPRECIATIVE INQUIRY WITH POSTIDENTITY TEAMS

Appreciative inquiry in postidentity teams is both more challenging and has the potential to be more rewarding than work with newly formed teams. In newly formed teams a Best Team Inquiry is always perceived as useful and appropriate. In plain language, it is simple and almost always a winner. In teams that have worked together for some time and will continue to work together for the foreseeable future, this is not always the case. I have found some success in using an appreciative inquiry intervention with ongoing teams in different ways, as will be discussed.

I suggest that the original purpose of appreciative inquiry—to create new, evocative, generative, and inspiring images that aid group evolution—operates quite differently in pre- and postidentity groups. In a preidentity group helpful images are those that create a vision of a team worth belonging to. The issue in the preidentity team is the team itself. In postidentity groups helpful images are those that point to something more than the team itself. Concerns are less about being a team and more about what the team will do. In postidentity groups, members are concerned with the team's need to survive and prosper in its environment, not just their own needs. Appreciative inquiry is experienced as useful and appropriate when it helps the team do that.

As a consequence, the BTI is generally not that helpful with postidentity groups, with a few exceptions. Instead, there needs to be an inquiry into the issues the group has constructed as meaningful to its purpose, flipped into the affirmative. This is the issue of "topic choice" endemic to appreciative inquiry, and the same risks and opportunities associated with AI in organizational settings apply. It's easy to say that if motivation is an issue the group can inquire into times of peak motivation. If unhappy customers is the issue, we can inquire into times of greatest customer satisfaction, and so on. Things are never quite so simple, however. Consultants often have to probe behind the presenting problem to uncover what kind of inquiry might unleash real energy. Unless there is some real interest, particularly by the group's leaders, in the topic of the inquiry, things get pretty flat fast.

In postidentity groups the inquiry often needs to gather stories from outside as well as inside the team. At the same time as the intervention is addressing the expressed need of the team, it is making an impact on the process by which meaning is constructed, turning the prevailing deficit group consciousness into a more affirmative group consciousness (see, for instance, Chapter 6). This is a well-documented intention of appreciative inquiry and I don't have much new to say about it. I would emphasize, however, that the leadership of the group must understand and support the attempt to shift the group's consciousness in this way or the intervention ends up looking, at best, like poorly organized benchmarking and, at worst, like a Pollyannaish waste of time. Benchmarking is studying the "best in class" of what others do so that you can adopt it. There is quite a discipline to it and if that is the purpose of the exercise, then I encourage doing benchmarking well. Appreciative inquiry, however, is about gathering, and understanding anew, stories of peak experiences in order to go beyond them. It is as much an intervention into the social process of the team, changing the meaning-making process and the self-identity of the team, as it is about influencing group outcomes and the content of the inquiry.

I have used the BTI with some success in postidentity teams in three specific and different types of situations:

1. A team that doesn't have an identified problem but simply wants to do some group maintenance.
2. Teams that are stuck in undisclosed resentments.
3. Teams stuck in a paradox.

Groups Desiring to Increase Effective Interpersonal Relations

One application of the BTI with postidentity teams is where the team, or the team's manager, wants to spend some time building relationships among team members. This kind of team-building request is often served by having members fill out a personality inventory and then learn about each other's styles and differences. Appreciative inquiry is a good alternative, especially if the team has already had a personality inventory type of workshop. If "teaming" is not all that important to the team, it might be better to have members describe their best experience in this organization, rather than their best team. Depending on the amount of time, other kinds of peak personal experiences can be included in the inquiry as well. I do not, however, recommend members talking about their best experience in that particular team. In times where I have done something like that, I have found that members will recall a similar experience and after two or three people have talked about it the process loses steam and members who haven't spoken yet have little to contribute.

Generally, I would suggest leading off a retreat with this activity. In this kind of format there is little need to explicitly do anything other than listen to the stories people tell. A postidentity group will know how to use this experience to further the group's survival and prosperity in its environment without the need to have this designed into the retreat. In a typical two-day retreat, time is set aside to work "issues." The way in which these get worked will be deeply affected by the prior experience of appreciative inquiry. It is likely to impact not only the content, but also the process of how the team decides what it wants to do and how it goes about doing it.

In this kind of environment the team is likely to construct a meaning for this process that is about relationships, intimacy, and celebration. I think that is a wonderful thing and would plan to organize the space and related activities to work with that to make it a bonding event.

One of the most powerful examples of this process I am aware of concerned the senior executives of a large utility. This group of eight spent a whole day simply listening to each other's stories about their peak experiences in the organization. Most of them had thirty or more years with the organization. Most of them had spent many years working together. Yet few of them had ever had such intimate conversations with each other. Even the consultants were amazed at the level of intensity and focus in the group, as each member physically went into the center of the room for at least an hour, told his or her stories, and replied to the questions of their peers. The impact on the group lasted well into the night, as members continued to deepen their intimacy over dinner and afterward. The internal consultants told me that use of more appreciative approaches began to be used by these executives in managing the organization after this retreat.

Groups Stuck in Undisclosed Resentment

I have had a couple of experiences of consulting to postidentity groups where a major theme was undisclosed resentments members had toward each other. In both cases these were groups of managers who had worked together for more than two years. Individuals were willing to privately tell me about their resentments but were adamant that they were not willing to talk about them at a team-building session. In these cases I believed that discussion of the resentments could lead to clearing up misconceptions and fuzzy expectations, but I was not allowed to tackle these issues directly. Clearly, a prolonged period where members have undisclosed resentments will damage a postidentity group and may reduce the ability of the group to meet the individuals' ideal social identity needs, causing it to revert to a preidentity state. As well, the energy that is repressed can cause the group to be less able to survive and prosper in its environment. In the past I have found this a very difficult situation to be helpful in.

The first time I used an appreciative inquiry in this kind of situation was out of frustration. I thought it might help members remember what kind of team they wanted to be in and start a virtuous cycle. The actual results were better than I expected.

I had been working with the CEO and his direct reports for about two years. The organization was in a remote, northern location and so all employees had strong community identifications as well as organizational ones. Most members of the administrative team had personal relationships outside of work. This organization was very prominent and visible in the community and this added pressure on the administrative team, whose construction of reality had the team needing to appear harmonious and effective to the outside community.

It had been nine months since my previous work with the organization and I had been asked to facilitate a two-day team-building retreat with the admin team. The CEO had described it as a pretty routine maintenance and planning exercise. I arrived two days before the event and spent the first day meeting with all the team members, whom I had developed very good relationships with. When I asked the head of production how things were going, he said "terrible" and went on to tell me how and why his relationship with the head of marketing, a formerly close personal friend, had soured considerably and how he couldn't understand things the head of finance was doing. I was surprised by the stories he told me, as they did not fit my picture of the heads of marketing or of finance. When I met with the head of marketing, she began by focusing on what had happened in the organization over the intervening nine months. When I asked her how things were going with production, she got tense and as we talked more about it she began to weep, describing the pain she felt over the loss of her friendship with the head of marketing and not knowing why. When I suggested she and he needed to get together and talk about it she refused, saying that she did not believe talking would help; it would only make things worse. When I talked to the head of finance, he told me how he felt the head of marketing and CEO were undermining him. When I suggested this was an important issue to bring out in the team-building session, he told me that there was no way he wanted that discussed and if I brought it up he would deny it was an issue. Both he and the head of marketing also had an issue with the newest member of the admin team, the head of materials, who was concerned that others inside and outside thought he had gotten his position because he was the CEO's hunting buddy. They didn't want that brought up either. When I went back the next day to the head of production to suggest he go talk about his perceptions of what was going on with the head of marketing, he could not see how that would do any good and reminded me that he had told me in confidence and would be very upset if I betrayed that confidence.

So the scenario going into the team-building retreat was that there were a lot of resentments, misperceptions, and confusions among this team of six and I was not allowed to talk about any of them. Given that, I had worked with the CEO the prior afternoon to design a day where the real issues might come out themselves, saying just enough to the CEO to make him aware things were afoot without violating confidences. We designed the day to start with task issues and hoped that socioemotional issues would surface, leaving time later to work those.

Unfortunately, the team members were quite adept at pretending that everything was just fine. The past year was reviewed, successes and failures noted, and opportunities and threats identified without anyone going near any of the issues bubbling under the surface. Toward the end of the day I was getting frustrated, as none of the socioemotional issues were surfacing, so I decided to try a BTI, hoping it would at least open up more intimate dialogue. I led the group in the first two parts of the intervention: telling their stories and listing the attributes of a great team. I told them their homework that evening was to think of things that others had done to make this team more like the listed attributes and to come back tomorrow ready to share their appreciations.

The next morning members came into the group with a lot of nervous energy. Then the head of marketing led off by saying that she had not been able to sleep all night because of how angry she was with the group and how little appreciation she was feeling. Others quickly agreed that they had found the exercise difficult for similar reasons. The issues that had been simmering under the surface came boiling up and the group spent the rest of the morning leveling and working through past hurts and resentments. It turned out most were due to misperceptions and misinterpretations of past behavior. It was a very cathartic session. As the session wound down, members felt that my intervention had failed and expressed some regret for not having done what I had requested. I thought that was pretty funny and we all had a good laugh as I described my undisclosed frustration of the previous day and my appreciation for what they had just done and how that had moved them much closer to the kind of group they wanted to be.

I look at this as a "paradoxical intervention" (Quinn & Cameron, 1988). In this case the intervention did not result in new, shared images of the team or its future. Rather, it created a cathartic release by forcing people into a paradoxical tension. By focusing on what they were not feeling—appreciation for each other—the issues that were causing the discordant feelings could not be contained.

It is intriguing to me that while appreciative inquiry led members to reappreciate each other, they first had to ventilate their resentments. It does not seem to me that it had anything to do with the "stories" people told—these were quickly forgotten—nor with the list of attributes the team generated—there was not a lot of life or energy to the list. It was the contradiction between the task they were being asked to do, the feelings they actually had, and the needs of this postidentity team as a team. They had constructed a reality where the team needed to appear cohesive and affirmative to prosper in its environment, which included all the employees in the organization and members of the community. The call to give each other appreciation, therefore, was totally legitimate within this reality. To not be able to appreciate each other was a threat to survival of the team. They could not simply brush it off as an irrelevant or illegitimate request, as a preidentity group might well do. Unable to avoid it, they were forced to confront the contradiction between their espoused and actual state. Fortunately, there was a lot of real appreciation for each other lying latent, and a clear wish to be in affirmative relation to one another, so that catalyzing this kind of process had a very positive outcome.

I am less sure what the impact would be in a group that did not see a need to be appreciative in order to survive and prosper in its environment. Again, the way in which a group socially constructs their purpose and needs heavily influences the meaning it makes of any event, and certainly influences the impact an appreciative inquiry will have on it. Of course, it could be that an appreciative inquiry will change the group's perception of what is required to survive and prosper. In fact, some might say that is the whole point. But I think there must at least be an initial bias toward appreciation and affirmation within the meaning nexus of the group, or at the very least the group's authority, for much impact to be registered.

Group Stuck in Paradoxes

The third and final example of using the BTI with a postidentity group does, in fact, alter the group's perception of its own needs, but it works in a very special instance: when groups are "stuck."

A perspective on groups that I find useful is that groups get stuck because they are enmeshed in a paradoxical dilemma (Smith & Berg, 1987). Paradoxes are endemic to group life and for the most part do not result in stuckness. Rather, they are experienced as dilemmas that frame a continuum of choice in decision situations. For example, "staff up projects to best utilize the talents of the staff" and "staff up projects to provide staff developmental opportunities" is a common dilemma in project management. In most cases such dilemmas are dealt with on a project-by-project basis, with succeeding decisions balancing off these mutually exclusive values. But when a group becomes stuck, unable to make a decision or take action, it is often because such a paradox is operating at a subterranean level in the group. This does not mean that members are not conscious of it (some probably are), but that the group, for whatever reason, is not able to talk to itself about it. Stuck groups can appear visibly dysfunctional or just normally mediocre. A postidentity group can be stuck in a paradox for quite a long time and as long as it is able to meet the demands of its environment can continue operating in a business-as-usual style. Sometimes the stuckness is only apparent in retrospect, after the group becomes unstuck.

I have found that using the BTI in a stuck group can reveal an image that resolves the paradox for the group. It is like a projective technique. The BTI provides a blank screen for the postidentity group to generate new images that the team needs to survive and prosper in its environment. In this case there really is a generative image that emerges from the inquiry, one that helps the group become unstuck. When a group becomes unstuck, there is a clear, visible change in its energy and behavior, and the group can be seen to move along the path of achieving its potential and accomplishing its purpose.

I first became aware of this using a Best Team Inquiry with a group that I did not realize was stuck until after the image that resolved its paradox surfaced and I observed the group go on in the following months to recreate itself into a much more effective and innovative team. Let me illustrate this with an example of using an appreciative inquiry with a group I was pretty sure was stuck.

A very large company I had worked with for many years had called on managers to experiment with creating self-managing teams. The company did not give much more support than that and attempts to create such teams were fragmented and spotty. In one part of the company a senior manager had looked for professional departments where a group of people had operated well together for a number of years and had professional values, and where the supervisor was due to retire. Once the supervisor retired, he was not replaced. Instead, the team was henceforth self-managing, and reported as a team to this senior manager, who had little time or inclination to supervise them.

This was a fairly successful department in this organization. Members were highly skilled, both technically and as business people. Their job was to come up with customized solutions to major customer needs that were more efficient than current practices so that they would cost less and undercut the competition. Problems were brought to them by in-house sales and marketing people and they would work with the in-house people as well as customers to devise creative solutions. Prior to the change to self-management I had some interactions with this team and found them to be in a strong postidentity state. They were cohesive, proud to be members of their team, and able to work team issues well. After the shift to self-management, problems began to brew. About four months into the experiment team members were complaining to the senior manager that "this empowered work team stuff just doesn't work," and were suggesting reviving the supervisory role. The senior manager, whose main objective appeared to be not to increase head count, asked me to get involved.

I began by talking to each member separately and what emerged was a series of complaints about problems getting work done. It was unclear at times who was responsible for what. The amount of time and effort going into group meetings had ballooned and this was annoying for everyone. People were afraid that the group was becoming less able to accomplish its purpose. Meetings had been held where all the issues they were describing to me had been hashed out and discussed. Plans for overcoming them had been made, including some pretty complicated resourcing processes, but they didn't seem to be working. It was clear to me that this group was stuck, but I was not clear what the core of the stuckness was about.

At that point I asked them to meet with me for one afternoon to try an experiment to see if by exploring what they each knew about effective teams they could develop a better process for managing their team. There were advantages to being self-managing and they were willing to try and make it work, so they agreed. That afternoon I led an appreciative inquiry into best team experiences. After a couple of members had told their stories, one member told the story of working on a charity fundraising drive with people who had been loaned, full time for three months, from their respective companies. Each person had pursued independent, creative initiatives in raising funds while at the same time fully supporting the initiatives of others. There was a program of activities to be done that had built up over the years and was fully documented for them. Over and above that, individuals pursued the group's core mission however they thought best.

This team reacted a little differently to this story than it had to others. Members were quieter and more withdrawn. The usual energetic enthusiasm was absent. At the same time, they did not seem to want to hurry on to the next member. It then dawned on me that this story offered a way out of an authority paradox (which, at the time, was one of a number of alternative explanations I had for their stuckness). The authority paradox occurs when members want to be authorized by the group to act on the group's behalf, but don't want to authorize others to act on the group's behalf. Members don't want others to obligate them to do things they have not agreed to, but want to be able to make decisions and take action without always having to come back to the group for authorization. A group stuck in the authority paradox is one where members can't do anything without getting approval of the group.

Noticing the possibilities, I then highlighted them by asking this person how the group was able to let others have free reign without fearing someone, due to inexperience or eagerness, would get them into a bind? He said, "We decided we had no way of knowing if we could trust each other so we figured we had more to lose by not trusting than by trusting." At this another member piped in, "So trust costs less." The image of "trust costs less" blended this group's bottom-line business identity with the essential element for the resolution of the paradox. Because it was such a novel combination of those words, it opened up new gateways to emotional issues in this group. They agreed that the "problem" was that they were trying to agree as a whole group before anyone could do anything that affected the group, making it difficult for people to operate. If members always had to "check in" before agreeing to anything, it was easier to have one person (a supervisor) to check in with than a whole group. They were able to explore what the "price of distrust" was. Some were angry about how much other's distrust had cost them. People were able to admit that they hadn't felt trusted, hadn't been trusting others, and believed trust would cost less. From there it was easy to decide on the "core program" and ground rules for what people could do without seeking the group's prior approval.

I made sure that the group stayed with this set of issues and ideas until the discussion wound down and then the remaining members were asked about their best team experiences. Interestingly, they often referred back to the preceding discussion in their descriptions and explanations. After the stories were finished, instead of listing attributes of effective teams I asked if there were any additional ideas about how to support trust costing less, and the group listed the new set of processes it would use and how it would try to manage future trust issues. The team became even more successful thereafter and came to highly value its self-management. A year later it was transferred to another division during a major restructuring and a supervisor was assigned to the team. They were able to reverse that decision and retain self-management status.

A BTI can help a stuck postidentity group by allowing for a generative image to emerge that offers a way out of the paradox. A common quality of generative images is that they jostle conventional thinking with uncommon word combinations like "trust costs less." In doing so, they offer opportunities to find synthetic resolutions to paradoxical dilemmas.

I am less confident that this kind of intervention would work with a preidentity group stuck in a paradox. I doubt the members of the preidentity group would (unconsciously) chose stories that aid the group to resolve the paradox. Remember, individuals in preidentity teams do not identify with the team and are not very concerned with the team's needs to survive and prosper. Only in postidentity groups are members truly concerned about the team's needs as well as their own. The meaning of the BTI in a preidentity group is most likely constructed as an opportunity for individuals to advance their interests and agendas. If an image emerges that resolves the group's paradox, it will probably only be by chance and will probably not have a lot of impact on other group members. But in a postidentity group any team-building intervention is construed as an opportunity to further the team's needs and interests. If an image that does resolve the group's paradox emerges, members will notice it even if they are not aware of what they are noticing. It helps a lot if the change agent has some hunches about what is causing the stuckness and stays alert to changes in group energy, searching for the brilliant idea in the stories being told.

The following is a summary for using the BTI with postidentity teams:

Team-Building Workshop
- Can be used instead of personality inventory workshop.
- Ask for stories from outside this particular team.
- Allow the team to use the material that comes out of the stories as it sees fit.
- Expect to build on a mood of intimacy.

Paradoxical Intervention
- Best used when people are very upset with the team but not willing to talk about it.
- Allow a good amount of time between listing attributes of great teams and giving each other appreciation so the pressure of the contradictions become too much to hide.

Overcoming Paradox-Based Stuckness
- Can be effective when a team is stuck in an undiscussable paradox.
- Useful to have some ideas about what the basis of the stuckness might be.
- Watch for big shifts in energy when stories are being told and pay attention to how those stories might offer a way out of the group's stuckness.
- Allow the group to follow its energy in discussing its stuckness, even if other members have not had a chance to tell their stories yet. Come back to them later.
- Hold conclusions and new agreements to the listing-attributes stage. Modify if it seems more appropriate to list something like "how we'll operate differently in the future."

CONCLUSION

The Best Team Inquiry is simple and effective in helping individuals in preidentity teams move toward greater identification with the team. This occurs less through design and deliver than through changing the perceptions and interpretations—the meaning—that members assign to each others' past and future actions, and through the opportunities to describe the kind of team and social roles members want in order to identify with the team. Postidentity teams, on the other hand, are more able to utilize the appreciative inquiry process to truly dream, design, and deliver phases of appreciative inquiry because members are concerned with the team's success.

For the most part, then, the inquiry with a postidentity team needs to be customized to an affirmative topic that captures the team's needs as constructed by its members. The Best Team Inquiry is not as appropriate with a postidentity team, but there are some exceptions. I have discussed three: group-maintenance team-building retreats, paradoxical intervention into a group with undisclosed resentments, and a group stuck in an unconscious paradox.

Teams offer an excellent microcosm for studying the effects of appreciative inquiry on the process of social transformation. I suggest that the distinction between preidentity and postidentity, which is so easy to see in groups, also operates at larger system levels. If this is true, then we should find that the impact of appreciative inquiry is quite different with social systems where individuals do not identify with the collective than those where they do. For example, using appreciative inquiry with multistakeholder groups, diverse communities in conflict, or fragmented organizations may, at best, aid these groups to develop a common sense of identity, helping to move them into a postidentity state. If I'm right, I'd expect the design and deliver phases of appreciative inquiry to appear less robust and inspiring and the follow-through to be weak. Indeed, a well-customized appreciative inquiry might not worry about spending too much time on these phases with preidentity social systems. Again, if I'm right, it is in postidentity systems where appreciative dialogue and dreaming can lead to powerful and evocative new ideas for how the collective can create a better future and the will to follow through will be found.

PART **II**

Renewing Organizational Vitality: Transforming Systems in Decline

4

Appreciating Appreciative Inquiry in the Urban Catholic School

William Van Buskirk

Since appreciative inquiry (AI) was originally proposed as a revisioning of action research (Cooperrider & Srivastva, 1987), it has demonstrated considerable power and a wide range of potential applications. For some, the approach is a generic intervention into an organization's social construction and visioning process (Johnson & Cooperrider, 1991; Ryan, Smither, Soven, Sullivan, & Van Buskirk, 1999). Appreciative inquiry, used in this way, produces an array of positive effects through providing an "interpretive ground" that allows for a broad rethinking of a host of specific practices and policies. In effect, appreciative inquiry provides a positive rather than a problem-oriented lens on the organization, focusing members' attention on what is possible rather than on what is wrong. Barrett (1998) sees this kind of broad, implicit "appreciative competence" embedded in excellent companies, such as Honda, Canon, and EDS. Other applications focus on specific issues. Bushe (1995) notes that a majority of appreciative inquiry projects focus on human resource issues within the company. He reports that an appreciative approach to the issue of sexual harassment, in which men and women studied the issue together, had remarkable results. Other specific applications that I have gleaned from colleagues include "turfism" and competition, management–union relations, and building a vision of service among elected officials.

The study of appreciative inquiry has also been somewhat limited by the fact that AI generates its effects in realms of organizational life that are not easily viewed. Whether broadly or narrowly focused, it changes the organization through changing the processes of valuing and social construction across many individuals and groups. These changes occur in the minds and hearts of organizational members, who may be guided or inspired by the experience to make changes in the organization. The system level at which appreciative inquiry operates is not always clear. It embraces seemingly microlevel change in individuals as well as strategic organizational change. There is a dearth of longitudinal case studies that connect the subtle microeffects of AI to enduring change. This report of an appreciative inquiry project in two urban Catholic high schools in Philadelphia attempts to make a contribution in this area.

AN APPRECIATIVE STUDY OF TWO
URBAN CATHOLIC HIGH SCHOOLS

In general, Catholic high schools have a remarkably consistent track record of successfully educating multiethnic, at-risk populations of urban youth.[1] This tradition has been documented in many studies and summarized in *Catholic Schools and the Common Good*, a book by Anthony Bryk, Valerie Lee, and Peter Holland (1993). The combination of clear governance structure, communal organization, academic curriculum for all, a tracking system that does not stigmatize, and an ideology that focuses on the development of whole persons has allowed Catholic schools to succeed where others have failed. However, deteriorating cities, immigration, the decline of Catholic populations in poor urban neighborhoods, and the decline of students who can afford tuition have called traditional ways of operation into question. Many school leaders believe that practices that have traditionally led to success (e.g., intense focus on academics, strict disciplinary codes) have to be altered to respond to the needs of communities more desperate than any the schools have served in the past. On the other hand, those who most value tradition sometimes resist change in the name of excellence. These tensions are felt most keenly by leaders in the schools, who must chart the course between traditional strengths and emerging needs. In different ways, each of the high schools faces this difficulty.

PROFILES OF THE SCHOOLS

In order to appreciate the impact of the project on each school, it is necessary to have a picture of each institution at the beginning of the effort. Since the principals have the unique responsibility for the day-to-day well-being of the schools, it is their views I present first.

Northeast Catholic High School (All Boys)

Father Michael Murray O.S.F.S. became the principal at Northeast Catholic (North) in July 1992. In September it was announced that the diocese of Philadelphia considered North as a candidate for closure due to declining enrollment. Murray became an advocate for the school with the diocese. He was successful and the school remained open. In retrospect, he realized that this episode taught him a great deal about North's culture.

There was a lot of emotional stuff! There was so much emotion around all of this! You heard things like . . . "but we've been here so long! The kids need us. The community needs us!" You didn't hear things like, "Well, we have a very solid building." This was all about philosophy of life. That's how we convinced the Diocese to keep us open. (Murray)

However, Murray realized that the school had "just dodged a bullet." Old ways of operating would need to change. He realized that "the demographics weren't going to get any better in Philadelphia" and that the school would have to become a more inclusive institution serving in a wider variety of ways (i.e., offering GED classes). If this were to occur, faculty would have to take more responsibility in strengthening and stretching the school. The old culture in which the oblates (the religious order that ran the school) were in charge and everyone else was a "hired hand" would have to change. These changes would affect the most minute aspects of the day-to-day operation of the school.

Against this need for change, Murray acutely realized his status as a "Johnny come lately." "This school has been around for seventy years. I'd been here for a few months." Many elements of the school's culture were baffling and his plans for change seemed to encounter resistance from unexpected quarters.

Father Murray's desire to participate in the appreciative inquiry project stemmed from his need to learn about the culture of North. That AI was designed to be a change strategy was also attractive, especially if it could "help the long term faculty to be less negative about change and its challenges."

Little Flower (All Girls)

Sister Joan Rychalsky became the president at Little Flower one year into the study. Like North Catholic, Little Flower was threatened with closure in 1992. The school's leadership defended the school by mobilizing the Little Flower Community.

> It was really something to see. Everyone got involved. Everyone had a role to play. The administration kept communication open with the Diocese. The faculty recruited students. The students wrote letter after letter to the Diocese begging to keep Little Flower open. Alumnae contributed money for a scholarship program. It all culminated in a prayer vigil to which we invited representatives from the Diocese. It was a very moving experience, and when we found out that we were going to stay open, everyone was ecstatic. (Sr. Rychalsky)

The upwelling of support from all members of the community exceeded everyone's expectations. The school's community of well wishers was much stronger than anyone could have guessed. This incident reinforced the notion that Little Flower "had something special," a unique "spirit" that they could call upon.

However, like North, the community was facing considerable need to change. According to Sister Joan, the school always had a real knack for building community within its boundaries, but lack of attention to alumnae and potential external partners left the institution vulnerable. Long-time administration and faculty had an intuitive understanding of the school that served them well when dealing with students, but did not provide the "talking points" for dealing with outside publics. Moreover, some faculty wondered if the "Little Flower spirit" wasn't in some ways an illusion. How would students respond to an honest attempt to inquire into their experience?

Little Flower was an enthusiastic participant in the study. The administration wanted to gain a more conceptual understanding of Little Flower's "spirit." They wanted to check their perception with the perceptions of other groups, and they wanted to use the data to strengthen relations with alumnae and external groups.

Administrations at both schools had definite reasons for wanting to participate in the study that were rooted in each school's recent history. Each principal wanted to harmonize the institution's traditions with needs to change, but each saw the task somewhat differently. At North, it was hoped that AI would support a more expansive view of the possibilities of the school, reduce conflict, energize a wide array of stakeholders, and prove instructive to the principal, who wanted to learn more about its culture and climate.

At Little Flower, the emphasis was on making the tacit explicit. Recent events had convinced many that the school housed a special culture, and the administration and faculty wanted to understand more about what they could do to enhance it. In addition, a more explicit formulation of "when the school was at its best" could energize nascent fundraising activities. Finally, both schools found themselves in a context of decline that unquestionably threatened their sustainability.

STRUCTURE OF THE INQUIRY

The study was managed through the interaction of three teams: a faculty team from La Salle University in Philadelphia and an inquiry team from each of the schools. The La Salle team was comprised of six faculty who self-selected into the project from a study group organized to discuss *Catholic Schools and the Common Good* (Bryk et al., 1993). The project was originally conceived as an attempt to replicate that study, but when members were exposed to the appreciative inquiry approach they enthusiastically changed their focus. The high school teams consisted of parents, alumni, teachers, students, staff, and administrators. Both lay and religious persons were on the teams at all schools, and all teams were racially diverse.

It was agreed that the La Salle team would take responsibility for training all participants, help "customize" the questionnaire, analyze the data, facilitate a workshop to develop propositions, write the questionnaires for the schools, and oversee the "number crunching." Meetings were scheduled with principals on an as-needed basis throughout the project. The teams at the schools would take responsibility for conducting the inquiry, transcribing interviews, and attending training and data-analysis sessions. The schedule of activities is summarized as follows:

Spring 1995: La Salle team approaches the diocese of Philadelphia for help in finding schools for the project. Diocese recommends Northeast Catholic (boys), and Little Flower (girls).

Fall 1995: Principals from all schools "buy in" to the project.

Fall–Winter 1995: AI interview training in schools. Two training sessions of two hours each per school.

Winter 1995–Spring 1996: Data collection at each school.

Summer 1996: La Salle team categorizes quotes and creates a booklet for each school.

Fall 1996: La Salle team conducts a second series of interviews at each school.

December 1996: Meeting at La Salle of all participants from all schools to digest results and to formulate propositions for questionnaire (meeting canceled).

Winter 1997: La Salle faculty visit each school to generate propositions and questionnaire items.

Spring 1997: Questionnaires filled out at Little Flower.

Spring 1997: Propositions generated at Northeast Catholic.

Spring 1997: Conference at La Salle with Peter Holland.

Spring 1997: Principals and La Salle team present findings to National Catholic Education Association Meeting in Philadelphia.

Fall 1997: Feedback of questionnaire data to Little Flower.

Spring 1999: Two-year follow-up interviews conducted with principals from North Catholic and Little Flower and members of the La Salle team.

From the beginning, the process did not go as planned. Virtually everyone was overwhelmed by the project's workload. Problems stemmed largely from lack of time and energy. Everyone had other duties that took away from their ability to manage and monitor the process. In spite of these difficulties, members participated with an enthusiasm that surprised everyone in the project. Training sessions that involved data gatherers in "practicing on one another" were moving experiences. Trainees discovered that appreciating their community in public tapped into unexpected reservoirs of energy. Members easily designed questions tailored for each school. Interviews were conducted with virtually no supervision, yet more than 200 interviews were conducted and transcribed. Although many of the activities did not go as planned, many reported that they learned "something valuable" about their school from the process. Leadership at all schools found the process valuable and recommended it at educational conferences.

THE DISCOVERIES

The data presented here are a subset of all that was collected. The data are presented based on their relevance to the primary tensions in each school. In general, the study affirmed that each school embodied the traditional excellence described in *Catholic Schools and the Common Good* (Bryk et al., 1993). This was not surprising, but this public affirmation of the schools' value would reenergize commitments and inform thinking throughout the two school communities.

At Northeast Catholic, where disagreement was common and tensions ran high, the project surfaced a "hidden consensus" that the school's handling of community and discipline was its most cherished characteristic. This consensus provided a reframing of disagreements, informed leadership efforts, and energized many to recommit to the work of the school. At Little Flower, the data were not about conflict, but about how the school's "spirit" was embodied in relationships and how it was recognized and understood by various stakeholders. The proliferation of stories about "the spirit in action" encouraged administration to aggressively market the school to outside interests and rejuvenated the vocations of many.

Northeast Catholic High School

At this all-boys school in Northeast Philadelphia a concern for order and stability is primary. As a school of more than a thousand boys in one of Philadelphia's more dangerous neighborhoods, the environment always threatens to disrupt the school community. All the adults interviewed, and many of the students, agreed that the maintenance of order was a prime consideration at North. Faculty and administration agreed that the school was at its best when there was a blend of strict discipline and caring that kept the school safe. Each element is considered here.

Appreciating Discipline

In exploring how North's members valued discipline, we discovered that four groups of stakeholders, while valuing it as a cornerstone of the community, understood it a bit differently. These are the religious order that runs the school, the faculty, parents, and the students themselves.

Members of the religious order that runs the school, the Oblates of St. Francis De Sales, saw discipline as transformational. Boys who began as "diamonds in the rough" go off to college in large numbers. North students are well known for their politeness to visitors and their community mindeness. To many oblates, having seniors and alumni returning with expressions of gratitude signaled when the school was at its best.

Attention to discipline stems from the traditions of their founder, St. Francis De Sales, a seventeenth-century priest. De Sales's philosophy stems from his idea of the "Christian Gentleman," who is capable of being strong and gentle at the same time. It is their attention to this ideal and their attempts to work it out in the context of the challenges facing the school that make running the school both a spiritual and a practical discipline: "The Salesian Gentleman is the center of everything. It's the icon, it's the uniform. It is to North Catholic what Iwo Jima is to the Marines. There are these images, there are these personalities . . . you have to marry them together" (quote from an oblate interview).

Faculty, on the other hand, value discipline through a practical, close-up, day-to-day involvement with their students. When discipline frays, they feel it immediately. Many of the senior faculty appreciate the school's almost military atmosphere. They value the "toughness" of the code, which calls for automatic expulsion for fighting or drugs and at least suspension for the use of profanity. They police the code vigorously, noting violations as "minor" as a loosely knotted tie or a shirt tail not tucked in. These infractions are often causes for detention and demerits: "It's the minor infractions that can make a difference. Policing the dress, the comportment. This is how you communicate the values of the place" (quote from a faculty member). Faculty see the disciplinary code as going beyond mere issues of control to the formation of character in the young men who come to them at North. Many have taught at North for twenty to thirty years and have seen the demand to "act like men" shape up unruly students.

Parents dwell on the changes they discover in their sons. Unruly fourteen-year-olds "become responsible" as a result of going to North. Many were struck by the mature behavior at ritual events for the whole community: "I thought the Baccalaureate Mass was beautiful. They were men. They were dressed as men. I was proud of my son. Teachers spoke to the students as men" (quote from a parent). Others note that even at public events, the faculty are alert to potential infractions: "I could see a sense of discipline that was so strong. There was an incident where the school's disciplinarian had quieted a noisy crowd at a basketball game by looking up at the stands. You could hear a pin drop and I said, 'Wow! This is the place I want my kids to attend'" (quote from a parent).

Many parents send their sons to North because of its reputation as a school with strong discipline. Yet it is interesting to note that parents know very little of what goes on inside North during the school day. Their appreciation for the discipline of the school relies on their earlier experiences (many family members had attended North in the past) and on what they hear from their sons. They are unanimous, though, in their trust of North's faculty and administration to handle discipline in such a way that their sons will "turn out" right: "My youngest son had a problem with physical confrontation. The school helped him with this . . . stopped the behavior and showed him how to handle himself" (quote from a parent).

Students have a more varied view of discipline. In focus groups, many seniors sound like oblates in their ability to articulate the philosophy behind the disciplinary code. Others, especially ethnic minorities (North is mostly white), are not so sure: "Yeah, I don't know. You can't wear jewelry here. I gotta take my earrings out. They don't have girls here. Its kinda boring. I only went here because my uncle went here and he insisted" (quote from a minority student).

In response to this statement, the focus group facilitator asked about racial slurs in the school. Were there any? The group responded as one: "No way, never happen here." Ethnic minorities were able to relax "once they walked through the gates." Even if the subway ride was difficult, they knew they could count on North to be a place of order where they could concentrate on what was really important. Even students who couldn't make the connection between a dress code and their own success admitted that whatever the school was doing, the orderly environment and close relationships with faculty were prized. To an experienced North student, the system was not something to be feared: "Actually detention isn't so bad. You get to do your homework there. You can be quiet and think about things. . . . After a while you don't want to step out of line too often because you value the relationships you have with the faculty and the coaches and you don't want to jeopardize them."

The disciplinary system at North relies on a consensus about the importance of discipline among groups who have different orientations toward it. North's consistent ideology allows teachers to "be on the same page" when dealing with their charges. As one teacher said, "In a building with a thousand boys, you don't want to be giving out double messages." The oblates' tradition of the Salesian Gentleman, the faculty's practical concerns, the parents' trust of the institution, and the students' evolving appreciation of the system as benign and fair needed to be in harmony. Many were concerned that changes facing the school threatened this consensus. The principal and his management team were rethinking some of the tougher elements of the system, while some incidents where the administration "refused to back us up" were reported by faculty. Neither students nor parents seemed aware of these difficulties, but the interviews surfaced a number of troubling incidents. We will return to this issue in the section on the impact of this appreciative inquiry.

Appreciating Community

Implicit in discipline is the issue of community. Without a sense of community, order is threatened. For most of our respondents, North is at its best when community is strongest. This theme of caring runs through all the groups at North: administration, faculty, students, and parents. Four themes stood out as keys to community: the faculty, student initiatives, connection to parents, and communal response to tragedy.

Faculty as the Core of the North Community

The faculty is both recipient and primary instigator of community at North. As the group who most directly interacts with all segments of the community, they are uniquely positioned to make all groups feel like they belong. North is at its best when faculty care for one another, create the context for students to identify with the school, and interact with parents.

The faculty do face-to-face teaching, help students with academic problems, set up and staff all extracurricular activities, oversee events for the public, hone in on students with personal problems, keep a flow of communication to parents, maintain the disciplinary code, and recruit at local grade schools. They do this with salaries that are a fraction of their public school counterparts. For many, North at its best is the energy and commitment of its faculty.

However, faculty respondents are quick to point out that they are beneficiaries of the communal atmosphere at North as well. A number of them said that one of the best parts about North is the atmosphere that surrounds the place: "I don't know what it is, really . . . but there is something in the atmosphere. Something that feels like sacredness. I wouldn't say this in front of others. I'd be afraid of getting kidded. But I think they feel it too" (quote from a faculty member). This atmosphere is created, in part, by the way community members support one another. Administrators have a history of supporting faculty in situations involving discipline problems. However, most faculty agree that the community is at its best when it is responding to a faculty member in trouble. There are many instances in our data where the faculty responded to a colleague by taking up a collection to cover hospital bills.

You have to get out of the way because people will throw so many checks at you.

A faculty member here. His wife died and he had a little infant. He just brought his infant to school every day, and the Oblates' house staff took care of him until the father met someone and re-married. That period lasted a number of years. We were a part of that young person's formation. It was a good experience for everybody. (quotes from faculty members)

Faculty report that they love to "make things happen for the kids." Student focus groups are lavish in the sheer number of incidents describing faculty befriending students. At the face-to-face level, they like the way in which their teachers "come down off their pedestal." "When you come to North . . . all the priests were cool. I haven't had a bad one . . . they wanted to be closer to their students . . . right, they realize more . . . they want to be more a teacher than a disciplinarian, a friend. They want you to learn" (quote from a faculty member).

This ease of interaction between faculty and student happens in spite of the faculty's vigorous enforcement of the discipline code. Faculty give of themselves. Students report many incidents of faculty taking time out after school or during the lunch hour to help a struggling student with a problem or a writing assignment:

Ms. McNally asked us in the first couple weeks how we felt about high school and stuff . . . you feel like a person. . . . When I moved up to the second track in the middle of the year, she helped me. She would ask before a test or any time, if you didn't understand just come see her. She would spend any free time she had. She would even give up her lunch time.

Students also like the ways in which faculty involve them in favorite projects. Faculty interests often become the stuff of field trips, either as part of the school day or decidedly extracurricular: "A lot of what we do involves including students into what we like already. We have a regular series of field trips where kids learn things about what it's like in the work world. Last week we went to the Mint. I want to take them to the airport" (quote from a faculty member).

For many faculty, face-to-face interactions with students are the best moments at North, whether in the context of the classroom or extracurricular activity. If students are beneficiaries of their efforts, they also provide much of the meaning that "keeps the faculty going." "Making a difference to the students is the best part of working here. When they come here they are so unsure . . . so vulnerable. They are so appreciative of everything you do, much more so than in previous years. Then you get to see how they turn out at the end of their senior years . . . so many success stories" (quote from a faculty member).

Students as Initiators

An important dimension to the community life at North is the extent to which the student body spontaneously joins in activities that support the life-giving properties of the institution. Many students talk about the sense of gratitude they feel toward the institution and many desire to "give something back" while they are still students: "I'm always coming back here. In the last school year, there were only six full weekends when I wasn't here. I visit daycare places with some faculty. They don't just make you work. They take care of you. They give you benefits" (quote from a student).

The most often mentioned incidents from faculty and administration involve situations where students get into serious family trouble. Students are sometimes thrown out of their homes, or their families disintegrate around them. They lose the capacity to pay tuition. They find themselves "out on the street." Students are sometimes more likely to know about these incidents than the faculty. Often it is a student who initiates the contact, either with the student himself or with the administration.

We have a senior who was kicked out of his house . . . living on the street, he never missed a day of school, never said a word about his circumstances. He disappeared about three weeks ago. We finally located him and it turned out that he could either afford to pay rent on a room or he could afford tuition . . . the kid was found but then disappeared again. His fellow students led us to where he was. He is going to graduate because his fellow seniors are paying his tuition. (quote from a faculty member)

Communication with Parents

Another dimension of community building at North is the extent to which the school tries to keep parents involved and informed. An informal tradition among the faculty involves phone calls to parents whose sons are having academic difficulties. Most faculty said that such calls were common and happened either at night or on the weekends. They spoke of this as a routine "part of the job." Occasionally, parents were also called with "good news," such as when a struggling student does well on a test. Parents report that these calls allow them to participate in their sons' education and feel involved in the school: "I credit the faculty with letting us know what is happening with our son. Mr. A. really talked to him and called regularly to keep us up to date" (quote from a parent).

Parental involvement in awards ceremonies, rituals, and extracurricular activities are another dimension of community life. Wherever possible, the school invites parents to participate in these activities. Parents report that activities such as ring masses and basketball championships allow them to bond with the school and their children at the same time: "I went to all the games. I had four boys at North. I got to have the experience of hugging them all on the court at the end of the season. When we lost the basketball championship we just sobbed. That was a priceless experience" (quote from a parent).

Finally, many parents spoke of the bond of trust they feel with the school. For many, the connection goes back two generations to parents and grandparents. For generations, the school has been an ally in the difficult job of raising a teenage son in the middle of the city.

Communal Tragedy

At times, in spite of everyone's best efforts, life turns tragic. In North Philadelphia, tragedies are common. During the years we conducted this study, four students from our schools lost their lives in street violence. In addition, student illnesses such as cancer and family tragedies occur on a periodic basis. What is striking about these incidents is the way in which the community "steps up" to them. In one incident, a young man from the neighborhood (who was not a North student) was killed in a street fight. The school sponsored masses and memorial services to help with the grieving process, and made sure that affected boys had access to counseling: "Last year we had a terrible tragedy in the neighborhood. One of the local boys, not a student at North, was bludgeoned to death on the steps of a Church. It was a terrible tragedy but in a way it brought us more together. We were more sensitive to one another and to the students" (quote from oblate administrator).

Summary

The interacting themes of discipline and community, as they weave through various academic, extracurricular, and ritual contexts, are the strongest elements in the North interviews. For most respondents they are completely interdependent. Without discipline, the order necessary to the development of community couldn't exist. Without community and the sense of connection, identification, and gratitude that it inspires, the code of discipline would be empty for most members. This interaction exists at our other school, but only at North is it the centerpiece of appreciation.

Little Flower

Like North, Little Flower faced a near shutdown in the early 1990s, and like North they were faced with a need to "do business differently" in a new era of declining enrollments. The experience of nearly closing left the school's leaders with a need to speak more clearly about the school to its various stakeholder groups. The spirit of Little Flower was felt by many, but Little Flower's principal,

Marie Gallagher (and later Sister Joan Rychalsky), sought to understand this spirit better in terms that were secular as well as religious.

At Little Flower, the term "spirit" was used alternately in a religious and in a secular sense, often in the same sentence. In the language of the school, spirit unleashed at a pep rally blends into the spirit felt at a religious service. For many, the school is suffused with this spirit. The challenge was to articulate it so that sympathetic outsiders could understand it and value it, and respond to the school's needs for support.

The experience of "practicing" the AI interview with the inquiry team was a highly emotional one. As students, faculty, and administration began to articulate to one another how they felt about their school, tears began to flow. Most of the interview content focused on relationships among the groups. As they began to identify topics, a consensus emerged in which members of the team wanted to see if others in the school felt as positively about Little Flower as they did. In this section, data are presented to show how Little Flower faculty, administration, students, parents, and alumnae concretely understood the many manifestations of the Little Flower spirit. We will consider how student–faculty relationships and student–student relationships build into a culture of support whose most visible elements are a code of discipline, extracurricular activities, and strong rituals.

Appreciating Student–Faculty Relationships

Students reported overwhelmingly positive responses about their relationships with faculty. They felt that faculty liked them and respected them. This made many of them feel special. For many faculty, the "specialness" was reciprocated, as many of their best experiences involved reaching out to students in trouble or sharing an interest with a student:

One of the students in my freshman class had a personality conflict with one of her teachers. The teacher asked me if I could take this student into my class to see if the change would have a positive effect. . . . After a short while I discovered that this student needed affirmation. Now this student is doing relatively well. She wants to give me hugs, and she seeks me out to talk when she has a problem or just wants some company. I am thrilled that I had something to do with her coming out of her shell. (quote from a faculty member)

Many stories involved faculty going out of their way to help with academic difficulties. Faculty would give up their "own time" to help out with a student who was having problems. Often relationships forged between student and teacher in freshman year will persist throughout the girl's career at Little Flower, providing an "anchor of belonging" for her in the school. Many of these incidents take extra time or energy, but are greatly appreciated by students. Other incidents are dramatic. Principal Marie Gallagher spoke of one such incident: "I almost threw up my hands. Thirty freshmen were failing math. I just put it out to the faculty as a problem and asked what we should do. The next morning there was a list with each student matched up with a volunteer faculty tutor."

Faculty are also accessible on a personal level. Students report that they care not only about school work, but for students as people. Students report that they can approach faculty with a wide range of issues. Girls dealing with pregnancy, family problems, or abusive boyfriends all find a willing ear. Students perceive that faculty are ready to meet with them "any time." Moreover, many faculty don't wait for students to come to them with a problem. Faculty told many stories of "seeing that a student needed help." Each year, some students with academic or personal difficulties are "found" by one of the teachers and supported to succeed:

Every year there are children who seem that they won't make it academically and yet someone finds them. For example, a freshman student with four failures was taken under the wing of the vice-principal who had her come to her office everyday and this student is passing every subject now. I've seen these kind of relationships every year I've been here—where students who didn't seem to have a chance were "found" by a faculty member. (quote from a faculty member)

This willingness to become available and intervene when necessary has taught faculty and administrators that one of the most important opportunities to "reach" a student is when she becomes a disciplinary problem. Acting out in class or in the hallways mobilizes a potent support network of concerned teachers and counselors. Over time, many have learned to see these incidents as opportunities rather than problems: "Many students only started to make progress when they got into trouble. When all the discipline and support swings into gear they see how much everyone cares and this can make all the difference" (quote from a faculty member).

Students report that faculty "don't just care about the work," but also about how they are doing as individuals. It often seems that no issue is too small:

Melissa had a bunny for which she needed a home. A peak experience for her occurred when Sister Claire Madeleine let her bring her bunny to school and keep it in the science lab for several days. In the end, another student adopted it. She thought it was great that Sister Claire understood her problem and was willing to help her solve it. (quote from a student)

Appreciating Student Friendships

For most students, the highlight of their experience at Little Flower was the chance to make friends with other students. The most common theme of the student interviews was the ease of forming friendships throughout the school. It was as if the school did everything it could to make sure that everyone connected to someone. For many, the anticipation of going to high school was daunting, but once they arrived at Little Flower, they experienced immediate acceptance. Transfer students are welcomed by peers, taught the alma mater, and introduced to the culture of the school by peers. Students with no friends find new ones: "I was the only one from my parish going to Little Flower. I met people at the bus stop and in classes. Friends were found quickly. All the activities make it easy to find friends" (quote from a student). Many students are passionate about the friendships they make at Little Flower. A majority of students agreed that they expected friendships at Little Flower to "last the rest of our lives."

Appreciating the Culture of the School: Diversity

If student friendships are to be strong, ethnic diversity needs attention. For many students at the school, life has provided only negative stereotypes of other groups. A wide range of activities at Little Flower breaks down these stereotypes and allows students to see that "everybody is pretty much alike." Activities such as International Cafe Day, where students get to try out foods from other cultures, help students get acquainted across ethnic lines and have fun at the same time. As artificial boundaries fall, new friends are made and the cause of understanding is enhanced: "I have met many new people with different backgrounds who have shown me what true friendship is. Through these friendships I have grown as a person. The friendships I have made have shown me different ethnic backgrounds" (quote from a student).

For many, extracurricular activities were places where friendships were made and diversity barriers overcome (e.g., white students belong to the black student league). Extracurricular activities are a chance for many students to expand the closeness of the Little Flower environment with the community. Visits to old-age homes, day schools, and community-service activities were often mentioned as "best experiences," as well as traveling to other schools for athletic events.

Most of the study's participants recognize that student-to-student friendships are not peripheral to the school, but are critical to how Little Flower accomplishes its work. Students mention that friends have been important to academic and social adjustment to the school. Older students often give important advice about what to do and not to do, both academically and in terms of discipline. Students tell of friends holding onto a girl who was about to get into a fight (which would have resulted in immediate expulsion).

Discipline

One of the highest priorities at Little Flower is the maintenance of a safe environment. The extraordinary bonding that occurs between faculty and students, and between students of different ethnic groups, implies an environment where everyone feels safe. The code of discipline protects this safety by specifying rules of dress and behavior. The no-drugs, no-alcohol, and no-fighting policies are most important. Students violating these rules are subject to expulsion. The school has a discipline board that hears and acts on individual cases. The tough rule on fighting with immediate dismissal has almost totally eliminated physical confrontation at Little Flower.

However, discipline at Little Flower is more than a matter of rules and infractions. Individual cases are heard out to try to assure fairness, and each case is viewed in the context of what it does for the individual as well as for the community. Hence, for many, it is through the discipline proceedings that they make valuable connections that enable them to stay in school. Administration and faculty work together to understand each incident in the context of the student's wider life. Consistent offenders often have difficulties at home, or have a difficult time making friends, or have higher needs for affirmation than others. Cases are looked at in depth to understand and intervene in these situations.

Sister Judy enforces a rule and then does a follow up to provide better understanding among the students. Many kids do not have expectations for themselves. Little Flower has a discipline board for those students who are getting too many demerits. The value of the board is that the kids see that the faculty and administration care about them. This experience has a positive effect on the students. Students often become more committed to attendance, school work after their discipline board. (quote from an administrator)

In general, faculty and administration try not to wait until a situation has reached the critical stage. Unruly classroom behavior is carefully monitored and discussed. Potential fights are addressed with peer mediation training and counseling. Wherever possible, the purpose of discipline in the maintenance of the school community is explained.

From the student's point of view, there is widespread understanding of the purpose of discipline and its role in keeping the school orderly. For many, the school is a bastion in a sea of chaos, so the rules and regulations make sense in terms of maintaining order. For many others, the experience of getting demerits or even facing expulsion is credited with "turning me around."

All you have to do is look at specific students and how far they've come. The discipline is fair and they receive personal attention. Many students wrote, in an essay . . . that they were going nowhere when they came to Little Flower. They said that if they hadn't gotten into trouble and received help, they would have never stayed in school. (quote from a faculty member)

One reason students accept the disciplinary code of the school is their desire to not be expelled from the community they have learned to hold so dearly. After multiple connections with teachers and peers and participation in activities, they have "something to lose" by expulsion. Moreover, the disciplinary code "gives them something to hide behind" when they need a reason "not to fight."

The "Spirit" of Little Flower can now be understood as the communal sense that arises from thousands of interactions each year between various members of the community. Administration has a tradition of responsiveness, supporting activities and events that give rise to the kind of nurturance that the school has developed. This positive sense was borne out in the questionnaire circulated to all students and most faculty. The findings of the interviews were overwhelmingly supported. A surprising degree of homogeneity extended across students, faculty, administration, and parents.

IMPACT OF THE AI STUDY ON THE SCHOOLS

In understanding the impact of the study, we wanted a point of view that encompassed the whole institution. As the leaders of the school and the instigators of the appreciative inquiry process, the principals were in the best position to give us this perspective. For the most part, the analysis in this section is taken from interviews with the principals two years after the project ended. It also draws on conference presentations at the National Catholic Educational Association meeting in Philadelphia and at LaSalle University in spring 1997.

The Impact on North Catholic

At the time the project began, Principal Michael Murray was concerned with running the Middle States Evaluation concurrently with the appreciative inquiry project. How would a school strapped for energy and enthusiasm which had just survived near closure, and which faced the challenge of needing to "rethink" itself, deal with not one but two evaluations running simultaneously?

I had this devil on one shoulder and an angel on the other. One was saying, "oh we can't do all this. We have to do the Middle States. But we don't have to do the Appreciative Inquiry thing." But I had a hunch that the Appreciative Inquiry assessment would be more valuable. That it was a sea change that needed to happen, a sea change in attitude . . . that the Middle States just would not bring about, wasn't designed to bring about. (quote from Murray)

The Middle States evaluation represented a "problem-focused" inquiry that Murray saw as another burden for the school to bear. In spite of attempts to raise morale in the recent past (the labor agreement with the diocese had been rewritten to emphasize developmental aspects), the orientation of the faculty was to ask, "What are they going to find wrong with us this time?" Some faculty imagined the process as threatening accreditation and, in a school that had recently been slated for closure, these fears seemed justified. At its best, the Middle States process produces a list of "bullet items" to be improved. At North such improvements included smaller class sizes, separate rooms for every department, resource rooms, more computers, more VCRs, a handicap ramp, rewiring the building, and better lighting. These demands would tax the institution still further.

Murray saw the appreciative inquiry process as a complement to the shortcomings of the Middle States evaluation. He hoped that appreciative inquiry would tap into latent energy and commitment to the school that would somehow obviate the burden of the Middle States "to-do list."

We just didn't do this on the side but we went to the faculty from day one. . . . We had this invitation to participate from LaSalle and the Diocese. . . . It was like a one two punch, but we treated it the same way you would treat a Middle States . . . setting aside time in faculty meetings . . . letting students know about it, letting parents know. . . . I tried to communicate from the getgo that AI was just as important as the Middle States. (quote from Murray)

Murray sensed a change in the atmosphere almost immediately. During the training sessions, some feared that participants "just would not talk." So large pizzas were provided as a kind of quid pro quo for the participants. They were promised that the session would end after two hours. After one practice interview participants felt the power of appreciating their school in a public way. Murray remembers that it was difficult to "turn off the faucets."

The power of AI for North resided in the mode of discourse it permits. In many ways it was the "shadow" of the Middle States evaluation. Where Middle States emphasized institutional tasks and problems, the appreciative inquiry stressed mission and positive experience. Where Middle States utilized problem-oriented data gathering and analysis, AI used storytelling as its primary mode of inquiry. Murray was amazed at how quickly the participants got to core issues fundamental to Northeast Catholic's identity. For many what was best about the school stretched back to previous generations, as they remembered teachers who had befriended them. The theme of witnessing the transformation of North students "from boys to men" was shared across administration, staff, faculty, and parents. It was also shared among new faculty and those who had taught at North for decades.

In the end, Murray thought, the two assessments complemented one another. The Middle States's to-do list provided a significant agenda for change, but the appreciative inquiry approach balanced it with a rich articulation of what is most valued by the institution's members at all levels. The dynamism of the AI project provided important energy and direction for the changes that needed to happen in the school: "Middle States says—what you need is outside you: funding, resources, etc. AI says you have within you whatever you need to address an issue."

However, to understand the impact of AI on North, it is necessary to delve into the nature of the transformations from negative to positive and to understand how this new energy relates to the problems facing the institution.

How Appreciative Inquiry Energizes North

In the two years after the initial AI intervention, faculty and administration continued to use the document as a touchstone in faculty meetings and in retreats. "What we are like when we are at our best, and what should we be doing about it" were common questions. For Murray this was a sea change in the culture of the school. Instead of being dominated by passivity and negativity, the faculty took on a new attitude that changed the school in many ways.

The core of this change involved, for Murray, a recontextualization of the appreciative versus the problematic. Heightened awareness of "what we are like at our best" both energizes the faculty and provides a backdrop against which new problems might be perceived. Problems do not "go away" as a result of the inquiry, but are perceived from a new and energizing context of positive rather than negative identity: "For the people participating in it . . . it fires them up—'let me tell you what it sounds like, what it tastes like, what it smells like' . . . this fires them up, changes their perspective . . . they see things they didn't see before."

Appreciative inquiry at North occasioned something like a figure–ground reversal in which deenergizing problems became reframed by a larger awareness that "we are all in this together and we are good. We've always been good." Again, Michael Murray's reflection: "AI flips the pyramid . . . in the sense that 'yeah, I'm a sinner. I'm burned out. I need new technology. I need ongoing education,' but that takes on a whole different meaning when it happens in the context of 'I am a good person. I do have something to offer.' . . . People see more light and less shadow."

As individuals experience themselves and their school differently, they begin to notice positive things about their colleagues that had remained implicit. AI is not just a matter between the individual and the organization; it evokes shared definitions of the situation within which individuals can situate their relationships. In connecting themselves to what is most positive about the school, they do so in the emerging context of what others think is most positive. They find correspondences that reinforce their intuitions and apperceptions as well as differences that become intriguing.

These transformations were not limited to the rank and file. Murray noted that AI changed his perceptions of faculty during the interview and feedback phases of the study. The process led him to realize how ingrained (and one-sided) some of his perceptions of faculty had become:

My experience with them in other settings would have led me to think . . . ómigod what is that person doing in this group? Everything about my experience with those individuals up to that moment would have led me to believe that they would not participate. People who go on and on in the faculty lunch room about all the injustices, hurts, baggage . . . their list of conspiracies. . . . There was a whole new dimension to them which I found very confrontational in the sense that while I might be used to the negative stuff, there is a whole other dimension that was just as perceptive . . . remembering all the very positive and wonderful experiences. (quote from Murray)

These positive surprises encouraged the school's leadership team to press for changes in their relationships with others. They realized that their own perceptions of the faculty might well have been part of the problem, as self-reinforcing loops between leaders and followers solidified unhealthy stereotypes. The wealth of positive material emerging from the study allowed them to be mindful of a pool of positive energy, even during moments of confrontation.

Finally, the AI project energized the whole community by helping members of different groups to find a common connection between their lives and the mission and traditions of the school. As individuals reflected on when the school was at its best, many stories went back twenty to thirty years and individuals who had long since died were recalled for their contributions. For example, the janitor in the cafeteria, a man in his seventies, was a young boy when the school opened and he remembered stories from the 1930s. Thus, in affirming the school, many affirm their pasts, which have been conditioned by the institution's mission and history, and which coincide with their own values and life experience. In this instance, affirming the best of one's personal experience and the best of the institution become one and the same thing. Past and present blend into a vital commitment:

None of that [Middle States recommendations] is going to work . . . unless we invest more passion in our relationships. That means trying to support and challenge one another to make real in everyday goals the ideals we expressed in these stories that impact us in ways that are sometimes not even conscious. Just because Father so and so or Mr. so and so who had this wonderful influence are dead, it doesn't matter. They epitomized the ideals of the institution. They challenge us to embody those ideals and create an environment. We do that less by the color of the paint and more by the quality of our relationships.

Some Practical Outcomes

Many cultural changes, such as those described at North, need to be reflected in practices to have any enduring effect. In the new affirmative climate, faculty and administration confronted a host of demands with a new attitude: "People started to say—'we can do this, we can take this on.'" Murray sees many such shifts, both dramatic and routine, all of which were made possible by the increased energy and commitment engendered by the appreciative inquiry process. He notices more widespread participation in such activities as marketing the school and recruiting students, and even in more routine activities, such as marking papers. Three such changes are the following: (1) recommitment to the FAST program (a program to aid students in academic difficulty), (2) the rethinking of discipline at the school (a topic discussed earlier), and (3) a new format for faculty meetings.

Recommitment to Academic Achievement

For years faculty members had seen the need to have a systematic approach to help North students who were in academic difficulty. However, energy was limited and even people who saw the need "did not feel up to the challenge of making it happen." Past attempts had involved a structural approach to the problem. Administrators tried to free up schedules of interested teachers so they could meet to discuss cases. However laudable the goal, this structural approach didn't work. After the appreciative inquiry project, "people got fire in the belly" and decided to meet to do what they could within the current structure. With this grassroots initiative, the administration again moved in to provide time to network during the course of the day so that the teachers didn't have to meet before or after classes. Energy supplied by AI allowed bottom-up initiative that supplemented the structural change attempted in the past. For many, the success of this program further affirmed the worth of the community.

Rethinking Discipline

Affirmation of the traditions of the school and the oblates themselves lent a new perspective to the disciplinary problems that threatened to split the administration and the faculty. Prior to the AI project, the faculty tended to take hard-line stances on discipline that favored prompt responses to any infraction. Minor infractions such as dress-code violations received detention and demerits, while more serious ones involving fighting or profanity received expulsion. Administration was seen by many faculty as "young and soft." In a few instances administration did not "back them up," and there was some concern for the orderly environment on which they all depended. In truth, administration did have some differences with faculty. They were concerned about the perceived fairness of the system and saw the mechanical administration of punishment as at odds with the traditions and mission of the school. These differences were largely implicit at the beginning of the study, and given the need for consensus on discipline, many people were uneasy.

In an environment where all members were finding connections between their best experiences and the mission of the school, the issue of discipline could be opened up. The key, according to Murray, involved "helping people to get in touch with, rediscover, uncover the theological or religious philosophy of the school in ways that were non-theological." At North this translated into a dialogue on how students (especially troublesome ones) should be treated.

As St. Francis De Sales says . . . "We're so busy trying to live like angels, we forget how to live like good men and women." That is the pillar of his spirituality. You live in the present. It's the only moment you have. It's a down to earth spirituality whose real claim is there is nothing so strong as gentleness, nothing so gentle as real strength. The fundamental basis is that the more human I am, the more I am in touch with the divine in me and then the more I can be in touch with it in others even though no two people package the Divine in the same way.

Salesian concreteness is also expressed in a respect for the complexity of specific situations. Disciplinary issues would be looked at in a more comprehensive fashion. The behavior of faculty members would come into the picture. In a few instances it was found that faculty, in the stress of the moment, had provoked student misbehavior. Offenses that would have brought on suspension in previous years were now forgiven.

AI put people in touch with a much broader tradition of discipline. One person said, "I remember the time when I thought he was going to yell and scream at me and he didn't. He put my head on his shoulder. As a result of that gentleness, that humility, he cut me a break but it didn't lead to a life of dependence. He overlooked it this time but I resolved never to disappoint him again." (quoted by Murray)

Murray and his fellow administrators took pains to work with individual faculty to understand the philosophical basis for their decisions (i.e., that they were based in some real thinking about tradition, fairness, and the needs of current students). Discipline gradually subsided as an issue of contention and a new consensus developed that incorporated a "situational" approach to the subject. Murray thinks that this revisitation of discipline led to a year at North that was virtually fight free, an unprecedented achievement.

Appreciative Inquiry has had an impact on revising the whole notion of discipline. As adults we can create environments where kids are more or less likely to fight. The principal can give a sermon or a talk but that's not nearly as effective as when teachers, both lay and religious say . . . "that's not acceptable. That's not how a Salesian gentleman would handle that." Or, "good job, that's how a Salesian gentleman would handle himself." This is how we can do something special with these knocked around adolescent, urban males in Philadelphia where, all too often, the back-hand compliment is king. (quoted by Murray)

Faculty Involvement

The more flexible approach to discipline was mirrored in changes in relationship between administration and faculty. Traditionally, this relationship was dominated by administrators who ruled firmly but benignly. This tradition did not encourage faculty to disagree directly with policies, and Murray saw this as a serious problem in a school where faculty energy would have to power significant changes. The most visible change in this relationship occured in the faculty meetings. Traditionally, these were run completely by administrators, chairs were arranged in a classroom manner, and issues were brought up by faculty by anonymously dropping a note into a bag. The administrator would then take it out and respond to it. It is not surprising that faculty meetings seldom dealt with anything important. After AI, faculty raised issues publicly on their own. Murray looks forward to the day when faculty will run their own meetings.

The Impact on Little Flower

At Little Flower, broad-based, passionate support saved the school from closure. However, in order to stay open, the school would have to recruit students in an era when the diocesan schools would be in open enrollment. Instead of relying on geographically drawn feeder patterns to supply students, Little Flower would have to attract students and money to help with enrollment.

Sister Joan Rychalsky, Little Flower's president, saw the challenge as capitalizing on the school's greatest strength, its spirit. Although the spontaneous outpouring of support during the closure incident brought the community together, the future task of selling the school to prospective students and alumnae meant finding a way to articulate it to outsiders: "Well the school was saved, and we had this wonderful experience of all pulling together, but we didn't have the specifics of it yet. The experience of AI allowed us to articulate all the things that were happening that were positive in the school."

In essence, the AI process allowed the positive energy generated by the campaign to save the school to reemerge; a "life-giving" force for continuity was nurtured. This time, instead of being a momentary response to immediate danger, it was "continuous." Appreciative inquiry allowed the spirit to be studied, articulated, and codified in terms of the many behaviors that generated it. Up to that point, the spirit of the school, while passionately felt, was a relatively tacit and private experience. It was easily accessible to individuals in the welter of positive interactions and values that characterized the culture, but it was hard to think about. The La Salle liaison to Little Flower put it this way:

It's not that they didn't know what they were doing. The traditions of Little Flower go back to its founding in the 40's. It's just that it was never that important to be all that self-reflective about it. People just went ahead, built their relationships with students and did their jobs. Appreciative Inquiry helped them to see what it was they were doing.

During the course of the inquiry, many teachers and administrators appropriated the language of AI. It was not uncommon to hear individuals talk about "what we are like when we are at our best" in ordinary conversation. Perhaps the most important impact of the project was to instill the idea that taking a positive view of the school was important to its vitality as well as to its survival:

The good was present, but AI helps you pick out all the many specific positive things . . . helps you appreciate the gift you have. . . . In a world of such negativity . . . all of a sudden you can be surrounded by the gift. We realize now that we don't work on the positive enough. That's what this concept encourages you to do . . . it makes you grow. (quoted from Sister Joan Rychalsky)

This personal transformation was widespread and mentioned by many of the faculty. For many, their experience of Little Flower's spirit was an individual one, lived out day by day in interactions with students. By making tacit, private values into an explicit public expression of who they were, AI helped everyone see the full extent of the school's spirit. It was reflected not just in one's own experience but in the experience of hundreds of others. Faculty gained access not only to their own experiences with students but to a full appreciation of the transformational power of the whole community. Individuals were able to see themselves in the stories of others, some of which went back thirty years:

That day when the students, faculty and some of the graduates got together and worked on propositions . . . that was such an exciting time. You felt such energy. . . . The students of today hearing what others recall of the 50's, 60's and 70's . . . they felt a sense of the tradition and that made them want to live it even more. Everyone was so excited. I saw awe in the faces of some of our present students. When teachers would talk about the school, students were impressed. . . . People need a sense of the past and the present, and how they fit in. (quoted from Sister Joan Rychalsky)

At this level, AI allowed the community to come together on two dimensions. People could see how the school spirit was widespread and interrelated. They could see how their own experiences were similar to those of many others in the school. A second kind of confirmation involved connecting to the traditions of the school. Many of the stories involved events that happened many years previously. Respondents got to see themselves mirrored in the past as well as the present. Sister Joan noticed a strong energizing effect on the Little Flower community: "You knew you were good. But you didn't really know how good. With AI we get to see the effect we are having on the whole community. Now we know we are good. And we work harder to be even better. . . . It's a kind of self fulfilling prophecy."

In helping to give form to the community's energy, AI provided a language that helped them identify implications for practice. One aspect of the data that was particularly strong was the importance of extracurricular activities as an occasion for positive interaction between students and teachers. Since many students had to work after school, faculty became concerned that this avenue was unavailable to many students. In response, faculty designated certain free periods as "activity periods," where students who worked could be involved. As the issue of diversity became highlighted, a diversity committee, consisting of students and faculty, was created. Members take responsibility for enhancing understanding throughout the school: "AI enabled us to identify all the things that were positive. These we carried on . . . but once in a while we found something that wasn't working so well. You could eliminate that" (quoted from Sister Joan Rychalsky).

Thus, the corpus of anecdote and analysis provided a background against which teachers could look at the school and decide what to change and what to keep. It was as if once there was a strong image of what the spirit was, there was enhanced clarity about what to do.

As president, Sister Joan emphasized the importance of "not putting the AI results on the shelf," but using them to communicate with various publics. The cache of stories, quotes, and quantitative data provided a language that its stakeholder groups could understand. Strongly articulating the school spirit in terms of concrete stories gave administrators encouragement and a language to approach other groups. The two most important of these were the alumnae and prospective students in local grade schools. "One of the things we asked when we were finished was . . . how can this help us now? . . . This can be a language to get a lot of people on board if you use it that way . . . if you don't close the book" (quoted from Sister Joan Rychalsky).

If the school was to survive, Sister Joan realized that the alumnae would have to invest in the school. It was they, after all, who had benefited from the school in the past. For many, however, there are barriers to getting involved. Many alumnae had graduated from Little Flower in "another era," when many of the trappings of Catholic education were different. For others, the image of Little Flower's neighborhood of Hunting Park in Philadelphia conjured up images of urban blight. To overcome these barriers, Sister Joan used both the content and process of AI.

First, she wrote the alumnae and thoroughly described the project, its structure, and its results. However, the crux of the campaign would not lie in descriptions of AI, but participation. Sister Joan began inviting alumnae to the school to spend a day with selected students who would tell them about "the school at its best."

I think my concept has always been, if we want our alumnae's support, we need to show them the product and where we are today. . . . They have a concept of what it was like. We are now considered an inner city school. That comes with its own stereotype. So, I invite four classes per year to spend a day with the students to see what makes Little Flower work. It has been enormously successful. It is an educational tool . . . it has led to being able to start this endowment. I've been able to use this experiment to tell our graduates about the good things we have identified. That makes them willing to invest in a good product. (quoted from Sister Joan Rychalsky)

Appreciative Inquiry has also been helpful in communicating to prospective students the virtues of the school. Wherever possible, current students and recent graduates are enlisted to make visits to local schools. Sister Joan notes that students who have been exposed to the AI process make very effective "ambassadors." "If we can communicate. well to our alumnae and to prospective students, we will do fine. The alumnae will contribute scholarship money for students who can't afford our tuition and the students will want to come."

Finally, the good news inherent in the school and documented by appreciative inquiry helps Sister Joan orient her management team, especially as it expands to include outsiders. Since the project has ended, the school has hired a development director and a director of recruitment. Results of the appreciative inquiry project were an important part of their orientation.

If you are aware of all the good things, it's the first thing you want to pass on when you meet new people. And if you're not aware of them then the good news isn't going to get out. I trained a development person this year . . . obviously you want her to know all the good things we identified. The AI report is part of our history now. I wanted to let her know how much the students perceptions and our perceptions are in synch. I've also used it as a training process. If you have a new development director you want that person to become aware of the good things . . . to continue the education of the alumnae.

As the endowment campaign begins to show success, confidence about the school's survival is high, and promoting the school has a playful side: "Just for the heck of it, I wrote Oprah to see if she would like to have us on her show. I worded it—'Kids who love their school'—whatta concept. . . . After a year and a half she wrote back. We didn't get on, but our kids want to tell the world about this school" (quoted from Sister Joan Rychalsky).

CONCLUSION: APPRECIATING APPRECIATIVE INQUIRY

This study allowed us to see the benefits of appreciative inquiry in two urban high schools through the unique opportunity to revisit the sites two years after an initial intervention. In these studies, appreciative inquiry was "at its best" as a pervasive intervention into the culture of an organization. Its power is exerted through three transformations: (1) it transforms perceptions of how individuals relate to their past experiences in the organization, (2) it transforms how they relate to the best experiences of others, and (3) it transforms how they relate to the most cherished traditions of the institution. To the extent that it successfully accomplishes these transformations it may have significant impact on a myriad of specific commitments and practices in the organization.

Individual's Perceptions of Self

One of the most common reactions to the appreciative inquiry interviews is a mixture of surprise and delight. Respondents are surprised at the impact that "just focusing on the positive" has on their energy, attitude, and understanding of the institution. Individuals at both schools went out of their way to tell us how enjoyable the experience was. We attribute this to a kind of figure–ground shift from negative to positive in which positive aspects of one's experience in the organization become explicit rather than tacit. This provides a heightened awareness of value and potential previously clouded by cultures of problem-centered thinking. This new vision of the organization engenders both safety and self-esteem.

In the moment of acknowledging the organization at its best, individuals also often experience their alignment and connection. The school at its best is something they can count on and be proud of.

Seeing the Best of Yourself in Others

Essential to the appreciative inquiry process is its social dynamic. As individuals talk with others, observe focus groups, and participate in feedback sessions, they see that their own transformation is not unique. Individuals separated by gender, ethnicity, age, organizational position, or even religious orientation begin to see commonalities. Seeing the best of one's self in others reinforces the image of the school at its best. If the first transformation is from tacit to explicit, here the private becomes public. This movement validates individual discoveries of the interviews. It allows participants to connect the best of their experiences to those of others. It allows for a spontaneous realignment of roles based on this emerging image of "the school at its best." As more and more people contribute, the vision, and actions taken upon it, become multifaceted, comprehensive, and shared.

Seeing the Best of Ourselves in the School's Tradition

As individuals share more of their experience, they begin to realize that many of these experiences are long standing and historical. Individuals who have died were mentioned at both schools. In a sense, they are still part of the school. They live on in its present members. In making these experiences explicit and public, AI unleashes the tremendous energy stored in them. At North they challenge people to live up to the standard they set. At Little Flower, they enchant the students, who see the best of their experience reflected in a much wider historical context. AI at these schools allowed people to "pull" cherished traditions into the present, "connect" them to current issues and conundrums, and "realize" guidance and rejuvenation that is more than implicit or private.

As these processes develop under the leadership of the school, a number of more practical effects can be noticed. School leaders shed their negative stereotypes of the institutions and begin to see the schools in terms of their strengths rather than their limitations. Through the contributions of so many stakeholders, they begin to imagine their schools in more expansive terms. As they realize "just how good we are," they are encouraged to seek support among critical stakeholders. As individuals begin to envision themselves in relation to the best of what is, they find more energy to contribute to a range of projects, both routine and innovative. Decisions to participate are made freely and spontaneously. Even long-standing conflict (i.e., the discipline issue at North), was reframed and re-solved in line with the appreciative images of the institution.

Leaders in this context can ride a wave of positive change rather than force it. AI in these schools provided sensitive leaders with a wealth of detail about the kind and style of changes that members wanted to pursue, change that is consistent with shared traditions of excellence. As images of "the school at its best" move from im-plicit to explicit, private to public, and connect to cherished tradi-tion, leaders have a new language, the language of the school at its best. At North and Little Flower the principals learned this lan-guage, let it guide them, and used it in their attempts to lead the schools. It may be that their religious ideology prepared the princi-pals for this kind of appropriation. In any case, they actively used AI as a vehicle for learning about their schools "in action." They opened their minds and hearts to an extraordinary degree. If ap-preciative inquiry helped create the context in which this happened, its most subtle contribution may also be its most powerful.

NOTE

1. The original study involved three Catholic high schools. In one case, the principal and other key leaders left during the two-year interval be-tween the inquiry and the follow-up. This made outcome data difficult to obtain and obviously influenced the use of the inquiry discoveries in that school. For these reasons and the limitation of space, the third school has not been reported here.

5

Creating Unity from Competing Integrities: A Case Study in Appreciative Inquiry Methodology

Charleyse Pratt

This chapter reports a case study where appreciative inquiry (AI) methodology was used successfully as an intervention strategy in a newly merged organization fraught with wounded relations and negative feelings. The case highlights the tendency of appreciative methodology to privilege positive aspects of organizational experience. As the story unfolds, a tension between this selective focus on the positive and the apparent refusal to honor negative dimensions of lived experience seems to compromise the integrity of the AI process. The case describes the challenge of blending these two integrities. A summary of the intervention process and methods and a review of the outcomes attributed to these methods are presented. A strategy of consolidating story elements into learning parables is described as a method to interpret and understand individual and collective realities.

BACKGROUND

The intervention described here occurred in an organization we will call Southview West Agency (SWA), situated in a small, midwestern urban community. It is an outpatient drug and alcohol treatment center certified by the Joint Commission on the Accreditation of Healthcare Organizations (JCAHO) and the State Department of Alcohol and Drug Addictions Services for treatment of alcohol, drug addictions, and associated mental health problems. Demand for these services had increased due to a declining economic environment in a community plagued with high unemployment. SWA evolved from the merger of two smaller agencies. One had provided services to alcohol-addicted clients for over eighteen years. The other agency had served chemically dependent clients for approximately seven years prior to the merger. Both agencies had solid reputations as providers of counseling and mental health services to employer-paid employee assistance programs in the area. Over time, more and more clients were dual-diagnosed with both alcohol and chemically related problems. Consequently both agencies had begun to offer many duplicated services. Funding for duplicated services was neither realistic nor likely in an increasingly competitive economic environment. A merger offered the promise of protecting the future of both agencies and addressed the threat of reduced funding under the auspices of a single, more integrated agency.

The merger changed the face and form of the agencies, and neither staff was pleased with the decision. Their displeasure became painfully apparent when staff from both agencies were colocated to a newly renovated facility. Integration of staff and services was extremely difficult, partly because of a perceived hierarchy among counselors and service providers. Counselors from the alcohol treatment agency viewed their services to be more legitimate, based upon the general acceptance of alcohol-related problems as a medical condition. Credentials for alcohol counselors required at least an undergraduate degree, clinical experience, and professional licensing. Alcohol treatment programs required approval of a licensed psychologist or medical doctor and were conducted under supervision in order to qualify for medical reimbursement by most hospitalization plans. Chemical treatment programs usually did not qualify for reimbursement under most hospitalization plans, as they were often considered social rather than medical problems. In addition, the chemical treatment agency utilized a "community-based" treatment model employing counseling staff indigenous to the community. These counselors had successfully completed a local training program for counselors of chemically addicted clients and had received certificates for limited counseling, based upon successful completion of the training, their own history of drug experience and recovery, and/or experience with family members in treatment.

The agency was renamed Southview West to avoid the perception of one agency being absorbed by the other. Under a new roof, the merged identity, purpose, structure, and procedures of the new agency were presumed to be united and common. However, treatment practices and administrative operations continued according to their divergent past practices and philosophies. Each staff group continued to operate as they had prior to the move, although now under one roof, in front of each other. One counselor described it as "planting old ways in new places." Board members also continued to operate with strong commitments to former agency affiliations, as evidenced by patterns of voting for or against actions aligned with favored interests of their former agency associates. It was obvious that although the agencies had merged legally and colocated staff to a new facility, they had been unsuccessful in blending the two organizational entities and cultures into a united or new whole. A new organization had not formed. The culture and essence of the two smaller organizational entities had survived the merger and were coexisting under new conditions.

Conflicting preferences for treatment models and counselor practices were a particular source of discontent and grievances. Contributing to the situation were perceptions of counselors from the chemical treatment agency who felt that their services and contribution were not valued by the more educated and licensed alcohol counselors. There was limited interaction between the two staff groups and those interactions were more likely to be combative than collaborative. In an attempt to bridge the professional relationships, the agency director insisted that a pair of counselors would facilitate twelve-step program meetings, one from each agency. The goal was to build capacity of staff while also building relationships. It was not uncommon to have counselors argue or disagree publicly during these meetings. Counselors from both staffs had begun to behave in ways that were experienced as "mean spirited" and discrediting others.

New hires quickly observed these rigid applications of former treatment practices by the two agency subgroups. A general lack of coordination and collaboration between warring factions led to anxiety, fear, and loss of enthusiasm. Under these conditions, staff members who needed guidance, support, or instructions were reluctant to make such a request for fear that it might be interpreted as a lack of competence. These optimistic professionals, who had been attracted to the merged organization by its potential to offer exposure to a range of client needs and corresponding services, soon lost their enthusiasm. Since the new entrants did not share history or identify with either of the former agency structures, they were faced with the choice of aligning with one of the competing factions or isolating themselves, trying not to become involved in the struggle. The merged organization had become a hotbed of negative emotion, with staff feeling frustrated by the dynamics of fear, isolation, conflicting practices, and questions about competence, little cooperation, and collaboration.

One unfortunate incident involving a board member and a perceived breach of confidence occurred just prior to the intervention. It was alleged that confidential and sensitive information about a staff counselor had been shared with personal friends of the board member. These friends of the board member were also clients of the agency. The staff counselor considered the disclosure to be scandalous, damaging to his professional reputation, and jeopardizing his credibility with clients. The apparent breach left the staff counselor feeling personally injured. Exaggerated accounts of the situation spread quickly and a variety of retaliatory actions by staff followed, in sympathetic response to feelings of betrayal. The executive director resigned under the weight of all these pressures. A growing fear of an exodus of competent staff in support of the protest of his departure loomed over the already troubled agency. Absence of leadership exaggerated the serious nature of the situation, which was already having a negative consequence on delivery of services. Morale hit an all-time low.

Other concerns also threatened SWA's future. The name of the agency, selected to avoid the perception that one agency had absorbed the other, did not reflect its purpose or mission. A revised mission and strategy for service had not been communicated. No advertisement or community announcement had ever been made. Members of the professional treatment community had become aware of the challenges of working at SWA through conversations with colleagues and clients. The agency had begun to be described as fragmented, inefficient, and poorly managed. Referrals from employers and other agencies declined, staffing levels were consistently low, and recruiting of staff became more and more difficult. Mandatory reports to funding employers, agencies, and regulatory boards revealed a pattern of understaffing and declining numbers of clients served. Pending grant proposals and funding requests were being challenged. From any perspective, the future of SWA was in jeopardy.

FRAMING THE APPRECIATIVE TOPIC

The outgoing chairman of the volunteer board of directors created the opening for appreciative inquiry and initiated contact with the author. He had learned about the AI process in a casual conversation with a colleague and hoped that this approach to intervening in the organization's process would lead to a restoration of healthy operations. The board, under his leadership, defined three objectives for the intervention. First, they wanted to understand the challenges of the agency more clearly from the perspective of staff. Second, they hoped to unify agency staff and board members. The third objective was to develop a clearer mission and concrete action plan to deliver efficient, quality services with high client satisfaction and positive outcomes.

Clarity of mission, task design, and roles are three essential factors for effective performance in human-service and mental-health treatment teams (Shaw, 1990; Perkins, Shaw, & Sutton, 1990). Clarity of mission refers to purpose and expected outcomes and the ability to prioritize a variety of tasks and activities that contribute to the organizational mission. The apparent difficulty in this area seemed to be a lack of integration incorporating elements of two organization missions into one inclusive mission agenda. Issues of task design were evident in the lack of understanding about changed relationships and coordination and distribution of new work and new organizational priorities. The SWA treatment teams needed more clarity about their collaborated task priorities. Treatment philosophies had not been adequately defined, and, therefore, staff counselors adopted preferred strategies. The "talked about" outcome of all this was an organizational nightmare of inconsistencies and duplications.

Physical boundaries of the two organizations had been altered with the move, but very few modifications had occurred in the former social and psychological structures. A sense of membership in former agencies had not transferred to SWA, since SWA itself was so vague and undefined. In order for members to have a sense of belonging, there must first be a "merged identity" to which to belong. There had been no process of redefining or extending organizational boundaries to engage or reorient staff as members of a newly merged team. In essence, what was hoped for was a process that would help to revitalize and unify the organization. The topic choice "unity" was derived from these desired objectives.

THE INQUIRY

Examination of the range of narrated accounts from various organization members enables a comprehensive, expanded view of the organization's multiple realities. Appreciative inquiry protocol helps these narrations become generative as well, by assisting the member in bringing forth a story of a positive experience and shedding positive light on best past experiences. The structured AI interview asks interviewees to recount details of a "high peak" or positive organizational experience. They are also asked to consider and describe things they value about themselves and to describe what makes them feel most engaged or excited about their involvement with the organization. The final question asks interviewees to offer two or three wishes for the organization with regard to the topic being examined; in this case, unity.

Twenty of the twenty-eight staff members and ten active volunteer board members were interviewed in person. Another four were interviewed by telephone. A structured interview protocol was designed for the staff and is shown in Figure 5.1.

A slightly different protocol was used for the volunteer board members. Since board members served voluntarily and staff was paid, there was reason to believe that their perspectives might be different and a different interview appropriate. Staff interviews were approximately one hour and were conducted on site, during regular operating hours. Interviewers' notes were transcribed and analyzed in two ways. First, data were analyzed for the identification of common themes and patterns of response. Common themes were cross-checked against more detailed reflective accounts and stories shared during interviews and observations made by interviewers. Emergent themes from interviews were synthesized and organized into categories. In addition, a variety of print media, including correspondence, flyers, handouts and other material, documents describing treatment philosophy and strategies, reports to funding agencies, position descriptions, quality assurance documents, bulletin boards, and other miscellaneous information were reviewed. The examination of documents served as a way to explore multiple voices that might differ from spoken interpretations (Hodder, 1995). The enduring nature of documents also contributes an historical insight to the inquiry. Feedback was presented at a full-day workshop session. This feedback workshop session concluded with action planning, establishing specific goals for thirty and sixty days forward.

THE INTERVENTION PROCEEDS

This intervention process evolved in four progressive phases that are consistent with the 4D model for appreciative inquiry:

1. Discovery: The process of learning about the best of "what is" in the organization, from hearsay to "he said" and "she said" to "we say"; integrating meaning from storytelling.
2. Dream: Actively visioning and imagining the best of "what can be."

Figure 5.1
Original Staff Interview Protocol

Name _____ Position Title _____

How long with agency _____ How long in position _____

Other positions held at agency _____

1. Think of a time when you felt the agency was operating at its best. What were the things that seemed to bring things together? Please be specific.
2. What do you value most about the work of the agency and the work you do?
3. How would you describe the unified mission of SWA?
4. Describe the work you do and with whom you work. What do you value most?
5. When is the agency most effective in achieving its unified mission? Please explain and give an example.
6. What are the greatest strengths of the merged agency?
7. How do you think you have contributed to the unified mission of the agency?
8. What makes you feel most like contributing to the team effort, working at the agency?
9. When do you feel that the agency operated most like a unified operating unit?
10. What else would you like to say?

3. Design: Being as we imagine; new storymaking.
4. Destiny: Constructing strategies and applying what has been learned to become what we dream about, daily.

Entering and Discovering "What Is"

Successful interventions require that the consultant or practitioner gain acceptance and build relationships with members of the organization (French, Bell, & Zawacki, 1994; Schein, 1988). We emphasized relationship building in the initial phase of the intervention by participating in a series of meetings to introduce the consultants and the appreciative inquiry process to members of the board. Our team of three was introduced to the staff during a walk-through tour of the facility. Later, a memo to staff and board from the board chairman provided an overview of the intervention, the objectives, and a brief description of the AI methodology and the intervention. The written document was provided to assure a cognitive understanding of essential aspects of the process. While the interviews were described in the memo as "voluntary," staff members were "strongly encouraged" to participate and assured that all information would be treated as confidential.

The discovery phase also involved the specific activities of watching and listening as interviews were confirmed and conducted in four full days of interviews over a two-week period. We observed that the floor plan of the new office facility contributed to the separation and isolation of staff. Offices were constructed on both sides of the building, with a long corridor down the center for access. Office doors were always closed. Closed doors had been the practice for client counseling sessions, but now the practice had been extended to protect the privacy of discontented coalitions and shield those who preferred isolation instead of coalitions. Closed doors darkened the corridor of access. It is amazing how unsettling the sound of a door being slammed can be in a professional office environment.

The interview team was assigned an office at the end of the corridor to conduct interviews. Early in the process we became acutely aware of resistance; staff had strong reactions to the tenor of the AI interview. They described the questions as "too positive" and unrealistic, giving rise to accusations that the intervention was a sham and would not produce meaningful data. We immediately became concerned that a lack of confidence in the data could result in a refusal to honor the feedback or to proceed with any positive action as a result. Despite our persistent and most persuasive efforts to give the AI process a chance, staff members were unable or unwilling to set aside their strong negative feelings, even for the purpose of a brief appreciative inquiry. It seemed impossible for many to formulate positive responses and consider provocative possibilities (wishes) for a collective future. They were emotionally entrenched—stuck—in the anger and injury of their experience, and their resistance was anything but passive.

QUESTIONS OF INTEGRITY

The intervention team discussed our interview experiences during the drive home on the first day. None of us had ever experienced such powerful resistance to the AI process. We realized that our understanding and modeling of one of the fundamental principles of AI—"to honor what is"—was being challenged. If the intervention were to proceed with any degree of integrity, we would need to find a way to honor negative experiences of the staff in the context of our positive AI process. The latter was also important because we wanted to honor and be honored for our commitment to an appreciative stance toward life in this system. This was an important discovery and a challenge for the interview team that prompted us to examine our stance and to modify the interview protocol. To protect the integrity of the AI process and the future outcomes of the intervention, we decided to modify the interview protocol to a more conversational, semistructured format and include neutral, open-ended questions (see Figure 5.2).

We agreed to ask a question and listen. Interviewees could respond in any way they chose, including making negative comments. We stopped resisting their resistance and incorporated these comments as part of the notes of the interview. After any negative response, we would engage in a conversation by acknowledging the intensity of a feeling or strength of an emotion we experienced in the answer given, and then ask another, more appreciative question. In almost every case, the process was transformed from a tense tug-of-war to a more liberated and relaxed but expressive interaction where each person felt honored. The tension involved a perception that what they wanted to tell us was not being honored by a process that only allowed them to talk about what we wanted to hear. They resisted the requirement to subordinate their experience to the desires and directives of the interviewer, interpreting this as yet another example of being devalued. People just wanted to be heard.

Interview data were analyzed and organized according to emergent themes, with the pattern of themes shaping into three categories. First were organizational issues, those things related to the formal or functional organization, mission, strategy, and structure of SWA. Next were operational issues, comments specifically related to individual performance and the delivery of services to clients. Third were relational matters associated with internal interactions (board–staff, management–staff, and staff–staff relations) and external relations (agency relations with community at large, recovering community, funding sources, and other agencies delivering similar services). Our attention turned to the search for methods and processes that would assist organization members to move past the past as separate organizational entities and move toward the future as a more unified agency. How could we help them honor their differences in ways that would create or reveal attraction to wanting to work together for a common, positive future?

Figure 5.2
Modified Staff Interview Protocol

Name _____   Position Title _____

How long with agency _____   How long in position_____

Other positions held at agency _____

1. How would you describe the unified mission of SWA?
2. What do you value most about the work of you do and the people with whom you work?
3. How would you describe the agency's current effectiveness in achieving its unified mission?
4. Think of a time when you felt the agency was operating at its best. What seemed to bring things together? Please be specific.
5. What do the agency and staff face as the three most significant challenges?
6. What are the greatest strengths of the merged agency and staff?
7. How do you think you have contributed to the unified mission of the agency?
8. What changes would you recommend in the agency, its operation, or its structure? Be specific
9. What makes you feel most like contributing to the team effort, working at the agency?
10. When do you feel that the agency operated most like a unified operating unit?

Please complete the following statements in your own words
A. I work at the agency because—
B. My talents could be more effectively utilized if—
C. I often wish that the agency would—
D. If the agency ceased to exist—
E. Most people in this community think the agency—
E. At the off-site meeting I hope we—

What else would you like to say?

LEARNING PARABLES

We used storytelling to facilitate conversational interaction and the theme of unity. We wanted to appreciate their stories of varied experiences as an interpretive recollection that not only reported what happened in their words, but used other words and imagery to stimulate thinking about more positive ways of interacting. This had to be accomplished without breaching confidentiality of any interview. An anecdotal illustration was created as a "learning parable" for each thematic category. This illustration was similar to what Phillips (1995) described as "narrative fiction," where selected elements of confidential stories are incorporated into a narrative account of a hypothetical organizational world. Using elements of several individual reports, the creation of learning parables protected the anonymity of speakers, presented a picture of the organization that was plausible and believable, and wove a pattern of truth that resonated with most of the people in the room. Learning parables facilitated the presentation of themes and offered interpretive explanations of the feedback. The empathic stories of fear, isolation, infractions, perceptions of betrayal, hard work, triumph, and success selected from interviews provided the details of significant organizational events. The learning parables permitted us to construct an image of an organizational world that incorporated scenarios from various individual stories to show the multiplex of experiences and affective aspects of the organization, including fear, anger, distrust, injury, pain, hope, sensitivity, professionalism, respect, and love, all of which drove much of the behavior in the organization. In this way, the concept of narrative fiction is expanded, as the parable includes specific illustrations, principles, or points of awareness that listeners can interpret as relevant to their own experiences. As we shall see, dialogue about the learning parables allowed organization members to engage in the sharing of information and insight as they collectively construct meaning for the learning parables.

The following is a sample learning parable incorporating these selected interview responses:

- When we were in our old agency, we had a clinical director who functioned as a manager and mentor. Here I operate in isolation; it gets confusing when I go to the hallway seeking help. Experience in other agencies is not really recognized.
- In spite of everything going on here, we are the only agency where a person can get help if he is dual-diagnosed. We have a good team of professionals. I wish we could just overcome our personal issues and start respecting each other and helping clients.

- They should be more open. Tell people what really happened. Stop some of the rumors and whispering. Start managing and stop writing oppressive memos.
- There are monsters lurking behind these doors. Clients are not the only ones who need help coping.

Learning Parable

It had already been three weeks since Jan (not her real name) had started her new job as counselor but she was still nervous and unusually anxious. Walking down the hall with a new client, inviting casual conversation, was a ritual her former agency director had taught her. The practice seemed to reassure new clients and calm their fears about starting up a new counseling relationship. Sobriety is an ambitious goal and a long journey with many false starts. Clients need every encouragement they can get to make it. They have to believe the counselor is with them in the struggle.

"Monsters and secrets lurk behind closed doors," the client said, observing all the closed office doors. "You can't fix what you are afraid to look at."

Jan's office was small, just large enough for comfortable placement of a desk, bookcase, files and two chairs. The walls were decorated with diplomas and certificates. One family picture was positioned on top of the bookcase next to a small plant that was obviously suffering from lack of sunlight and water. A very small window provided a view of the parking lot. An inside window on the other side of the office offered an obstructed view of the corridor with only tiny openings between the posting of agency policy memos, 12-Step meeting notices, community program flyers and poems. You could not see out and no one could see in. It was a dark place to find hope.

Jan ushered the client to a seat in the office and proceeded to close the door.

"Leave it open," he said anxiously.

Surprised at the tone of the directive, she advised him that closing the door was important to protect confidentiality.

"Leave it open," he repeated, and continued, "I don't know about protecting my confidentiality but I know a closed door shuts me off from everybody else out there that can help me beat this problem. Closing that door leaves me here with just you. With all due respect to you, nobody ever succeeds or gets sober with only one person helping him. I know this for sure, you got to find a way to keep the door open."

BEING WHAT WE IMAGINE:
FROM STORYTELLING TO STORYMAKING

A full-day appreciative, feedback workshop was designed and conducted at an off-site location to permit the group to work on group process with limited interruptions or distractions. Twenty-six staff and board members attended. Agency operations were suspended for the day, except to respond to emergency situations. The session began with a welcome and brief review of the introductory memo from the board chairman that described the AI process. We reminded the group of its intentional focus on the positive. We reviewed the sequence of activities in the intervention and discussed the decision to modify the interview protocol to acknowledge and honor the diversity of positive and negative experiences. Themes were presented on a flip chart, including selected quotes from the actual interview responses. Learning parables were used to explain and interpret themes and to create an understanding of the situational context or manner in which respondents had offered information about the theme.

Dream is the second D of the AI 4D model, where images of a possible future begin to take shape in the minds and imaginations of the organization members. Activities used in the feedback session design were selected to allow members of the staff to not only imagine but also actually experience the dream of a new positive future. Learning activities created the forum for the staff to engage with one another in new, positive ways. In this sense, the session became an adventure in search of new ways of engaging to bring out the best in each member. It was an active, unified search for new "life-giving" forces to redirect the negative energies of this warring system.

Experiential learning activities helped us to simulate and demonstrate the existing ability to work collaboratively and collectively. In a sense, it was the construction of a "unitary reality" accomplished artificially through the focus on a single group task. I have defined "unitary reality" as a temporal sense-making of collective singularity that joins individuals and synthesizes their actions and interactions, for a time, not all time. The experience of unity, however long or short in duration, has everlasting consequences, as does each step along a path to an imaged future. Temporality has particular importance in the achievement of unity, as it enables our understanding of an "experience of unity," not as some ideal future state of permanent harmony, but as frequent experiences of limited duration. As episodic experiences of unity become more frequent, enabled and facilitated by our learning from experience, the cumulative effect is accelerated movement of individuals and organizations toward a more sustained harmonious state of being. We had great success with two specific activities in this regard: the jigsaw puzzle and the unity quilt.

Two-hundred fifty jigsaw puzzle pieces were spread out on top of a small table at the back of the room. The group was invited to assemble the puzzle before the conclusion of the session. No other instructions were given. A picture on the cover of the puzzle box provided the vision of the outcome the group hoped to achieve. The absence of specific roles and responsibilities did not hinder their collective effort, as ambiguity became the challenge and not the problem for this task. Intrigued by the challenge, they became unified in the task of completing the puzzle, as they began to discover and design their own process.

The jigsaw puzzle activity provided an initial basis and experience of forward movement in the group. People shared various strategies for completing puzzles of this type. Others listened attentively, valuing input from others in a continual movement toward and away from the table. As more pieces were joined to form the picture, more and more staff became enthusiastically involved. When the puzzle was completed, the room erupted in applause, everybody hugging and jumping in celebration. After the celebration, we discussed our process, recounting the experience of our collective, unified success. Formed as a product of collaborative authorship, this new story outlined everyone's actions, intents, and feelings, including explanations of behaviors. They achieved a collective work through unified effort, and in the process established the outline and model of a new organizational story. Recounting the story became an exercise of collective storytelling, first creating and then telling their story, their way.

The successful process of solving the jigsaw puzzle offered metaphoric, conceptual, and concrete evidence of future possibilities. We were then able to use this concrete experience in discussion to replace the learning parables. Collectively and conceptually, they began to imagine and articulate unified possibilities for events in the future, moving beyond the negative past. This experience of unity and collective interpretation of contributing events provided a powerful concrete illustration and evidence of possibilities for the future. We had begun the process of altering the course of this organization and moving toward unity. This unified experience, the collective storytelling about it, and the earlier expressions of apology helped to break new ground in a landscape of healing and organizational restoration.

The unity quilt was the final activity. Each person was given a six-by-eight-inch swatch of craft felt and instructed to work individually to design a personal swatch. The completed personal swatch was to be a representation of the individual designer. An assortment of craft supplies was situated around the room; this required participants to move around to negotiate use of selected items. They were free to use any resources available, with the understanding that all material on the swatch should remain a part of the final product. After one hour of design and construction, the group formed a circle near the table with the completed quilt. Each person presented their swatch as a "reintroduction" of themselves to the group. Introductions completed, swatches were placed on the floor with each adjoining another until a collage of individual expressions formed the "unified" whole quilt. Again, they applauded the success of their effort and the beauty of what they created together.

The collective reflective account of the quilt construction differed slightly from that of the jigsaw puzzle, reflecting even greater insight. The group was able to contrast the difference between assembling multiple pieces of a puzzle, detached and outside of self, and joining more personal pieces of a quilt that represented a part of a newly constructed identity in this group. The group reflected upon the questions, "Who am I?" "How do I wish to be known by this group?" "How shall I attach myself to this group?" The reflective responses to these questions and the process of reintroductions with new alignments with others, also being reintroduced and realigned, seemed to allow the privilege of a new start, a more positive beginning.

EMERGENCE OF A NEW LIFE-GIVING FORCE

An unexpected dynamic in the process occurred as the workshop evolved. After the presentation of emergent themes and learning parables, people began to share other stories. They told about experiences of being isolated and unsupported, feeling disrespected, embarrassed, and not valued. These experiences helped to explain their feelings of pain, injury, and embarrassment. Unlike the interviews however, these accounts were presented in sensitive and caring language and tone. After hearing these disclosures, some participants actually apologized publicly to others for past actions and behaviors. The room was flooded with a new quiet emotion that we all felt and seemed to understand.

As the day progressed, we began to notice people engaged in conversations with individuals outside of their usual, bounded social network. As we listened, we became aware that new stories and public apologies had generated these new engagements and changed conversations. Apologies had become life-giving forces born from an acknowledgment of another's pain. Public apologies seemed to provide a bridge from the negative past to a more positive future by accepting responsibility for past behavior with an implicit invitation to reestablish relationships on the basis of changed expectations: hopes in place of fears.

We credit the modified interview protocol for seeding this break-through, as it demonstrated the "being" of valuing by providing the space for staff to be heard and honoring the undivided integrity of human experience that is both negative and positive. Learning parables served the group by making the variety of their human experiences available via an intentional construction to provoke thinking about new positive possibilities. Experiential learning activities simulated and demonstrated new, more positive ways of being and engaged the staff in active new storymaking. Through these experiences, the staff began the process of creating positive new memories to replace negative old ones. Not all matters were resolved during this time, but the acts of apology as the acknowledgment of another's pain were generative life-giving forces that clearly helped to liberate the group from its prison of a warring web of negativity and division.

Realizing Dreams and Designing the Future

Through the flip charts taped to the walls that captured the essence of the negative past, the jigsaw puzzle, and the unity quilt still prominently situated in the center of the room, the room had been transformed into a mosaic of historical, present, and future realities. We sat quietly for long periods in the midst of these kaleidoscopic realities. Before us were the catheterized themes of a negative past generated from an appreciative process that honored both positive and negative dimensions of lived experience. The jigsaw puzzle represented the evidence of possibility in collective action when the vision is clear and contributions varied and free. The unity quilt, more than anything, offered more personal but tangible evidence of a new beginning. The quilt's complete mosaic form illustrated a finished work accomplished from the contributions of many, a unified and collective work. The honoring and inclusion of their diversity had contributed to a beautiful piece and a new peace and wholeness in organization. We sat, taking it all in. Through the appreciative process of honoring the undivided human experience and discovering ways to join ourselves, people had felt valued. They reported feeling that having their experiences listened to, heard, and honored was affirming. They were then ready to move on.

Finally, the work of the third and fourth Ds of the 4D model, planning action for the organization's future, felt easier to accomplish through our active and intentional learning processes. A long and intense discussion helped us to come to the conclusion that change is possible, but would also be gradual. We also reached a consensus that the work of creating a new organizational future had definitely begun on this day.

The day-long session ended with a natural movement into the third phase of the appreciative inquiry model: design. The group formed a circle and a large group dialogue ensued. There was some abbreviated storytelling wherein the content of the stories had changed from a discussion of negative things that happened months earlier to the more positive experiences of collective visioning and collaborative work of this day. This ending dialogue session about a shared future produced several short-term action steps, some agreement about measurements, and a unanimous commitment to continued meetings, as a whole, until they achieved the more positive future they had begun to imagine together.

GENERATIVE LESSONS LEARNED

My attention is drawn to two aspects of this case that reveal both the challenge and the strength of the appreciative inquiry process. First, I consider the undeniable expression of negativity from people who are experiencing pain. We experienced the expression of negativity by the staff in this intervention as a determined refusal to suppress intense feelings of injury or painful experience in favor of an intentionally directed positive focus, prescribed as essential to the AI protocol. I offer my reflective account of how the process was modified in order to honor the integrity of experiences of participants, without denying my sense of integrity as it relates to "being" in an appreciative space with another. The modifications enriched the process and helped guide us to a path of unity.

Next, the use of storytelling as an undivided description of lived experience in the organization to provide deeper understanding of organizational experience is discussed. Through their eloquence and colorful interpretation, stories and parables provided thick descriptions of events and opened windows to view the organizational reality from the personal, lived experiences of its members. In this intervention, unified (undivided) stories that reported positive and negative experiences seemed to provide respondents with a vehicle through which to describe and make sense of their experiences, free from organizational sanctions or restrictions. The integrity of lived experience in the organization, described in storied accounts, offered insightful explanations of reality and provided a framework for excellent reflective analysis and a new understanding of events.

Honoring the Undivided Experience

Early in the process, appreciative inquiry interviewers were immediately confronted with the reality of negativity expressed in intense, often angry accounts of experience. The staff resisted our guidance to frame interview responses in appreciative terms. Reacting to the tenor of the AI interview, respondents described questions as "too positive" and unrealistic. Persistence by interviewers to solicit positive things about what was going right was met with a tenacious resistance to the point of refusal to answer any questions. One person arrived at the interview and announced, "If you don't let me answer the questions my way, I am not going to stay. Why should I sit here and just tell you what you want to hear? If you really want to help, you should listen to what we have to say."

The methodological imperative of appreciating or valuing only the positive seemed paradoxically limiting. It required the denial of expression of their feelings of negativity, which were "real" to respondents, in order to achieve the goals of the intervention and organization. This form of "emotional labor," where individual interests were being welded to the managerial interest of the intervention, was being resisted by the staff (Van Maanen & Kunda, 1989). They were unable (or unwilling) to exert the degree of emotional labor needed in order to set aside strong negative feelings about oppressive memos, disrespectful interactions, and lack of leadership and guidance. It is also entirely possible that we, the interviewers, were unwilling to exert a similar emotional labor initially, being protected from doing so by a structured, positive protocol. A complex mixture of intense emotions had been festering since the merger of the two organizations and was not to be denied. Consequently, it was evident that feedback or conclusions drawn from the inquiry that did not reflect or value the range and intensity of emotion would likely be considered by them as an inaccurate representation, not relevant or reflective of their "real" lived experience. Feedback is a critical element of any intervention process. It is a useful way to orient the group as to what process issues may exist. In order for the feedback to be useful or effective in this regard, however, it was essential that the data stand the test of valuing and appreciation, subject to the examination of those interviewed (Schein, 1988). It was important, therefore, to honor these expressions of negativity and include them in the process of discovery in order that the dream and design phases of the process were not compromised.

Sense-Making: Merging Integrities and Realities

The process of reconciling reactions to our interview protocol and the appreciative methodology was not an easy one. Our conscious decision to use the AI methodology as an intervention strategy was challenged now by an obvious lack of appreciation for an important dimension of human emotion and experience that was negative. It was a contest of integrities; a tension between the intentional, selective focus on the positive as a guiding principle of appreciative inquiry and the honoring of lived experience that includes both positive and negative dimensions. On the one hand, an intentional focus on the tacit but nonetheless real positive aspects of the past of these two agencies seemed totally "right" for this situation. On the other hand, refusal to acknowledge or include the reported negative responses seemed to marginalize an important dimension of human reality and compromise the integrity of foundational guiding principles of the appreciative stance to value "what is."

Stephen Carter (1996) offers a definition of integrity, with three essential dimensions of the root word "integer" that refer to a sense of wholeness. First, he emphasizes the significance of discernment of what is right and wrong. Next, it is important to take action on what you have discerned. Finally, it is important to say openly that you are acting on your understanding of right from wrong. Using Carter's definition, we felt compelled to acknowledge the dissonance of our own feelings during our empathetic engagement with the interviewees. To selectively disallow a category of responses would serve to decertify an important dimension of interpreted experience, rendering less important the structures of significance to this group. Alternatively, the appreciative process enables presentation of both negative and positive aspects of lived experience in an organization. The need for members of this organization to speak their truth in reality and be heard was significant. A requirement that negative experiences, as significant dimensions of human experience, be suppressed or denied or framed only in "appreciative terms" clearly privileged the process of AI over people, and subtly implied a lack of appreciation of an important part of their reality. This acknowledgment required action. A modification of our approach to the appreciative intervention was in order, as it was impossible to advance a conception of "valuing and appreciating" while ignoring the reality of emotions that reflected anger, injury, and wounding. Moreover, to Carter's third point, public sharing of our need to value and appreciate these integrities rather than to methodologically explicate the positive was compelling. The workshop discourse turned more positive as organization members observed and experienced our struggle to honor and value "what is" while moving toward the possibility of a more positive future state.

Power of Storytelling and Storymaking

A growing body of literature speaks to the value of storytelling in organizational analysis and intervention. Boje (1991) maintains that organizations are themselves storytelling systems and considers storytelling a key part of organizational members' sense-making and meaning making. Storied accounts of lived experience provide a mixture of rational and emotional interpretations of fantasy and reality. They make intricate details of one's life experience accessible to others in public discourse and enlarge our perspective with a layered account, as the narrative shifts backward, forward, and sideways through time, space, and various attitudes throughout the story. Articulated stories communicate and sharpen the collective or shared understanding of experiences through the telling and retelling of multiauthored stories (Boyce, 1995), and contribute to the building of community through common sense-making (Weick, 1993).

The unexpected outcome of public apologies and expressions of painful experience through storytelling created a sacred-like space of safety or collective centering for sense-making into which we were all gently drawn. I believe the catharsis of negativity actually began with the articulation of personal experience during the appreciative interviews. Modification of the interview format had itself begun a life-giving process, as it encouraged acts of authentic disclosure, with interviewees reporting their own truth, free from the demand to prove or defend a negative point of view. Details offered in stories and accounts of experience contributed valuable insight about personal values, attitudes, and behaviors previously not available in a conflicted environment where communication was limited and censored. Learning parables formed from these stories became a medium of communication that publicly and positively interpreted perceptions, emotion, and behavior that had previously been locked behind the wall of negativity. Parables offered the opportunity for multiple interpretations and various constructions of meaning. They were incredibly evocative in their power to promote understanding through articulated insight and public expressions of internal logic. With new information and insight available, members of the organization drew from and added to the storied interpretations, thus enhancing and expanding the understanding of the collective experience.

Important to this process was the appreciative stance of the interviewees, which honored the range of the dimensions of human experience. With the exception of one long-standing conflict, apologies were given and accepted. In the exceptional case, an agreement was made to continue the dialogue, working toward a resolution, after the sessions. Expressions of apology usually followed the pattern of referencing the list of emergent themes, which remained visible and prominent. Next a speaker would offer some anecdotal explanation as to why certain comments had been made. Then the speaker would offer an expression of regret for causing pain or injury to others. The ease of tensions, which had lasted for years, was begun. It was a dramatic demonstration of the power of the positive to overcome the presence of negativity. The hopes and dreams of a more positive, unified future not only seemed possible, but we had actually begun to experience them as a new organizational reality.

EPILOGUE

Returning to the objectives of the intervention, we were able to assess our success. One important objective was to understand the challenges of the agency and staff more clearly from their perspective. This was accomplished with the modified protocol and an interview process that honored the accounts of experience as reported. Another goal was to unify and revitalize agency staff and the board. The difficulty in this area seemed to be a lack of assimilation of purpose and missions, incorporating elements of each to create a new inclusive merged agency mission. The success of the jigsaw puzzle activity helped illustrate the importance of vision to accomplish tasks and mission. Participants commented that once they had seen the picture on the cover, it helped them to gain a sense of what to do and how to contribute to a successful, unified outcome. The valuing of a living vision and mission had begun in this group.

A new executive director was appointed two weeks after the session. He immediately involved staff in a participative process to develop a revised vision. The staff participated in meetings to establish work plans and communication strategy for clients and the community. Treatment teams became more clear about their priorities through the development of a broad, clear treatment philosophy. As a result of the intervention, and more specifically the feedback-workshop experience, position descriptions were reviewed and revised to align with the new, merged vision and mission. While it would be naïve to conclude that all boundaries have been removed, it is safe to say that the evidence of forgiving and healing offers new hope for unity, based upon communication processes demonstrated that day, in that group.

The experience of this application of AI speaks to many aspects of interventions to promote positive change in organizations. It highlights the tendency of appreciative methodology to privilege the positive aspects of organizational experience and calls our attention to the need to honor the multiple and undivided realities of human experience in organizations. As a practitioner, I have often felt more loyal to process than people. The experience and outcomes of this intervention assures my sense that honoring of the whole contributes to, rather than diminishes, the quality of the appreciative process and affirms the power of the positive to prevail and to heal in organizational processes.

Through the sharing of this case, the telling of this story, I hope also to provoke a closer examination of the use of appreciative inquiry processes in organization revitalization, restoration, and unity, particularly where radical and dramatic changes have occurred. To the extent that the telling of this story heightens awareness of the wholeness of people in their experience and the creative and varied ways those experiences are expressed, the practice of appreciative inquiry is strengthened.

6

Generative Metaphor Intervention: A New Approach for Working with Systems Divided by Conflict and Caught in Defensive Perception

Frank Barrett and David L. Cooperrider

Under conditions of intergroup and interpersonal defensiveness, how can an organization engage in dialogue seeking to create a common vision and a positive image of a collectively desired future? This dilemma has been faced by many managers and organization development (OD) consultants who have worked with groups paralyzed by anxiety, defensiveness, and negative attributions. Too often we have failed to understand the nature of human cognition that leads to the formation of negative stereotypes and self-perpetuating attributions. Our efforts to transform defensive routines, when attempted at all, have conventionally been problem focused. Direct efforts to solve such problems often heighten the very problems they attempt to solve: When attempts are made to make people conscious of their negative attributions toward others and of their defensive attributions in relationships, they all too frequently respond by becoming more defensive. How is it even possible then to foster dialogue among competing members of an organization whose impressions and judgments of one another have been well ingrained? We propose two remedies in this chapter:

1. Working at a tacit, indirect level of awareness through constructing a generative metaphor that deliberately fosters formation of new impressions and judgments allows new meanings to be given birth.

2. Building an appreciative context rather than a problem-solving context helps generate the positive affect required for building social solidarity and a renewed capacity to collectively imagine a new and better future.

This chapter is divided into four sections. First, we explore the dynamics leading to an experience of "stuckness" in a downward spiral of negative attribution and defensive posturing. Second, we introduce the concept of generative metaphor and argue that such metaphor invites new openings for fresh perception, especially when a deliberately supportive or appreciative environment of inquiry is constructed. Third, in the main body of the chapter, we illustrate the use of generative metaphor in a case study. Finally, we conclude with a set of propositions about how appreciative inquiry (AI) into a related domain or generative metaphor can liberate a group in ways that more conventional OD problem-solving methods could not begin to affect.

THE NATURE OF GETTING STUCK

When people are threatened with anxiety, there is a strong human tendency to deny parts of the world. When, for example, one feels threatened and begins to prepare oneself for a stressful event, one tends to bias many pieces of information as confirming the appraisal of threat. The active denial of the world to allay the threat of anxiety takes many forms, including avoided associations, numbness, flattened response, dimming of attention, constricted thought, memory failure, disavowal, and so on. Once judgments and theories about others have been formed, those judgments have a tendency to persevere even in the face of totally discrediting information, especially if one is engaged in forming a causal explanation to account for the impression or theory one has formed (Anderson, Lepper, & Ross, 1980). The simple process of explaining why one has a certain theory about someone may in fact have the unintended consequence of strengthening the impression and making it more resistant to change, even if the information upon which it is based is completely discredited. For example, imagine a situation in which a traditional team-building intervention is being done with a group of managers who are divided by competition, jealousy, and "turfism." A direct intervention, as advocated by many conflict-resolution theories, would call for managers to articulate why they see one another as troublesome or problematic. Following the perseverance effect in social cognition theory, once one puts forth a causal explanation for one's belief the belief is actually strengthened. Therefore, if one were to say one sees a coworker as crabby and unapproachable because the coworker is selfish, moody, and insecure, the chances would be greater that merely because one formed and articulated this causal explanation one's belief about the coworker would be stronger. One becomes even more convinced that the coworker is selfish, moody, and insecure.

What happens when people perform behaviors contrary to the stereotype we have formed? When people do perceive behavior in one another that is inconsistent with the original schemas, they may notice the inconsistency, but it often tends not to alter the original impression. Research has shown that while evidence that disconfirms an impression is noticed and remembered, the original impression itself is not altered. When subjects were shown information that was atypical of a previously formed stereotype, it actually facilitated their recall of the original stereotype. Seeing a basic incongruency may require more information processing, but actually facilitates recall of the original impression. So, for example, imagine again that one has a well-formed image of one's coworker as selfish, moody, and insecure. Even if the coworker were to engage in action contrary to this image (e.g., the coworker offers to take one out to lunch, or makes a large contribution to charity), one would process this atypical information, but the original stereotype would likely remain—and in all probability the negative image would paradoxically be strengthened. One would tend to explain the core incongruency in terms of the stereotype (recall that the act of putting forth an explanation will strengthen the original schema). So, to continue, one might then say to oneself, "He [or she] is only taking me to lunch because he [or she] wants something," or "He [or she] is contributing to charity because of feeling guilty about being so self-oriented." Thus, if we were to appreciate the nature of this dynamic when applied to traditional OD, we would see that many of our activities, such as diagnostic action research or encouraging direct and candid "confrontation meetings" among differing groups, may unintentionally reinforce those very dynamics they seek to amend.

Nobody has synthesized the processes of selective perception better than Goleman (1985), who argues that (1) the mind often protects itself against anxiety by dimming awareness, (2) this cognitive process creates a blind spot, a zone of blocked attention and self-deception, and (3) such blind spots occur at every level of system, from individuals to groups, organizations, and societies.

Similarly, it appears that one's present affective state or mood largely determines what one is able to perceive, learn about, or recall from memory. According to the work of Alice Isen and her colleagues (Isen, Shalker, Clark, & Karp, 1978), mood, cognition, and action form an inseparable triad and tend to create feedback loops of amplifying intensity. Studies have demonstrated, for example, that people who are "primed" into a negative mood state are able to recall significantly fewer pleasant memories of their past than people in a positive mood state. Likewise, it has been shown that a negative mood state cues a person to think about negative things (Rosenhan, Salvoey, & Hargis, 1981) and increases a person's capacity for perceiving mood-congruent or negative things in self and others (Isen & Shalker, 1982).

Hence, what we see from this important research is the natural human tendency to form judgments and notice traits in others based on previously formed categories or current mood states. Further, these categories and mood states are often primed and made ready to guide perception through social interaction. This process of cognitive cuing, which is part of the natural process of enculturation or socialization, often remains outside of a person's or group's awareness. Further, once impressions and judgments are formed, as in the halo effect or pygmalion dynamic in the classroom, they tend to persevere. Furthermore, when the context is marked by feelings of fear, threat, anxiety, and protectiveness, the dynamics of perception become even more entrenched. Under conditions of fear and anxiety, individuals and groups will dim awareness and deny what is going on in the world. Hence, people often guard against seeing the very things that might allay their fears. To understand this paradox is to understand one of the central challenges of working with systems divided by conflict and caught in defensive perception.

GENERATIVE METAPHOR FOR OPENING PERCEPTION

With all these forces acting to constrict awareness and attention in ways that people seem ill prepared to control, under what conditions can their well-ingrained interpersonal perceptions be expanded: How can they get unstuck? How, as OD practitioners, can we intervene to help groups out of self-perpetuating defensive strategies without the direct and often reinforcing confrontation of these defensive routines? To answer these questions, we discuss the concept of generative metaphor (Srivastva & Barrett, 1988) as a way of supporting the cultivation of fresh perceptions and the acquisition of new schemas of others. First, we being with a discussion of important properties or principles of metaphor.

Principles of Metaphor

Metaphor Is an Invitation to See the World Anew

Metaphor presents a way of seeing something as if it were something else. Metaphor transfers meaning from one domain into another and thereby enriches and enhances both domains. Metaphor acts as a way of organizing perceptions and provides a framework for selecting and naming characteristics of an object or experience by asserting similarity with a different, seemingly unrelated object or experience. For example, in the metaphor "man is a wolf," the ravaging, predatory nature of man is given focus; whereas the metaphor "man is a flower" focuses more on the delicate, beautiful nature of human beings blooming to fruition and going through seasonlike changes. Metaphors are, therefore, filters that screen some details and emphasize others. Further, metaphor acts as a subtle transaction between contexts, as an entire set of characteristics can almost spontaneously be transformed from one set to another to create new contextual meaning. For example, in the metaphor "man is a wolf," one's picture of man acquires more colorful detail: he is seen hairy and on all fours, saliva dripping from his mouth, with piercing and ferocious eyes and long fangs awaiting his prey. Also, in the interaction between domains, the wolf begins to take on human qualities: One sees the wolf as purposeful and intent, having feelings and thoughts.

Because metaphor can instantaneously fuse two separate realms of experience, it is transformative. As Nisbett and Ross (1985) suggest, metaphor is powerful because of its capacity of semantic and cognitive reconstruction:

Metaphor is, at its simplest, a way of proceeding from the known to the unknown. It is a way of cognition in which the identifying qualities of one thing are transferred in an instantaneous, almost unconscious flash of insight to some other thing that is by remoteness or complexity unknown to us. The test of essential metaphor . . . is not any rule of grammatical form, but rather the quality of semantic transformation that is brought about. (p. 4)

The potential for semantic transformation is what makes artists, poets, leaders, and scientists alike so attuned to the power of metaphor and aware of its potential for directing perception, enriching awareness, and transforming the world. Good metaphors provoke new thought, excite us with novel perspectives, vibrate with multivocal meanings, and enable people to see the world with fresh perceptions not possible in any other way.

Metaphor Facilitates the Learning of New Knowledge

In confronting radically new knowledge, metaphor can be useful. As anomaly is created, an experience is apprehended that is outside one's present frame. It is through immersion in the experience, active thought experimentation, testing, and correction that expansion of cognitive frames begins to occur. Thus, for the young science student who is cognitively blocked in trying to grasp the structure of the atom, the metaphor "the atom is a solar system" could indeed be useful. The student might begin to "see" neutrons and electrons revolving around the gravitational center. He or she might then engage in such active thought experimentation long enough to allow a new understanding of the atom to emerge.

Metaphor Provides a Steering Function for Future Actions and Perceptions

Social order and social structure are not preordained, but are achieved through members' construction of reality. Metaphors provide the social group with a whole set of categories through which the social group interprets the world. In the nineteenth century, for example, Marxist theory operated according to an embryonic metaphor. Social orders were seen as proceeding from the "womb" of preceding others, with transformation periods likened to the "birth" of a new order. The state of capitalism was seen as carrying the "seeds" of its own destruction. These metaphors spawn categories and terms that drive people to initiate actions congruent with the metaphors informing their beliefs. Another example of how a group's or society's root metaphors can provide a steering function for future action is that of U.S. involvement in the Vietnam War. It can be argued that this involvement was connected to the cognitive categories that emerged from one root metaphor: the domino theory. Once the United States began to see communism taking over countries, causing them to topple one after another, policy makers were left with little choice but to stop this "evil" momentum.

Metaphor Invites Active Experimentation

This experimentation is in areas of rigidity and helps people overcome self-defeating defenses. Milton Erikson's work in psychotherapy provides perhaps the best example of this principle (Haley, 1973). Erikson's approach is to circumvent the patient's areas of resistance and to work with the neurosis indirectly and metaphorically. Learning becomes transferred to the area of difficulty, and "suddenly" the patient is able to change previously rigid perceptions and behavior. Erikson discusses, for example, the case of a couple having sexual difficulties. Rather than confront this delicate area directly where patients resist revealing their insecurities, he begins to work at the metaphorical level. He proposes that the couple enjoy a long, leisurely meal, taking time to enjoy the succulence and sweetness of the food rather than rush through to satisfaction. Together they discuss their eating habits: The man's tendency to rush to the main course of meat and potatoes, the woman's preference for leisurely enjoyment of the appetizer, the atmosphere, the pre-meal activities, and the preparation. Erikson then deliberately instructs the couple to engage in another meal and this time to prolong each course and attend to their positive sensations. Such experimentation begins to have an effect on their sexual relationship: Learning is subtly transferred to the area of difficulty and the couple begins to change their behavior. Defensive routines are not confronted head on; they are circumscribed. Problems are not identified, discussed, analyzed, or even challenged. In fact, Erikson is careful to avoid such discussion, because the couple, as he explains, are least in need of further "education" about the unfortunate mess their lives are in. They already know about it. Thus, it is active experimentation and involvement in the metaphorical domain that helps the couple overcome resistances in the area of rigidity. Imagine, for example, what would happen if Erikson used a direct problem-solving approach with the troubled couple. Suppose he were to sit down and face the man and say, "So what seems to be the problem you are having in bed with your wife? We must discover the causes of this dysfunction because it appears you're not making her happy." Such an approach would challenge the man's self-esteem and in all likelihood trigger defensiveness, insecurity, embarrassment, and painful self-consciousness. Under such conditions of threat, it is unlikely that either person would be open to learning or rational behavior change. Rather, each person would begin to look for reasons and excuses to explain his or her behavior. Perhaps each would even begin to blame the other and possibly experience a worsening of the sexual relationship.

Generative metaphor, then, is an invitation to see anew, to facilitate the learning of new knowledge, to create new scenarios of future action, and to overcome areas of rigidity. There is a subtle, indirect component to generative metaphor. Fresh insights are transferred instantaneously, almost unconsciously, bringing about semantic and perceptual changes.

A CASE STUDY: THE MEDIC INN

The Medic Inn is a 380-room hotel facility with two dining rooms, a bar, several meeting rooms, and a large ballroom. It is owned and operated by the Midwest Clinic Foundation (MCF), a large tertiary-care center with a 1,000-bed hospital. The Medic Inn was privately owned and operated by a hotel chain until it was purchased by MCF in 1981 to offer lodging and food to patients and their families. MCF recently expanded and built a new, large clinic facility on the east side of the hotel, and with the expansion the hotel was also renovated: A large, elegant lobby was built, the dining room was renovated, and the top floors were converted into elegant, high-priced rooms especially designed to serve foreign dignitaries.

While changes were made in the physical facilities, MCF retained the managers of the hotel to operate it. As one MCF administrator put it, "We're not in the hotel business and we really know nothing about running one, so we decided to keep the people who were on board." The authors were originally hired in 1984 to do a benefit, compensation, and job audit through the human resources division of MCF. As an entry intervention, however, we proposed to do an employee attitude survey. We met with the four top managers of the Medic Inn, and they belatedly agreed to our proposal to conduct a survey of all 260 employees.

The managers of MCF were suspicious of us from the beginning. It soon became clear that their suspicion and distrust extended to the Medic Square Hotel Company, the for-profit group of administrators set up by MCF. In conversation with the general manager, it became apparent that he was afraid of losing his job. We conducted an employee attitude survey and continued to work with the group in team-building sessions and by facilitating various task-force meetings. What became increasingly clear after almost fourteen months of working with the group was that the management group was divided by interpersonal and interdepartmental conflicts and had a history of little cooperation. The four top managers were aware that the administrators of MCF wanted the Medic Inn to become a four-star facility, a designation granted to high-quality hotel and restaurant service facilities. Since the Medic Inn had a long way to go to achieve this status, this goal added pressure to the group. It is difficult in a short case description to give a flavor of the degree of interdepartmental conflict, but we cite a few examples to help clarify the climate.

Among the top four managers—the general manager, the manager of food and beverage, the rooms manager, and the accountancy manager—there was a history of backbiting and what they referred to as "sandbagging" one another. When the four held their weekly planning meetings, the meetings were laborious, and they had a difficult time arriving at a decision. What follows is one example of the kind of exchange that occurred between them. This dialogue comes from a meeting that occurred approximately two months before the intervention we describe in this chapter:

JOHN (general manager): What's changed since we started these regular meetings?

TIM (manager of food and beverage): Nothing.

FRED (manager of accounting): I agree. All we do is bicker.

Long pause.

RICK (manager of rooms): There's more separation between the Food and Beverage Department and the Rooms Department than ever before.

Long silence.

TIM: A year ago we agreed to move toward a four-star status. We've taken care of some of the physical things and it looks nice, but we haven't taken care of the people things. We still don't have a common goal. And before we even try to talk about a common goal, I want to hear a personal commitment from people. I don't feel it, I don't see it. Sometimes I hear people say it. But I wonder how deep people's commitments are to this. I don't know where Rick is.

RICK: Could we keep this discussion on a business level and keep personal relationships out of it?

TIM: The way some of the departments have been run, I'm not sure everybody even wants to be part of this team.

In private conversations, the four managers were even more candid about their frustration with one another and their hostility. One said of another: "Tim thinks he's better than everybody else. He blasts and sandbags people behind their backs."

Among the next level of managers—thirteen middle managers who reported directly to the four top managers—interdepartmental conflict was also evident. This is how some members described the group.

The people are confrontive and insecure. It seems like people are involved in too many power plays instead of just working together. Ron [a food service manager] and Fredricka [a rooms manager] can't even talk to each other. They're supposed to work together to plan the new construction of the 17th floor dining room, and every time they try to discuss something they end up yelling at each other. I think they actually try and make each other look bad.

I think people are jealous of each other here. It seems like food and beverage managers get raises all the time. They get taken care of. We [room managers] are ignored when it comes to raises and promotions.

Members were defensive, and some felt that their efforts to help and cooperate were treated with suspicion and interpreted as intrusions. This frequently led to the withdrawal of energy.

The other day I told Fredricka about the party of 30 we are catering a week from Thursday. I tried to talk to her very carefully and gently. I asked her if there's anything we could do to help. She bit my head off again just like I knew she would. She goes, "Nobody ever tells us anything. You think I don't know how to do my job here or what?" Stuff like that. It makes me want to just avoid her.

The interpersonal tension and competition that existed became an obstacle to people's capacity to generate a vision and strategic plan for the future of the Medic Inn and what needed to happen to make it a four-star hotel. Most members found it difficult to generate ideas and struggled with a pessimistic response and deficiency orientation.

When managers met to discuss the future plan for the Medic Inn, there was little sense of hope or belief in their own efficacy to create the future. Many members generated passive, cynical accounts, often belying a fear that MCF would withdraw support for any strategy they enacted. As one manager put it, "MCF has not given us a vision. I don't trust the plan they talk about. They keep calling to get new numbers. That shows how insecure it is. It's a game they keep rewriting. . . . It will just be a cost decision and they will keep spending it [money] until someday they'll say, 'This has gotten out of hand,' and I'll be gone."

Members continued to generate similar scripts of impending doom. During planning sessions, accounts of fear and debilitating thoughts emerged:

FRED: They've given us a blank check.

KARL: We get money way too easy. No one rejects anything we ask for. Doesn't that bother anybody? Am I the only one who's bothered by it?

RICK: I agree. I' m just waiting for the hammer to fall. . . . I'm afraid they're going to wake up and discover this thing can't work like this. There is no way. They're going to pull the plug on us.

The group needed to engage in dialogue in order to develop consensus about goals and a vision of what was possible in becoming a four-star, excellent organization. And yet there was an inherent dilemma: How could a group of people divided by competition and turfism engage in dialogue with one another? Further, how could a group with depressed aspirations talk about how it could become a four-star hotel? When they looked at themselves and at one another, they saw only deficiency and unmet expectations. It was as if the worst was always expected; it just hadn't happened yet.

As consultants, we were faced with a dilemma: The traditional problem-solving approach in HR and OD would call for us to analyze the dilemmas in the group, feed back the problem themes, and ask the group members to face the issues and generate solutions. So ingrained is the problem-solving mentality that most OD consultants and action researchers are scarcely able to envision alternatives. The language of the field continues to be guided by a deficiency model of the world (Cooperrider & Srivastva, 1987). It is as if the field itself revolved around a root metaphor that says "organizing is a problem to be solved" and therefore OD equals problem solving; to do good action research is to solve "real problems."

When organizations are approached from the conventional deficiency perspective of the discipline, all properties and modes of organizing are scrutinized for their dysfunctional but potentially solvable problems. According to Levinson (1972), therefore, organizational analysis is done to "discover and resolve these problems. . . . The consultant should look for experience[s] which appear stressful to people. What kinds of occurrences disrupt or disorganize people" (p. 10). Similarly, French (1969) advises that the OD practitioner look for problems:

Typical questions in data gathering or "problem sensing" would include: What problems do you see in your group, including problems between people that are interfering with getting the job done the way you would like to see it done? And what problems do you see in the broader organization? Such open-ended questions provide latitude on the part of respondents and encourage a reporting of problems as the individual sees them. (pp. 23–24)

As consultants to the hotel we were faced with a dilemma: Traditional problem-solving approaches would have called for us to (1) identify the key problems of the group (the "felt needs"), (2) analyze the causes of the problems, (3) feed back the problem themes, and (4) ask the group members to candidly face up to their issues and generate collaborative action plans. We decided that it would be counterproductive to do this. Members already knew about the tensions in the group. They already had multiple logics and compelling theories to explain and justify the current state. In fact, it occurred to us that the last thing the group needed at this point was further education—a more sophisticated education—on the dilemmas and seriousness of their plight. To face these issues and to develop elaborate analyses of the causes did not seem to be productive, and in fact might well have only heightened awareness of the tensions, constrained possible new perceptions of one another, and depressed aspirations even further. As in the myth of the two-headed hydra, we were beginning to believe that any one problem directly eliminated would be quickly replaced by two more. Our task was to break out of the current frame altogether.

Rather than ask the group members to directly face their tension, to become introspective, and to look at themselves and at their own problems, we proposed that they become active inquirers, focusing on a domain outside their own. In the rest of this section we outline exactly what we did by discussing the four stages in what we now call the Generative Metaphor Intervention Process (GMIP), including (1) journey into metaphor, (2) poeticizing the world, (3) possibility expansion, and (4) return to the original domain.

Step 1: Journey into Metaphor

In an effort to enable the group to break through its ingrained schemas, interpersonal stereotypes, static perceptions, and dimmed awareness to protect against intrusions of anxiety, we proposed a generative metaphor for the organization; that is, we constructed a situation in which the system could creatively focus attention on another domain, in this case that of another organization. Our choice of metaphor (another organization) was guided by two considerations. First, it was felt that, by definition, the metaphor needed to be related to but sufficiently different from the Medic Inn itself. To develop a transaction across contexts, we needed a refocusing of the group's attention on something new and potentially evocative. Second, there was the challenge of stimulating interest: What was it that would capture the group's excitement on a broad and collective level?

The solution was to find an organization in the same service industry, but one whose mission, market niche, and level of performance departed dramatically from those of the Medic Inn. Significant as well, it was felt that the journey into metaphor should in fact be a journey. The task was to cultivate a sense of adventure to help shift the group's frame of reference away from historical reality and into the realm of anticipatory reality. The idea was to use the journey into metaphor as a way of refocusing attention not only onto another physical domain, but onto another temporal domain as well—in this case, away from the strictures of the past toward the unbridled opportunities of the future. Following our earlier discussion, an anomaly must be introduced that stimulates active thought experimentation and subsequent expansion of cognitive frames.

The introduction of anomaly began with a prescription to the top three levels of management. We proposed (1) an immediate elimination of the many interpersonal problem-solving meetings that were taking place, and (2) the creation of a representative task force to plan a collective journey to Chicago's famous Tremont Hotel, one of the finest four-star hotel properties in the country. At the same time, we acknowledged the many interpersonal and intergroup difficulties throughout the Medic Inn, but suggested these be "put on hold," that time would probably have to take care of things. We argued that at this point the group did not need not to solve all its problems. It needed first to experience becoming a "learning system," free from the day-to-day task of running the hotel. From that point on, we resisted all attempts on the part of the Medic Inn managers to draw us into a problem-solving mode. We deliberately guided conversations away from the areas of most difficulty and consciously began stimulating and nurturing conversations that resonated with a sense of excitement, adventure, and positive anticipation about the journey to come.

Step 2: Poeticizing the World

Arrangements were made with the Tremont Hotel. The visit with thirty managers from the Medic Inn would take place not immediately, but in five months. We reasoned that the sheer anticipation of the trip and the idea of a significant adventure together would prove to be as important as the journey itself. Having placed a sense of collective positive anticipation at the foreground of the group's consciousness, we wanted to keep it alive as long as possible. As it turned out, this element—the creation of a positive anticipatory ethos—became a powerful effective force in the building of social solidarity. We reasoned that it would be out of such strength—this new sense of connection—that the Medic Inn would later be able to grow beyond its current deficiencies and difficulties.

The design of the journey into metaphor called for a five-day visit. The first day was to include a brief site visit of the Tremont Hotel and then an eight-hour workshop on a unique method of organizational analysis called appreciative inquiry. Day two was to feature an organization-wide analysis of the Tremont, conducted by the thirty Medic Inn managers. Their task, put briefly, was to enter the field setting to make as many observations and conduct as many interviews of Tremont staff as possible in an eight-hour day. As explorers, their focus was to be selective. Their task was to cognitively bracket all seeming imperfections and deficiencies at the Tremont in order to discover those factors that exhibited fundamental strength and value in terms of the system's people, its management process, its culture, and methods of organization. Deliberately appreciative in nature, the inquiry into the new domain was to revolve around a number of core questions.

1. What were the peak moments in the life of the hotel—the times when people felt most alive, most energized, most committed, and most fulfilled in their involvements?
2. What was it that Tremont's staff members valued most about themselves, their tasks, and the organization as a whole?
3. Where excellence had been manifested, what were the organizational factors (structures, leadership approaches, systems, values, etc.) that most fostered realization of excellence?
4. What were the most significant embryonic possibilities, perhaps latent within the system, that signified realistic possibilities for an even better organization?

The overarching aim of the organizational analysis workshop was to reawaken the Medic Inn management team's "appreciative eye." Building on the philosophy of appreciative organizational inquiry (as outlined in Cooperrider & Srivastva, 1987), we emphasized learning how to perceive organizations as creative constructions, as entities that are alive, vital, and emergent. More than a method or technique, the appreciative mode of inquiry was presented as a way of living with, being with, and participating in the life of a human system in a way that draws one to inquire beyond superficial appearances to the deeper life-generating essentials and potentials of organizational existence. The appreciative eye, we proposed, is what allows one to value that which has fundamental value; it allows one to see what Bruner (1986) speaks of as the "immensity of the commonplace," or, in Joyce's reverent phrase, "the epiphanies of the ordinary." During the training we contrasted the conventional problem-solving model with the stages of appreciative inquiry (see Figure 6.1), and did some skill-building role plays to prepare the group for appreciative interviewing. Most important, a context was formed through philosophical discussion of appreciation as a way of knowing and relating to the world. Diverse quotations (as cited in Cooperrider & Srivastva, 1987) begin to give a flavor of the spirit we were working to cultivate:

Figure 6.1
Training Notes on Appreciative Inquiry

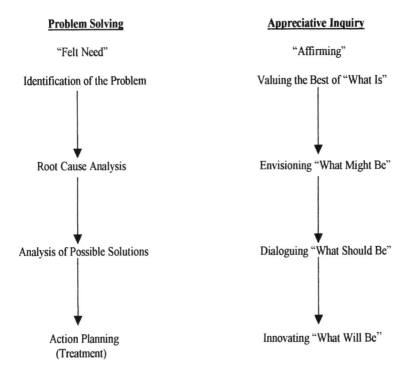

Problem Solving	Appreciative Inquiry
"Felt Need"	"Affirming"
Identification of the Problem	Valuing the Best of "What Is"
↓	↓
Root Cause Analysis	Envisioning "What Might Be"
↓	↓
Analysis of Possible Solutions	Dialoguing "What Should Be"
↓	↓
Action Planning (Treatment)	Innovating "What Will Be"
Basic Assumption: Organizing Is a Problem to Be Solved	Basic Assumption: Organizing Is a Miracle to Be Embraced

[Appreciation] thus makes immortal all that is best and most beautiful in the world. . . . It exalts the beauty of that which is most beautiful. . . . It strips the veil of familiarity from the world, and lays bare and naked its sleeping beauty, which is in the spirit of its forms.

Shelley

As soon as man does not take his existence for granted, but beholds it as something unfathomably mysterious, thought begins. . . . Ethical affirmation of life is the intellectual act by which man ceases simply to live at random.

Schweitzer

The most beautiful and profound emotion one can feel is a sense of the mystical. . . . It is the power of all true science.

Einstein

If I were to wish for anything, I should not wish for wealth and power, but for the passionate sense of the potential, for the eye which, ever young and ardent, sees the possible. Pleasure disappoints, possibility never. And what wine is so foaming, what so fragrant, what so intoxicating, as possibility!

Kierkegaard

One final note here is important. As participants began to experiment with the appreciative mode, we observed a relaxation of tensions, a new climate of lightness and freedom, playfulness and laughter, and a shift from the language of problem solving to the language of learning (e.g., "I wonder . . . what I'll discover about the Tremont's front desk operations"). Part of the relaxation of tension was due to all the participants' attention being turned away from themselves as a group. The new common gaze was on the Tremont. At no time did we suggest to the Medic Inn managers that they might begin to look at themselves appreciatively. The entire emphasis was on bringing attention to another domain.

Step 3: Co-Creation of Possibility

The next day began with immersion in the experience. It was a day of data collection, active experimentation, and attention to the details in the metaphor domain. Again, the purpose of this approach was to help the Medic Inn group become a learning system—to help them learn about themselves—but in a subtle, indirect way by immersing themselves in the life and detail of another system by using an appreciative mode of inquiry.

Arrangements were made for the Tremont staff to meet with members of the Medic Inn staff. The Medic Inn group conducted interviews with their counterparts as well as members from other departments. So, for example, the Medic Inn banquets manager interviewed not only the Tremont banquets manager, but also the rooms manager. They not only interviewed staff members, but because they stayed at the Tremont as guests, they were instructed to note in their journals as many other features as possible. They collected numerous details, for example, on how service was delivered, how their beds were made, how the washrooms were cleaned, how food was delivered, and how employees talked to one another and to guests. In addition to noticing physical layouts, they collected data on how employee meetings were run, who attended and what issues were discussed, and how training programs were conducted.

The following day of data analysis was designed for dialogue and reflection on the experience in the related domain. After dividing the Medic Inn managers into mixed subgroups, we asked for reports on every discovery. Indeed, the managers were keen observers. The groups generated list upon list of a myriad of factors that were found to be associated with organizational excellence. And the data were inspiring. Said one manager, "I can't believe the things that housekeeping does. What they do in terms of employee recognition and involvement is so simple—but it works. Their room exhibitions are something any hotel could begin immediately, at no cost!"

The managers of the Medic Inn were beginning to give full voice to their own highest aspirations and values. During the "report-outs" it was not uncommon for people to "wander beyond" their data. Extrapolating from the best of "what was," the Medic Inn managers began to envision "what might be." For five and one-half hours the group discussed its most interesting and exciting discoveries. The energy level was high. Communications were flowing. Then the group members were given one more important task: They were to take the best of what they could find at the Tremont and use that to create a visionary portrait—a genetic blueprint—of the ideal four-star hotel operation. This portrait was to be shared the next day with all the Tremont staff in the form of a feedback meeting. It was to be given to the Tremont as a "gift."

A key point is that the Medic Inn managers were not merely articulating their findings. They, in concert with one another, were creating new values and new possible ways of seeing organizational life through the act of valuing. Equally important, the attention was again focused on another domain. Among other things, this encouraged greater creativity in the envisioning process. Because it was not "their vision" for their hotel, the group members were freed from their habitual cynicism, doubt, and obstacle identification. Nascent ideas were given a chance. People experienced being listened to and heard. The group had become an aesthetic forum for sharing and crafting new meaning. It had become a safe place, even if only indirectly, for people to share their aspirations, dreams, and images of possibility.

What became increasingly clear as the members were engaged in this exercise was that, given this task, they were able to make private aspirations public ones. There were few obstacles due to defensiveness or negative attributions toward one another, ostensibly because the subject matter related to something other than themselves. In the meantime, they were becoming less strange to one another and less constricted in their exchanges. Indeed, people were beginning to experience more connection than disconnection, more consensus than dissensus, and more things to value about one another than to devalue.

In one unexpected transaction, for example, the two managers who were most at odds agreed publicly to "bury the hatchet." They literally had not spoken to each other in over six months. The group applauded as the feud was put to rest with an open hug. One of the two broke out in uncontrollable laughter, exclaiming that he couldn't believe he agreed with almost everything the other person said.

Step 4: Designing the Shared Future

On the last day, we suggested that the group members direct their attention to their own organization and envision and imagine what activities and plans they could engage in to begin to achieve excellence. Again, we were surprised at the unexpectedly high level of energy and the number of creative ideas that people generated. Unlike the group process exhibited before the Chicago retreat, this one left us feeling as if we were observing a totally different collectivity. Members were able to wish, to imagine possibilities for themselves. Whereas before they saw only deficiency in one another, they now talked about one another's potential as we led them through a role-negotiation activity. For example, the dining room manager, who had frequently been at odds with the housekeeper, sent the following message at the end of the workshop: "I never realized how much we take your work for granted. You have a tough, thankless job . . . and by the way, you're a nice person." Through renewed interpersonal ties such as these, discourse took on a whole new rational tone and substance. Broad consensus was reached on five primary dimensions of what would constitute a four-star hotel. At the end of the retreat, after discussing details of uniforms, behavioral norms, and policies, the group formulated, for the first time, a mission statement for the Medic Inn. Aspirations were liberated and a whole new sense of hope was stimulated. As one participant summed up, "The decisions and strategies agreed to here will completely change our future."

In the rest of this chapter we look more closely at the consequences of the generative metaphor intervention by looking at specific changes in the discourse of the groups in the months immediately following the Tremont retreat.

CONSEQUENCES OF THE GENERATIVE METAPHOR INTERVENTION

Any group, in a sense, is held together by a collective image or script that anticipates possible action. Prior to the Chicago retreat, the Medic Inn management group subscribed to a deficiency script for possible action. They did not imagine that it was possible to plan a positive future for themselves as a group. The horizon of meaning marked by this script triggered the negative images and schemas that managers held of one another. As a result of the generative metaphor intervention, a number of transformational consequences can be discerned.

First, there was a liberation of aspirations and expressions of preferences for the future. One consequence of the generative metaphor intervention was that it altered the collective horizon of possible meanings, expanding members' beliefs about the kind of actions possible in creating the future of the hotel. Following the Tremont experience, members began to put forth new notions of possible action in tentative, metaphorical language. At the first planning meeting following the retreat, members began to discuss what the Medic Inn should "look like." They began to propose what the bell stand and front desk should look like. An entire list of renovations and alterations was proposed by the group. There emerged a "four-star" language to reflect images of uniforms, behavioral norms, policies, and procedures. Members from different departments who previously would barely speak to one another began to develop a common language as details for physical revisions and personnel moves were discussed.

Once this common language grounded the group, there were expressions of hope and liberated aspirations. Members began to make reference to possible futures and abandoned the previous script of cycles of vengeance that had locked them into referring to past behavior. Members began to express preferences and wishes for the hotel's future.

"You know, I'd like to see more energy from the employees . . ."
"What got me really was the coffee club they started [at the Tremont] and I wondered, why wouldn't we do something like that if we could."
"We could meet monthly if we decide and . . ."

Such talk represents a liberation from old static structures. For this group, it can easily be argued that discourse of this kind marked the beginning of its empowerment to create–recreate the sociocultural world in alignment with its values. But first, something else needed to be addressed.

There needed to be a reinterpretation of the past in terms of ideological conflicts rather than in terms of interpersonal tension or personal deficiency. Members began to reframe the conflict-ridden past as a symptom of a "divided house" that lacked a common vision (note that even the choice of language—"divided house"—presupposes that members have developed an image of what a "united house" looks like). Reframing the past in these terms triggered a process whereby members began to attribute causality for interpersonal tension to a larger social–ideological framework. Conflicts among individuals could no longer be seen as resulting from personality deficiencies that reside inside of members. Rather, they had come to be seen as manifestations of an ideological split between departments and department managers. A forthcoming example illustrates this point.

Members began to imagine that future planning for the hotel should be a collective endeavor rather than something top managers do. It became legitimate for members to confront and hold one another to the commitments made by the "Chicago Group." Whereas frequent references had previously been made to those "know-nothings on top who have their heads in the sand," there emerged a new script for who could legitimately enter the dialogue and planning sessions. A new language emerged that remained active for years after the intervention. Members continued to use the term "Chicago Group," conjuring up reminders of the commitments made and the possible actions proposed by different departments. Not only was it deemed legitimate for the sixteen managers to engage in the planning process, but it became legitimate for a middle manager to confront one of the top managers in the name of the Chicago Group. When members exhibited what was considered dysfunctional or unsupportive behavior, they were often challenged. After two monthly meetings, one of the members was dissatisfied with a top manager's directions and addressed him: "I don't know how we're supposed to do that. What about Chicago? Have we forgotten about Chicago?"

Six months after the Chicago retreat, an interpersonal conflict between two managers from different departments surfaced in regard to how a customer complaint had been handled. The issue was discussed at a meeting of the Chicago Group, and as the conversation progressed it became clear that other such recent incidents reflected a difference in ideological interpretation. As the group began to discuss the troublesome area, they began to discover that the two manager's differences were emerging from the different ideological signals they were receiving from their top managers. Finally, one member addressed the group: "It's becoming clear that Kelly thinks what he's doing is right and Felicia thinks that what she is doing is right. And they're not getting this out of thin air. It must be a difference between you two guys [she points to Tim and Rick, the heads of food and beverage and rooms departments, respectfully]. You guys need to get your heads together."

The top management team was appalled, and after a short discussion in private agreed that negotiation was needed and planned an off-site retreat for the next month. When the time came for them to address the issue at the retreat, there was a new urgency in their voices. As Tim put it, "The Chicago group noticed something and they're right, we're marching to two different drummers. We have to straighten it out. We owe it to them, actually. We'll look like fools if we don't."

To cite another incident, eight months after the retreat, Tim, the food and beverage director, was overheard making a statement criticizing the service delivery in the rooms department. That afternoon at the regular staff meeting, Jean, the front desk manager, confronted the group: "I overheard a remark today made by one of the food and beverage managers that somehow the Rooms Department is holding this hotel back. Excuse me, but I thought we went to Chicago just to stop this kind of thing—to be a team. If someone has a complaint about how we are doing, he should bring it up in the open."

On the surface, this incident looks like a return to the old divisiveness and turfism. But upon closer inspection, we can see some key developmental differences. First, members now have a shared script for what it means to talk openly to one another, to explicitly challenge one another's tacit assumptions. Prior to the Chicago retreat, there was no script to imagine what a conversation called "confronting the departmental split" or "challenging a top director" might sound like. Second, members now have a denotative language ("Chicago," the "Chicago Group," "team") that carries rich connotations. When one member says, "What about Chicago?" there are a whole series of reverberations of meaning triggered for each member, tied to a previously unimagined picture of a team working toward a four-star rating. Third, previously disjointed members were able to jointly create scripts for possible action. They were now able to put forth possibilities that were not contingent upon eliminating competing interpretations. Whereas previously subgroups would bond by creating negative attributions of outgroup members or other subgroups, members could now bond around possible common futures. People previously seen as incompatible had become imagined as belonging in the same room.

Last, there was a reframing of the purpose of the hotel. Eventually, through continual dialogue, the group's critical reasoning began to take shape. For approximately ten months the group continued to meet around strategic plans and to propose unique social and physical changes at the Medic Inn. The data collected from the Tremont continued to act as a subtle conduit to trigger ideas and necessary actions. Members, however, began to debate about the appropriateness of instituting some of the Tremont features at the Medic Inn. The Tremont, after all, was a luxury hotel designed to serve downtown business guests. The Medic Inn was built to serve the medical needs of patients and guests at MCF.

Questions were raised around certain details that pushed members to reflect on the unique purpose of their hotel, and on such issues as the need for a swimming pool, the need for a valet parking service, the appropriateness of twenty-four-hour room service, and the appropriateness of building a first-class restaurant that might exclude middle-class guests. Each of these ideas was debated, and some were approved while others were discarded as "inappropriate for a hotel that was built to support a medical facility." As differences emerged, members began to differentiate between the Tremont and the Medic Inn and to propose a unique purpose for the Medic Inn. Finally, members came to the conclusion that the traditional market-driven thinking that drives the Tremont and other hotels did not apply to the Medic Inn. As one manager put it,

Let's face it. We're unique. We can't think like the Tremont. We're not here to make a profit from business guests. According to strict-profit sense, they shouldn't even give money to build anything in this hotel. But we're beginning to realize, we're not in the hotel business. This isn't a regular hotel. We're here to serve the Medic Foundation and the participants.

Eventually, fewer and fewer references were made to the programs at the Tremont Hotel as members began to create a unique sense of identity for the Medic Inn. The imaginative expansion that began in Chicago continued beyond even the consultants' expectations. To cite just one example, the group instituted a program in which employees elected their peers to sit as a "jury" and hear appeals and grievances employees had about their bosses. Employees who felt they had been unfairly treated could argue their cases before this jury, which had the power to overturn any previous decisions. The mere proposal of such an option would have been inconceivable to the cognitive ecology of the group prior to the retreat.

DISCUSSION AND CONCLUSION

In an environment in which managers feel a sense of insecurity and competition, they are likely to have developed schemas that include negative attributions of one another, category traits that frame one another in a negative light. We know from social-psychological research that these schemas and theories that explain others' behavior are not easily changed, even when evidence contradicts the traits we have attributed and even when we notice a behavior inconsistent with those traits. In fact, some research suggests that once we assign a trait to another, our noticing inconsistent behavior actually strengthens and reaffirms the original trait we have assigned. Furthermore, cognitive psychology research has shown that when we are under stress—for example, when we fear being verbally attacked by another or fear losing status or a job—we assume a protective stance. In such a state we often feel cognitive intrusions of the imagined stressor event, anticipating the negative event as part of our defensive posture. As we guard against these intrusions and the symbolic reenactment of the stressor event, we pay a price: dimmed awareness and preselected inattention. We choose to notice certain stimuli and disregard others. Given an environment of insecurity (such as the one described in this case), we can begin to appreciate the intrapsychic forces that would encourage one to relegate another into a restricted frame, thereby placing the self at a safer distance. We can begin to appreciate how attention becomes almost prefocused, how a competitive environment would encourage negative attributions toward others, and how positive gestures, when attempted, may not get noticed. Given these dynamics, we put forth the following propositions:

1. *To enhance genuine dialogue toward building innovative and creative ideas for the future of the organization, an environment must be created that supports the possibility of cognitive reappraisal and new schema development by members.* This should be a deliberately supportive (appreciative) environment that encourages members to direct attention away from familiar stimuli and habits that would cue familiar schemas.

2. *Generative metaphor is an invitation to see the world anew and can be used as an intervention into intergroup and interpersonal conflict.* The generative metaphor is a vehicle whereby learning is "suddenly" transferred from one area of strength to an area of difficulty, enabling problems to be "solved" without direct engagement with the problems.

3. *Metaphor is generative to the extent to which it serves to break the hammerlock of the status quo,* serves to reorganize perceptual processes and ingrained schemas, helps provide positive and compelling new images of possibility, and serves as a bridge for nondefensive learning among participants in the context.

4. For groups and other larger collectivities, *the generative potential of metaphor depends not only on its content, but also on the processes of inquiry and interaction that are engendered.* Processes of coappreciative inquiry heighten the generative potential of metaphorical intervention. Coappreciative processes of inquiry will heighten the generative

potential of metaphor because, first, appreciation is a poetic process that fosters a fresh perception of ordinary life. Unlike the evaluating stance of problem solving, which is based on the assumption of deficiency, appreciation refers to an affirmative valuing of experience based on belief, trust, and conviction. Second, coappreciative inquiry processes create a learning environment that fosters empathy, hope, excitement, and social bonding among people around desired values. Third, the appreciative mode engenders a creative stance toward life by drawing people to inquire beyond superficial appearances into the life-enhancing properties of organizational existence. Through affirmation of the best of "what is," the appreciative mode ignites envisioning into "what might be." Coappreciation inspires the collective imagination and thereby opens the status quo to the joint creation of new possible worlds.

5. *By regaining a sense of unity and participation in the joint creation of reality in a related but distinct domain, groups will be able to grow beyond their historical difficulties through an almost unconscious learning transaction between contexts.* Generative metaphor is frame expanding, facilitates new knowledge, strengthens a group's sense of efficacy, and provides a group with a new, transferable ability to manage the subtle dynamics of building relationships and bonding around common vision.

Generative metaphor enables groups to overcome defenses and liberates energy. In part, such liberation is achieved by cutting through constrictions of habit and cultural automaticity in perception. Generative metaphor is, therefore, poetic in nature. It is an instrument for seeing the world in new ways and in new combinations: It opens our lives to an expanded range of possible worlds. The poet's function, argued Aristotle, is to describe not the thing that has happened, but the kinds of things that might happen (i.e., what is possible). The poetic process helps us appreciate the fact that many futures are possible and that human realities are both discovered and created. As Bruner (1986) has elaborated, the function of the poetic is to open us to the hypothetical, to the range of meanings that are possible. Through AI, we helped to stimulate within the Medic Inn group an artistic vision capable of seeing and creating possible worlds.

We are in our infancy when it comes to intervention theories and practices that (1) operate out of affirmative or nondeficiency assumptions about the organizations we work with, and (2) emerge out of respect for the subtle and sophisticated mechanisms of indirect communication forms, which are in fact found in highly effective groups and growth-promoting relationships. If for no other reason than this, there seems to be ample justification for looking seriously at the case presented in this chapter. The case, which is offered more as exploratory illustration than proof, will be especially justified if it stimulates reflection on our basic assumptions about human nature, helps expand our options for action, and generates new inquiry into the affirmative and indirect sides of human-systems change and development. The application of appreciative inquiry to generative metaphor interventions promises to take us outside the dominant assumptions driving current organization transformation efforts. It truly puts us in front of alternative notions to guide our work, such as the metaphorical challenge that organizations are, in essence, miracles to be embraced.

NOTE

This chapter is an edited version of an article previously published in *Journal of Applied Behavioral Science 26*, 219–239, 1990. It is reprinted here with the permission of the authors.

PART III

Building Enduring Collaboration: Transforming Organizational Culture

7

Imagining Inclusion:
Men and Women in Organizations

Marjorie Schiller

Studying gender and workplace diversity issues is a natural application for appreciative inquiry (AI). AI enables us to build on positive experiences between genders, to relate those experiences to current situations, and to develop "positive possibilities" from what may have been negative situations. At its core, AI identifies and studies stories of successful interactions among men and women. These successes, over time, can become the positive reinforcement for changing the gender culture of an organization. In this chapter I will discuss two cases that illustrate effective applications of AI in understanding, addressing, imagining, and (in one case) transforming corporate gender cultures.

As workplace members, we operate in a milieu where the diversity of gender, plus other recognizable and unrecognizable differences, presents infinite opportunities and challenges. Working relationships raise issues that go to the depth and richness of cultures. These issues go far beyond the hot-button challenges of sexual harassment in the workplace and the "glass ceiling" that prevents significant numbers of women from reaching their full potential. They extend to how to attract, retain, satisfy, and support both men and women working in innovative, productive teams; how to truly value and incorporate the diversity of backgrounds that reflects the emergent labor pool. Diversity defines the communities of organizational life, including race, gender, religion, age, physical ability, sexual orientation, personality, organizational position, ethnicity, class, culture, and all other community differences that influence human experience. It is the essence of this diverse working population that leads to infinite opportunities and challenges within an organization.

Two international businesses, Bell Atlantic (formerly NYNEX and now Verizon) and Avon Mexico, used appreciative inquiry to gain an understanding of the cross-gender relationships within their organizations. Although they are similar in methodology and intent, the following cases differ in impact. In undertaking the process, they both

- Identified and studied existing, high-quality work relationships between men and women.
- Mined positive examples of men and women working together, ultimately focusing on the behaviors, systems, and other actions that encouraged these relationships to flourish.
- Compiled data to understand what was effective, and used the resulting themes to shape a mutually constructed vision.

The difference in outcomes between the two illustrations has to do with lasting consequences of applying AI in both settings.

BELL ATLANTIC:
FRAMING THE CORPORATE GENDER CULTURE

Bell Atlantic decided to study men and women working together who displayed the highest productivity. The company had a long history of investment in organizational diversity. In the early 1980s, New England Telephone, Chesapeake Bell, and several other Bell operating companies offered a seminar called "Men and Women Working Together." Bell Atlantic supported a four-day affinity-group workshop called "Focus on Excellence: A Seminar for Management Women." Bell Atlantic also concentrated on developing minority managers through affinity-group training and cross-cultural seminars. The company further demonstrated its commitment to diversity by supporting the Minority Managers Association and the Association for Management Women. Both of these groups continue (with new names) at Verizon. They have recently been joined by more affinity groups representing other communities of interest. Training on compliance with the legal issues that resulted from affirmative action legislation was added to the skill-building and sensitivity–awareness training. Bell Atlantic offered awareness and compliance workshops about sexual harassment.

This consciousness raising about possible legal problems between men and women at work was followed by an appreciative inquiry into relationships between women and men in the organization. A member of the Men and Women's Advisory Committee explained, "We wanted to look beyond the law or just what's nice, and look at if, why, and how valuable business relationships happen in our company, because that's what affects the bottom line." Another member said, "We have had sexual harassment training and now we should know the laws and what not to do; we want to talk about more than that." Through AI, Bell Atlantic wanted to (1) expand the arena of conversation to understand successful relationships of men and women working together, (2) generate models for success, and (3) move the organization to optimize opportunities from employee experiences.

At the helm of the organization was Fran Austin, president of Telesector Resource Group (TRG), a corporate subsidiary of Bell Atlantic. A decisive, direct communicator, he had a reputation for maintaining excellent working relationships with a number of women in the organization. Austin knew Bell Atlantic had to go beyond the legal issues of what was inappropriate and beyond the sensitizing and awareness training the company had already completed. "I like Appreciative Inquiry because it is cost effective. We conduct the interviews, not outside consultants," Austin explained. "Since it's essentially a positive process, it won't hurt the people who work here." Austin brought in a mixed-gender consultant team consisting of the author and David Cooperrider to lead the company through the AI process.

Introducing the Process

The appreciative inquiry introductory training and development of the interview protocol took place in a two-day seminar. Significantly, Fran Austin was a full participant for both days of training. Other participants came from a cross-section of the organization, including a high percentage of senior-level people. Participants were introduced to appreciative inquiry philosophy and its theoretical basis. They learned AI methodologies, practiced creating appreciative questions, developed interview questions, and set strategy to begin the process. In all, a twenty-person Men and Women's Advisory Committee, chosen by Fran Austin, developed the questions and guided the process. The committee represented a cross-section of the organization, with equal distribution of male and female membership.

The company newsletter posted requests for examples of good working relationships. Employee response was overwhelming. People wanted to talk about their good experiences. Respondents to the internal newsletter request for people who had high-quality, cross-gender work relationships were then asked if they would like to tell their stories. Those that did want to share their positive experiences were selected as interviewees. The interviews were designed to specifically analyze the components of high-quality, cross-gender relationships. The men and women who were members of the advisory committee interviewed most of the fifty male–female working pairs who responded. These colleagues, in male–female pairs, interviewed other internal male and female business "partnerships." The interviews were designed to specifically analyze the components of high-quality, cross-gender relationships. Questions included "When have people felt really empowered in this organization?" "What are the organization's best practices?" and "What supports or strengthens male–female relationships at work?" Throughout the interviewing process, teams conferred and refined questions and protocol. In the end each team submitted typed copies of their interviews. Responses were then grouped by question and coded by Susie Commoford, a Case Western Reserve University graduate student in the organizational behavior Ph.D. program. The data were analyzed for common language and emergent themes.

Three Ways to Relate:
Discoveries from the Appreciative Inquiry

At Bell Atlantic, interviews and conversations revealed three predominant styles or "gender cultures" that individual women and men used in their one-on-one relationships with the other gender. These gender cultures were defined as the norms, values, and beliefs that members of an organization have about male–female relationships, their differences, and the quality of opportunity, appropriate conduct, and manners. The three gender cultures were labeled Traditional, Gender Blind, and New Equality.

Traditional

A Traditional gender culture defines relationships with clear, historically imbedded, gender-based roles for each partner. In this culture, women characteristically look to men for direction and approval. How men and women should behave at work generally mirrors what the people who raised these men and women said about the opposite sex. As one Bell Atlantic employee said, "This has been a difficult challenge for me because society raised people in the past with different values. Females were looked on as being mothers, wives, and grandmothers not competent workers."

Gender Blind

Here, the intent is to view relationships as generic, with gender being an irrelevant factor in the workplace. Gender Blind was the most politically popular gender culture at Bell Atlantic. The belief is that decisions should be based on performance. Ability and potential should be the only relevant factors. The goal is to put people on a "level playing field." In the Gender Blind culture, language is "politically correct" and people are careful about what they say and to whom they say it. Many women at Bell Atlantic liked this culture because they believed it represented progress. "It's a step up. You don't get the dirty jokes or pictures, and there is more respect," one woman said. Most men in this organization believed this orientation is what the women wanted and what the company expected. It felt safer, it felt legal, and it felt practical, particularly in times of corporate cuts and downsizing. Several men said, in effect, "I don't think of my colleague as a woman. I think of her as a person." Interestingly, none of the women interviewed made similar remarks about men. The Gender Blind culture suggests that differences are irrelevant and that it is inappropriate to notice them. The underlying assumption is that we are all alike and that any comments to the contrary are politically incorrect and potentially rude. While some women preferred Gender Blind to Traditional, for many men and women it lacked truthfulness, and they felt constrained by having to be "politically correct."

New Equality

New Equality was the novel, emerging organizational culture at Bell Atlantic. While there were fewer examples of it, those who experienced New Equality relationships were very excited about them. This model proposes that men and women, working in partnerships, are simultaneously equal and different. Some experienced this simultaneity as a stretch: "It calls for mental aerobics," one interviewee said. New Equality suggests that women and men bring separate, distinct gender-related experiences to relationships, and that this diversity adds value. The emphasis in New Equality relationships is on being comfortable with one another, while at the same time recognizing each gender lives in a very different culture, with its own behaviors, customs, language, rituals, and unwritten rules. New Equality partners believe an understanding of both men's and women's perspectives enhances what each person brings to a task. It emphasizes energy and synergy. The following is an excerpt from an interview with two mid-level managers who work together:

SHE: There is a freedom to demonstrate and utilize our differences. We use talents from all over the world to the benefit of the job. We have fun.

HE: Ultimately you step back and say there is something to be gained from diversity. I think there is clearly a different perspective or a different attitude. If we had all males or all whites, you wouldn't get as many different perspectives. . . . I'm convinced that if we could be clones, we would not be happy.

New Equality relationships allow men and women to mess up and say the wrong things. New Equality allows for the authenticity that is required when men and women work successfully as partners and colleagues. Every person's full involvement in coconstructing a project is possible when people feel free to be truly themselves.

Working Amidst Different Gender Cultures

Men or women who have in the past had successful experiences while embracing a Traditional gender culture face a brand new coconstruction of the relationship when their working partner is operating out of a New Equality culture. Men who have had comfortable experiences with women who stayed only in support roles or women who had special access and privilege with male colleagues find it's a new ball game when the working partner is operating out of a different gender culture. Where men and women working together operated from the same gender culture, there was more agreement about how to relate to one another. When a person operating from the New Equality culture worked with a colleague operating from a Traditional gender culture, the results were more complex, even hurtful and misunderstood. Without clear mental models, people are left to make their way through confusing assumptions. As an example, Mary, a recent college graduate, told the following story:

I worked on a team for about three months, and then I did what I thought was recommended in my management courses—I asked someone who had been with the company for 20 years to help me understand the way things really work. I stopped him in the hall and I said to him, "Joe, you really know the ropes around here. Can we have lunch together and could you fill me in?" He crooked his finger and took me into a corner of the corridor and said, "I think you need to know, I'm married."

Mary was embarrassed and felt ashamed. "What did I do wrong?" she asked. There is no clear answer to Mary's question. Her construction and interpretation of the situation was very different than Joe's.

It is not surprising that good relationships and pockets of each gender culture were found in the business units throughout Bell Atlantic. Most people said they exhibited behavior from two or more cultures in any workweek. However, individuals, specific relationships, work groups, and the larger organization often were characterized by a predominant style. Understanding the organization's gender culture, and how an individual's personal style in dealing with the opposite sex related to that culture, became key to productive male–female work relationships.

Key Characteristics of High-Quality, Cross-Gender Relationships in the Workplace

In addition to broadening our understanding to gender "cultures" at Bell Atlantic, the interview stories and data revealed overarching core factors that "gave life" to positive male–female relationships at work.

Theme One: Communication

The men and women who were interviewed saw themselves as good communicators: They knew that communication is a key characteristic of those who enjoyed good cross-gender relationships. They recognized that high-quality relationships are "earned." Interviews showed that men were more likely to focus at the level of the content of the message, while women, although focused on content, also tended to deliver their messages to build the relationship or "talk rapport." The interview data showed good communicators to be proactive and aimed at seeking out each other's views. Here are some quotes from the interviews:

"We have had disagreements, but each one of us has been willing to be open and to listen to the justification each brings to the arguments."

"She challenges me to think differently."

"She lays out the issue on the table, then we flow through ideas. Eventually we come to the point where things fall into place."

"I try to be in the other person's shoes and to listen more than talk."

Theme Two: Partnering Skills

The ability to work well with colleagues was labeled partnering. The most significant factor in labeling someone a good partner was the perception that he or she could do the job. Capability was assumed as the first criteria for a desirable partnership. They identified key elements of partnering skills as recognition that power issues do exist, developing strategies to deal with unequal power, and recognition that personal attraction may be an issue for some people. Here are a few quotes from the interviews:

"We treat each other as equals. Each is part of the team and nothing is beneath either of us. The traditional parts aren't even considered."

"There are times people come to him because they are more comfortable with a man. Occasionally it is vice-versa. I appreciate that he is open and acknowledges the reality of what is going on."

"There was a cadre of people who cautioned me that she was attractive, and they were concerned rumors would happen. I worried about the rumors. Now I feel comfortable. Part of the problem is we don't know how to deal with issues of being natural with one another."

Theme Three: Leadership

This theme was the outcome of several key words around leadership that continued to come up in the interviews: dedicated, positive outlook, honest, "walking the talk," trusting, focused, and the willingness to learn. Here are a few quotes from the interviews:

"I try to create a learning environment. I don't have all the answers. I try to create opportunities to make personal discoveries."

"Take pride in success, learn from failure and learn from a lot of people at different levels that helps me grow in my leadership skills."

"Our best management practice is our ability to role model for the whole organization. We act as a team."

Results and Lessons Learned at Bell Atlantic

What worked? With the information and the stories collected, participants in the appreciative inquiry process developed five characteristics of the New Equality cross-gender relationship, which they defined as the highest-quality relationship for men and women in their workplace. The characteristics were respect, trust, honesty, sense of humor, and high work standards. In each case, the stories and experiences of the participants defined the deeper meanings of these characteristics. Multiple key factors that drove or strengthened each characteristic were also defined. From this information, the team reviewed the three most significant characteristics of high-quality cross-gender relationships at work (communication, partnering, leadership). New individual competencies, new training opportunities, and new ways of thinking about work and working together were developed to support the vision of the "new" corporate environment.[1] Individuals reported that the AI way of thinking and asking questions affected other parts of their lives, including profoundly changing their relationships with their families. "This works," said a human resources manager. "I tried AI at home with my kids. Now I'm ready to try it at work."

What didn't happen? Changes in Bell Atlantic's gender culture ultimately were not sustained. There are several possible explanations. First, Fran Austin retired and the head of corporate human resources left the company. Therefore, both visible champions of the initiative were no longer available to carry the message throughout the organization. The loss of these senior advocates of the appreciative inquiry process affected the next phase of work. While there was interest, there was no momentum for moving forward and no funding for continuing cross-gender initiatives designed by the initial participants. Second, the organization had a history of "flavor of the month" programs that cycled in and out. With the exception of individuals directly involved in the AI process, appreciative inquiry may have been seen as just another methodology, rather than an ongoing way of working together. As a result, people were wary of commitment to culture change; they surmised it might not last long.

What could have been done differently? In hindsight, the outcome may have been different if leadership and ownership for the AI process was cultivated on multiple levels throughout the organization. While turnover and resulting politics are unforeseeable, they are common facts of corporate life. Since the individuals directly involved in the process were favorably affected by it, this could argue for an up-front commitment and budget allocation for a more sustained effort. AI is an iterative process that requires repetition and reflection to develop an appreciative vocabulary and to ask new kinds of questions.

AVON MEXICO: CHANGE THROUGH COMMITMENT

Avon Mexico is one of the most profitable subsidiaries of Avon Products, an international direct-sales organization. In the Mexico City headquarters, 3,000 employees support a 250,000-member sales force. The CEO (called affectionately "El Jefe," The Chief) is known as a strong leader. He is articulate and highly influential. He enjoys unquestioned authority and is respected as a leader who is genuinely committed to optimizing women's contributions in the company. El Jefe's objectives for Avon Mexico were aligned with corporate values and made the best possible "bottom-line" sense. He was also committed to building more productive and mutually supportive relationships between men and women. It was important to the CEO to foster a culture where everyone sought to know and understand the other's point of view, not only as men and women but also as individuals.

Mujeres y Hombres Trabajar en Equipo (Men and Women Working in Teams) described Avon Mexico's appreciative inquiry into cross-gender relationships. Its purpose was to address issues of gender equity. Its objective was to live its corporate vision to serve the "wants, needs, and aspirations of women around the world." Employees in the study wanted the internal organizational structure and systems to be congruent with the corporate mission in the external world.

In support of the objectives of its parent division to increase the number of women executives, Avon Mexico wanted men and women to work together in teams at all levels, including the most senior. An internal Avon Mexico team of three members from the human resources department expanded to include representatives from sales, publicity, and external affairs. The chief executive officer and the international corporate director of human resources also served as full-time team members. Five of the eight members of the "core" team that planned the appreciative inquiry program were Mexicans.

Introducing the Process

The CEO warmly endorsed appreciative inquiry and recognized the power and worth of using positive models. He enthusiastically participated in a two-day introductory session. The first of several AI workshops included company officers, "influencers," and opinion shapers. Participants were introduced to appreciative inquiry philosophy and its theoretical basis. As in the case of Bell Atlantic, they learned AI methodologies, practiced creating appreciative questions, developed interview questions, and set strategy to begin the process. Additional AI workshops included interviewers from all parts of the company. Through these AI workshops, Mujeres y Hombres Trabajar en Equipo trained male and female partners to conduct interviews with other male and female partners. The first interviews revealed that the questions needed refinement; some were seen as redundant, others did not evoke enough stories. The working team redrafted the questions from what had been learned from the first round of interviews. Three core questions were as follows:

1. Describe your most positive working experience with a man (or a woman).
2. What were the conditions that led to this situation?
3. What would be your three wishes for future men and women in this company?

The CEO, the director of human resources, and other members of the planning team, including U.S. consultants Marge Schiller and David Cooperrider, worked together to draft a set of "possibility statements" based on the interviews. The resulting propositions were brought to a summit meeting for all of the interviewers and other stakeholders to revisit the outcome.

It was almost a year after the first workshops that the large group summit was held. A key developer of the possibility statements, the CEO served as the leader of a summit meeting of more than a hundred people who worked with the draft possibility statements and refined them so they really fit peoples' aspirations. The possibility statements addressed the following topics:

Mission and Strategic Orientation	Decision Making
Being a Learning Organization	Communication
Organizational Structure	Human Resources and Career Practices
Team Skills	Rewards
Style and Culture	External Relations
Understanding and Awareness	Image and Self-Esteem

The resulting possibility statements led to new programs and initiatives at Avon Mexico that included

1. Creating a new database of employee skills and aspirations.
2. Basing salaries on ability and job performance equally for men and women.

3. Sponsoring specific lectures and workshops for women to value themselves and build self-esteem.

4. Developing gender awareness training.

5. Requiring all Avon Mexico task forces and managing teams to have male and female membership.

Change began immediately. From the very first interviews, the culture began to reshape itself. For example, one of the core propositions (possibility statements) was that men and women would be represented at all levels of decision making. Because of the clarity of this possibility statement, a decision was made on the spot to invite the two most senior women in the company to attend all officer meetings. In less than a year, the first woman officer was appointed. As soon as a core proposition was conceptualized and clearly articulated, behavior appeared to naturally follow.

Appreciative Inquiry and Cultural Sensitivities

In reflection, aspects of the Latin culture seem particularly suited for using appreciative inquiry in talking about gender at work. People are generally relationship oriented. They invest time in building the rapport necessary for high-quality professional relationships. The impact of women in the workplace was evident. In Mexico, the status of women is continuously evolving. Applying the discoveries in the Bell Atlantic case, I would say that Avon Mexico moved from a Traditional culture directly into the New Equality gender culture without using the interim Gender Blind model. The company was respectful of Mexican culture and traditions. While a Gender Blind way of working might be more appealing to both men and women in the United States, many Mexicans dismissed it as unreal, dishonest, and somewhat silly. This conclusion was reflected in the interviews and in our inquiry. One senior manager said, "Let me see if I got this straight. I have always loved women and enjoyed being around women and what you are telling me is 'that's all right.'" The director of human resources added, "He was probably thinking that in our company this would be the wrong thing to say. People are going to have feelings whether or not we acknowledge or legitimize them. Avon is saying differences are wonderful and fine. Enjoy them."

Avon Mexico provided leadership in stressing women's self-sufficiency, higher participation in the paid workforce, independence, sharing in responsibilities, equality of rights and obligations, and changes in the mentality of both men and women. The college students from Mexican universities who were invited participants in the summit meeting confirmed the evolutionary movement toward equality. They reported that young women and young men have very different relationships and live in a very different world than that of their parents. Thus, there were some concerns about whether or not the U.S. consultants and Avon corporate staff from New York would respect and understand cultural differences around gender. The appreciative inquiry process of using positively framed questions and inviting the variety of voices that represent the total system shortcut those concerns. By focusing on what worked best, cultural differences were revealed and could be talked about in a positive context. Potential denial or defensiveness that might have arisen was rendered unnecessary.

Translation: A Benefit to Understanding

During the training session for the group of interviewers (who called themselves "pioneers"), the consultants and presenters spoke in English with simultaneous translation. Initially, the translation requirement felt awkward and time consuming, but, in fact, translation proved to be a great asset to learning. By slowing down the process, participants had time to clarify questions, to solicit examples, and to internalize ideas. Untested assumptions were minimal, clarifications were frequent, and understanding was high. The assumptions inherent in fast conversations were systematically examined and questioned. For example, one woman asked, "When we say teams what do we mean? Whom exactly are we talking about?" There was a lot of note taking and significant periods of silence. Perhaps these reflective times contributed to a higher level of internalization of appreciative inquiry concepts.

There were other language challenges for the group. Some of the appreciative inquiry terminology (for example, "provocative propositions") did not translate into Spanish appropriately. The consultant team changed the language to "provocative possibility statements." The men and women participants worked well together. Most of them found that "thinking out loud" gave them new information about themselves as well as others. Participants liked the experience. There was laughter and an informal atmosphere. It was pleasant, and people learned. One Mexican manager summed up the experience like this: "The questions opened up all kinds of possibilities. It was useful. People were positive in their attitude; they were open to tell what was happening. The answers were related to job, family, and social life. They want to know what is going to happen now. They want to share these thoughts."

Results: Owning the *Philosophia*

At Avon Mexico, appreciative inquiry was never just a method. From the beginning, it was embraced as a *philosophia*, a guideline for living and behaving and a vision of the future that people wanted for the company. Consultants served to get things started and provide resources. Women now participate more fully in collaborative efforts from the manufacturing floor to the executive boardroom. The first female member of the executive committee was appointed within six months of the appreciative inquiry.

There were equally significant changes in communications, strategic direction, organizational structure, style, culture, and relationships that evolved out of this appreciative inquiry initiative. The positive energy generated naturally grew to embrace a wider set of issues than those originally defined in the gender inquiry. After the consulting team left Mexico, The CEO wrote, "A thousand flowers are still blossoming as a result of our work." The director of human resources reported that "Mujeres y Hombres Trabajar en Equipo" was never a project; it is a process that continues. Some people have left and new people have replaced them, but the work goes on. For Avon Mexico, it is now a way of doing business.

A Well-Deserved Award

For its efforts in successfully addressing gender issues, Avon Mexico received the 1997 Catalyst Award. The Catalyst Award honors the business world's most effective initiatives for women's advancement. Selection criteria include identifying a proven success model that sets the standard for other North American organizations. One thousand people honored Fernando Lezama and key members of the Avon Mexico and Avon International staff at a banquet held in New York City. Lucy Laredo, the first woman officer at Avon Mexico, was in attendance. In 1999 Ms. Loredo was named general manager of Avon, Ecuador.

CONDITIONS FOR A SUCCESSFUL
APPRECIATIVE INQUIRY INTO INCLUSION

Appreciative inquiry provides the positive structure for organizational growth via a constructive framing of the right questions. It discovers and makes known to the whole organization what is already working well and builds on that solid foundation to form pictures of the desired future the organization holds for itself. It encourages organization-wide participation and ownership of the process and results and is a highly practical and constructive medium for creating organizational change. Appreciative inquiry is a natural way of approaching good working relationships that move across the worlds of race, gender, age, religion, geography, sexual orientation, physical abilities, organizational position, and other differences and commonalities. Inclusion makes it possible to attract, retain, satisfy, and achieve the highest productivity from today and tomorrow's workforce. The following are some considerations for an appreciative inquiry into women and men working together:

1. Consider the diverse cultures in your own organization and your own relationships. Search for the elements of your culture that already promote high-quality cross-gender relationships and help you and your department reach your goals and prepare for the future.

2. Consider what kinds of organizational support will be necessary to conduct an appreciative inquiry. Consider the form that will best suit the organization, whether it is a large-scale intervention or starting with a single organizational unit.

3. In introducing appreciative inquiry, pay attention to cultivating internal ownership for the process and results and what will help your organization move beyond the "flavor of the month" mentality.

4. Take time to define the topic of inquiry so that it is of a scope worthy of people's attention. Focus on topics that engage and energize people. In formulating the appreciative questions, slow down the process to enable people to test and clarify assumptions and fully internalize the appreciative inquiry philosophy.

5. Provide forums to talk about what is working in male–female relations. Go beyond problem-centered discussions. People are enthusiastic in their response to real-life models of excellent men and women who have good work partnerships.

6. Encourage conversations in which people use their best experiences to imagine a preferred future. From these specific stories, develop a clear, shared, articulated vision of how men and women can work together successfully, capitalizing on both differences and similarities. Then, support the "new" relationships through revisiting policies, practices, and reward systems, and recognize, reward, and learn from high-quality male–female work partnerships.

FINAL THOUGHTS

AI is as much about possibility as it is about positivity. In both the Avon Mexico and Bell Atlantic cases, the work was affirming and not based on shame or guilt. In some dialogues negative feelings were verbally expressed, conversations were open, and there was an acceptance of people's ability to grow and change. Although

...ı may be interpreted as primarily focusing on always being positive, it is the inquiry that creates a bridge to new possibilities. That explains why the first questions we ask one another are fateful. When people are asked appreciative questions, they find the answers within themselves. In asking the questions, we legitimize the quest for our own answers. It is in this place where acceptance and the generosity of the human spirit flourish.

Finally, in the spirit of asking "fateful questions," can "he said" and "she said" become just "we said"? If we want to promote workplaces that offer opportunities and experiences that draw the most from our women and men in the workforce, let's stop only studying the battles. It is not enough to pretend to ignore or defend our differences. It is not enough to simply tolerate them. Instead, let's work together in our organizations to identify what is succeeding; how the beautiful differences between us are actually working to our and others benefit. Let's analyze why, and then let's imagine the possibilities of exploring what success really is and replicate it again and again. If men and women can be in such a continuous appreciative inquiry, then we can "be" inclusion.

NOTE

1. Report is available through the author: M. Schiller, 49 Rockwood Road, Hingham, MA 02043.

8

Appreciative Inquiry and Culture Change at GTE: Launching a Positive Revolution

Diana Whitney, David L. Cooperrider,
Maureen Garrison, and Jean Moore

The intent of this chapter is to reflect upon the process of culture change at GTE, the focus of our work and learning for the past three years. This is a story about a highly successful large-scale change effort that draws into question many of the traditional theories and practices of change management. It is a story of "grassroots change," change that is emergent and generative rather than programmatic and directed. It is about the power of voluntary effort to bring about positive change within a large, well-established bureaucracy. We hope it is a story that invites you the reader into the journey and toward your own revelations and understandings about the philosophy of positive change and the practice of appreciative inquiry for large-scale organization-wide change.

It has been three years since the introduction of appreciative inquiry to GTE. As we reflect back over this time, we realize that there have indeed been ups and downs and bumps along the road. In recalling highpoints, the times when we were most engaged and excited working with members of GTE, many come to mind—the first distance learning (satellite broadcast) appreciative inquiry training program, the union–management partnership launch, the appreciative inquiry call center initiative, the Zealots program—

each a success on its own and a formidable part of the systemic culture change.

Upon reflection, however, it is the approach taken to culture change, with its grassroots revolutionary focus, that has held our attention for nearly three years and continues to enliven us as students of organization life. We continue to learn from stories of the "wild flower" initiatives sprouting up and growing naturally throughout the organization, and from stories of the positive impacts of appreciative inquiry upon the organization and its members. The approach taken to culture change was founded upon four principles. Designed into each culture change initiative, these principles created a context for change that was at the same time an image of the ideal organizational culture and a living practice of that image. Briefly, the four principles are as follows:

1. *An unquestionable commitment to front-line employees.* Over and over again we found ourselves asking what we could do to demonstrate our confidence in front-line employees to do the right thing. In addition, we sought to be partners with front-line employees in creating the needed transformation. We wanted to relate in a way that gave life to employee self-sovereignty and invited their best to come center stage.

2. *A willingness to invite and innovate new forms of cooperation.* We began with an extraordinary stance toward cooperation among those contributing to the culture change effort. The change team consisted of public affairs, human resources, and organization development staff who worked closely with senior management to ensure quality and sustainability. Throughout the company there was a commitment to new forms of organizing based on cooperation rather than hierarchy. We took up the challenge of helping the organization image and practice cooperation, partnership, and unity in all that we did.

3. *A "storytelling" narrative model of organization culture.* Early in our working together it became evident that we all recognized the power of stories to guide human life personally and collectively. It was Tom White, president of GTE Telops, who gave us a rallying cry for the culture change process when he said, "Culture is the stories we tell ourselves about ourselves, and then we forget they were stories." We built upon this idea in numerous ways: storytelling as the theme of the annual President's Leadership Awards ceremony, a "success stories" column in the company newspaper, a study of the organization's inner dialogue, the ratio of positive to negative stories told about the company by members of the company, and a storytelling focus to training and learning.

4. *A commitment to appreciative inquiry as an organization-wide, integrative change process.* Approximately one year after the introduction of appreciative inquiry to the organization, the organization's Culture

Council decided to use appreciative inquiry as the integrative approach to culture change. The Culture Council decided not to create appreciative inquiry as a stand-alone program, but to use it as the core methodology for change in all company initiatives. As a result, appreciative inquiry has been woven into numerous programs and processes, including front-line employee training, management and leadership training, the union–management partnership initiative, an organizational improvement process for call centers, the positive change network, and a diversity initiative.

BACKGROUND

As of 1999, GTE has merged with Bell Atlantic to form Verizon, the largest telephone company in the United States, serving both commercial and retail customers, with broad international reach and growth potential. Like all companies in the telecommunications industry, GTE has weathered great change in recent years. By mid-1995 it had undergone major reorganization and consolidation, a substantial acquisition, process reengineering, and significant downsizing. The prospect of new national telecommunications legislation was looming and every indicator pointed to more change ahead. All employees, regardless of position, were experiencing the effects of massive change with no end in sight.

In the summer of 1995 the senior executives of GTE Telops gathered for their annual conference. With the recognition that opportunity and risk run hand in hand in the newly competitive, increasingly high-technology telecommunications industry, the mood at the onset of this conference was one of cautious optimism. With the awareness that customer-driven market opportunities could only be realized by a fully engaged workforce, this team gathered to hone its leadership capacity. It was during this conference that appreciative inquiry was introduced to the GTE Telops leaders. Conference feedback ratings showed appreciative inquiry as the highest-ranked session in the entire conference. The seeds of positive change were sown. It was not yet evident, however, how fertile was the ground.

In February 1996 the senior leadership team found the results of the annual employee opinion survey disturbing and responded with a call to action. Management scores were up in six of nine categories. Nonexempt employee scores were up in seven categories. Hourly employee scores were up in only two categories, while flat or down in seven of nine categories. Knowing that GTE hourly employees serve in excess of 90 percent of GTE's customers, the Telops senior team was in agreement: Something had to be done to positively engage front-line employees. The goal was clear: to ensure a connected, committed, and passionate front-line workforce, knowledgeable about the business and dedicated to customer service, by focusing resources on the front line. The ground was tilled for systemic culture change.

INVITATION TO A POSITIVE REVOLUTION

The senior team's favorable reaction to appreciative inquiry led the internal change management team, comprised of organizational development and public affairs consultants, to choose appreciative inquiry as the process for bringing about the much-needed organization change. David Cooperrider and Diana Whitney joined the team as external resources. The goal was to introduce appreciative inquiry to the organization, beginning with the front line, and to support its use across the organization in a way that enhanced employee engagement and business success. What initially appeared as a call for an organization-wide appreciative inquiry quickly became an invitation to participate in a positive revolution, the momentum of which has been created and sustained by employees throughout the organization.

The first fateful question emerged: How can we engage the positive potential of all 64,000 employees toward the transformation of the company? The focus was clearly on changes needed at the front line to enthusiastically and effectively serve customers. The external consultants submitted a proposal using the company's communication technology for companywide education and inquiry. The change management team went back and forth between the idea of a companywide inquiry and the idea of building critical mass and receptivity to positive change through training of front-line employees. We discussed the possibility of a companywide inquiry. We were excited by the potential of a 64,000-person inquiry. We considered a strategy of face-to-face interviews, focus-group interviews, and on-line interviews. Some wanted to launch a nationwide inquiry as the leverage process for change. Others believed it was important to build a critical mass of awareness about appreciative inquiry within the organization before launching a whole system inquiry. We chose to build critical mass by introducing appreciative inquiry to employees as a process they could use, as they believed warranted, to help them be more effective.

We knew that our first initiative would indeed be fateful. Committed to the continuity and sustainability of this endeavor, we chose what we thought would be a moderate first step: front-line employee training in appreciative inquiry. Little did we know that we were about to unleash a positive force so powerful that once liberated it would multiply on its own, enhancing learning, cooperation, and customer service as it went.

BIRTHING A POSITIVE CHANGE NETWORK

This was the birth of what is now called the Positive Change Network. Initially called the Zealots Program, it started as a two-day appreciative inquiry training for front-line employees. When asked what he would like to accomplish with this program, Tom White replied, "I want every employee to be a 'zealot' for this company—an enthusiast whose cause is the satisfaction of our customers. I am the first GTE zealot and I want a whole company full of zealots." Even though we were uneasy about the word zealot, his enthusiasm struck a cord in us. Had we envisioned the role of organization change as behavioral transformation we would have gone no further. Believing as we do—that within all people and organizations there is a positive core, a source of positive potential that is brought to life when recognized and evoked through inquiry—we proceeded with a sense of bold possibilities.

We clearly wanted whatever we did to recognize and invite front-line employee self-sovereignty. We wanted to avoid the all too familiar empowerment trap. Having senior management tell front-line employees they are empowered does not an empowered workforce make. We did not want to prescribe to people how they should behave. And we certainly did not want to impose appreciative inquiry on anyone. We wanted in every possible way to demonstrate confidence in and commitment to front-line employees. As a result, we decided to introduce appreciative inquiry and to invite participants to explore applications and practices in their own areas of work, rather than prescribe a standard set of follow-up actions for everyone. At the end of the workshop people asked, "What are we supposed to do now that we've been through this session?" The answer we gave, with some concern that we were not satisfying peoples' need for clarity, was, "It is up to you. Use these ideas and practices however you'd like and only if you find them useful in your personal life or your work life." As a result, people began to realize that the future of the company is indeed their responsibility, that the images they hold and the questions they ask—be they positive or negative—do make a difference.

One further question emerged as we prepared for the first Zealots training. What do we say when asked, "What is a zealot? What does a zealot do? And more specifically, what does the company expect of zealots?" We knew that the habits of discourse are such that if asked these questions during a question-and-answer period, senior managers would answer them, and that no matter how good the answers, it would be a losing position in that it would set up the hierarchical discourse pattern where employees ask and executives tell. This would undermine all we were attempting to bring forth.

We thought about the transformation desired. Our image of an organization at its best is one where self-sovereign front-line employees have full voice, where they comfortably share best practices with one another and with management, where they inquire into the myriad ways that customers are satisfied, and where they openly talk about what is needed for them to better serve customers. And so we decided to experiment. What would happen if we turned the executive–employee relationship around and in this case have front-line employees tell senior managers what it means to be a zealot and what zealots need to thrive and succeed in GTE.

The result was indeed a highpoint of the first Zealots workshop. As the wrap up of the session, senior executives came to lunch to hear what the zealots had to say. Six groups of zealots had prepared presentations addressing questions such as these: What is a zealot? How can we best grow zealots throughout the company? What communication vehicles will help zealots stay connected? What do zealots need to thrive in GTE? And what do zealots do? The enthusiasm was high as lunch was served to the tables of zealots, now joined by two or three executives at each table. Zealots talked about appreciative inquiry and the value they saw it having for the organization, and, when asked, described their plans for taking AI back to their work and their homes. Lunch ended and it was time to hear from the zealots.

The first group to present surprised us all by asking everyone in the room, including in some cases the company president to whom they report, three or four levels removed, to stand and recite "The Zealot Oath," a pledge they created in answer to the question, "What is a zealot?" They assured everyone that zealots were here to stay and that they would make a positive difference in the company.

The Zealot Oath
GTE Employee Zealots Always Act With:
Zeal
Enthusiasm
Attitude (We're Can Do)
Leadership
Openness
Trust
I solemnly affirm to support and display, daily,
my personal commitment
to the ZEALOT Way.

Each presentation built on the enthusiasm of the previous ones, while also making the business case for liberating the "power of the positive" through appreciative inquiry. Tom White concluded the session by asking for additional questions or comments. Even the number-one zealot was surprised by the question that followed. One participant stood and quietly asked Tom White and the senior managers present if they were ready for the positive revolution that had just been born. He went on to say that people want to be recognized for what they do well, they want to learn from the best practices of others, and they want to be the easiest and best company to do business with in the telecommunications industry. He said that now—with the power of AI to study our best and to build on it—there is no stopping us.

GRASSROOTS INITIATIVES FOR POSITIVE CHANGE

We wondered if, indeed, that would be the case, until we began hearing stories of how this first group of zealots were using appreciative inquiry and the tremendous impacts they were having. For example,

- One customer-service representative created an interview guide and, by herself, interviewed over 200 customers to discover just what it is that they value about GTE service.
- Another participant asked the internal consulting group to help her conduct a full-cycle (4D) AI in her organization of about 300 people.
- Several people presented an overview of AI to their work teams, which included appreciative interviews about teamwork.
- Others began the practice of starting meetings with good-news stories.
- A group designed an interview guide and interviewed customers about images of quality service.
- Several initiatives focused on measuring service successes rather than service failures.

It quickly became evident that the change management team could (and perhaps had to) support the zealots by building a communication architecture that presented evidence of their successes throughout the company. They needed a vehicle that allowed them to share stories with one another, that enabled them to learn from one another, and that fostered cooperation among them. Articles about the zealots appeared in the company newspapers, a zealots' intranet address was established, zealots' conference calls were used to gather input for executive decision making, and computers were set up so zealots who worked in the field could stay connected and contribute.

Thousands of people throughout GTE were introduced to appreciative inquiry and trained in the basics of topic selection, crafting appreciative questions, and conducting interviews. In the first year, 800 employees attended the zealots' AI training sessions. Hundreds of people were involved in learning appreciative inquiry as frontline facilitators, and even more learned about it at annual leadership retreats, where some of the authors were keynote speakers.

There were numerous appreciative inquiries underway within the organization. Zealots and others who had learned AI along the way had spontaneously generated several inquiries on teamwork, customer service, and communication. There was an inquiry guide developed by a team of zealots wanting to conduct a simultaneous inquiry throughout the entire organization. Any of the zealots who so wished could conduct interviews. The topics chosen were quality, teaming, ownership, inspirational leadership, and fun at work. Over 100 zealots participated and over 400 interviews were conducted. The lessons learned from these interviews were supported by an intranet site for stories and best practices. It became clear that the positive revolution was growing, as was the sense of contribution and enthusiasm among those who were participating.

CHANGING CULTURE THROUGH STORYTELLING

It is through the stories we tell about an organization, its employees, its leadership, its customers, and its ways of operating that an organization is known. An organization becomes real to us through the stories we tell and the stories we hear about it. We give life and meaning to an organization as we engage with others in talking about the organization, the work it enables us to perform, our visions, plans, and customers.

James Hillman (1996), noted Jungian psychologist, in his recent book, *The Soul's Code*, draws attention to how we construct our sense of childhood and childhood identity through the stories we tell and read.

Because the "traumatic" view of early years so controls psychological theory of personality and its development, the focus of our rememberings and the language of our personal storytelling have already been infiltrated by the toxins of these theories. Our lives may be determined less by our childhood than by the way we have learned to imagine our childhood. We are, this book shall maintain, less damaged by the traumas of childhood than by the traumatic way we remember childhood. (p. 4)

This suggests that the stories we tell about who we are—more than a set of personality traits, or even our past experiences—truly constitute our identity. The same may be thought about organizations. Organizations are created and exist in the narrative processes of inquiry, conversation, and storytelling among members, customers, and other stakeholders.

Organizations are made and imagined through narrative processes. This view of organizing suggests that the keys to organization culture change are the organization's narrative processes. The collective conversations that go on within and about the organization can be considered a form of "inner dialogue" or organizational "self talk." Research shows that healthy people, healthy marriages, and healthy organizations demonstrate a positive inner dialogue. That is, the sum total of conversations is more positive than negative by a ratio of at least two to one for individuals (Cooperrider, 1999) and five to one for couples (Gottman, 1994) and organizations.

Dan Young, assistant vice president within human resources at GTE, starts front-line employee meetings on culture change by asking participants to share their definitions of organization culture. Generally, participants describe organization culture in two ways. Some offer a behavioral definition à la Deal and Kennedy (1982): "It's the way we do things around here." Others describe culture in terms of deeply held values that guide decisions and actions: "It's our core values and how we use them for decision making and it's the way our values are lived in our relationships with one another and with customers." Dan Young replies that these are common definitions of organization culture. He then asks in a light voice, "How many of you think we really can change our core values and behaviors? Furthermore, how many of you want to?" Not many hands rise in affirmation to either of his questions. Dan concurs: "I don't think we can or should change our values, but we can change the stories we tell about ourselves. And that's what we mean by culture." He goes on to emphasize how often we tell stories about problems and complaints, and how seldom we tell stories of success, customer satisfaction, or a job well done. He challenges participants to change the stories they tell about the organization, their colleagues, and even themselves. That, he assures them, will change the culture of GTE.

Creativity, innovation, and positive change stem from an affirmative, narrative-rich environment. In many organizations today, human communication means memos, reports, and—at best—negotiations. All are forms of communication that tend to be reductionist and linear. They do not encourage "out of the box thinking," nor do they enhance the generative capacity of the organization. Narrative forms of communication such as storytelling and inquiry, on the other hand, invite exploration, ignite the imagination, and satisfy the human need for connection and cooperative meaning making.

Our image for the GTE culture change process was to create a narrative-rich culture in which the ratio of positive to negative stories was at least five to one. We approached this in a number of different ways:

1. We taught appreciative inquiry with a focus on storytelling. We developed a unique module on transforming negative discourse to positive discourse. Training was provided for the zealots, for front-line core-course facilitators, and as part of the launch for a union–management partnership initiative.

2. We created opportunities and processes for collecting and sharing "good news" stories. One executive volunteered to be the center for all the stories. They came into his office and he sent them out to other groups in the organization, to be shared and replicated when appropriate. He began all his meetings by reviewing success stories and discussing "root causes of success." Many were passed on to the company communication department for publication in the newsletter.

3. Storytelling was embedded into various processes in the company. For example, the President's Leadership Awards program focused on storytelling about the winning employees, their teams, and customer service.

4. We added open-ended questions to the company employee survey and tracked the ratio of positive to negative images, stories, and comments. We collected responses to questions such as, "Assume for a moment you have a crystal ball that can see into the future, realistically, what kind of company will GTE be five to ten years from now?"

5. We created a parable—a storybook—about appreciative inquiry as a teaching tool for all employees. Through these and many other activities, we focused the attention of GTE employees throughout the organization on their power to positively impact self-esteem, identity, and success—their own, one another's, and the organization's—through the quality of their conversations and the stories they construct, share, and spread.

THE UNION–MANAGEMENT PARTNERSHIP

Two years into the effort the winds of change circled around us in some very unexpected ways. GTE went through a major reorganization. The culture change initiative continued and indeed served as a centerpiece for communication to employees about the reorganization. Focus on front-line employees continued as business units were reconfigured to meet the competitive market environment. In the process, some executives used appreciative interviews to select their new teams and to quickly build cooperative capacity in their new organizations. Membership on the change management team changed. The overall initiative, however, continued seamlessly, with appreciative inquiry at the center. GTE was awarded the ASTD Culture Change Award for 1997. For many of us it was indeed an exemplary process and a career highpoint.

And then the winds of change blew stronger. It seemed that the company's two major unions, the Communication Workers of America (CWA) and the International Brotherhood of Electrical Workers (IBEW), were curious about the culture change initiatives, especially the Zealots Program.

During this time, the CWA and IBEW national leadership and GTE leadership were working on a new partnership. They were meeting with the Federal Mediation and Conciliation Council in Washington, D.C., to craft the purpose and principles of their partnership. The company soon realized that the culture change efforts that had once been organizationally (managerially) empowered also needed to include union involvement and ownership.

David Cooperrider and Diana Whitney were called to Washington to attend a meeting of the Partnership Council. Union and company leadership alike greeted them with skeptical curiosity: How, if at all, might AI be used to support the newly conceptualized partnership? Comments were made like, "We don't know what appreciative inquiry is but it seems to have caught on in the company," "We don't know what appreciative inquiry can do but we sure know that what we have been doing for the past decade isn't working anymore," and, of significance, "We are committed to being a company that values its unions; and unions that support their businesses. And we need all the help we can get." After a very candid and wide-ranging meeting, it was agreed that leadership—union and management together—would be given an opportunity to learn about appreciative inquiry and to vote on whether to use it as a cornerstone for the new partnership. The consultants were asked to come back the next morning with a draft agenda for a two-day meeting to introduce appreciative inquiry to 200 union and management leaders from across the company and country. It was not the only sleepless night that led up to the meeting and vote. The next day the agenda was thoroughly discussed and approved. A team of CWA, IBEW, and GTE people was designated to organize and host the meeting, which was held about three months later.

A total of 220 people showed up in Dallas: 120 union leaders and 100 company managers. During the first evening, the air was thick with old hurts, current frustrations, and a determination to see the good and the just prevail. The next day started with some nervousness, but we managed to set the context and get people into interviews with their union or management counterparts within the first thirty minutes of the session. The subsequent day-and-a-half training session went well. The 220 people sitting at tables of eight gradually relaxed into the ideas and practices of appreciative inquiry. And then it was time for the vote. Dan Young, then assistant vice president of organization effectiveness, took the stage. David Cooperrider and Diana Whitney went to the back of the room and waited in great anticipation of the vote. Dan Young gave the group thirty minutes to discuss whether appreciative inquiry should be used to build a new relationship among unions and management at GTE. The groups' task was simple: to cast a table vote of yes or no.

Thirty minutes later, Dan Young called the question. He asked each table to voice their vote and their reasoning. What we heard was surprising: "Table One votes 100-percent yes on the condition that every employee in the company has access to learn appreciative inquiry." "Table Two votes yes, and asks that union stewards and coaches [front-line supervisors] attend training programs together." Tables three, four, five, and so forth—until all twenty-some tables were heard—said yes. The conditions for success were laid out in the process: full participation, partnership at all levels of the company, and a focus on initiatives that benefit employees, customers, the unions, and the company.

We quickly went into action to design and host the partnership kick-off meeting. A Partnership Summit involving 250 people would be the first introduction of the Partnership Council and the purpose and principles they had drafted. It would give local leadership an opportunity to chart their course for the partnership. The unions' training and development staffs, the company's labor-relations staff, public affairs staff, and organization effectiveness staff; the Federal Conciliation and Mediation consultants; and the appreciative inquiry consultants were now a team. Appreciative inquiry served as a backdrop upon which to design the summit, provided a common language, and guided the organizing process for the meeting, allowing the partnership principles and the work of local teams to be in the foreground.

NOTEWORTHY RESULTS

The results have been unprecedented. The local support for the union–management partnership was contagious. Local Partnership Councils formed to provide direction and to ensure that, whenever possible, local decisions are made in partnership. Efforts already underway became showcases for how to address essential business issues, such as overtime, the company's use of contractors, and workforce retention in call centers, through real partnership.

As local Partnership Councils formed they asked for support from human resources, organization effectiveness, and labor relations. Information, training, and consultation programs were put in place to respond to the requests for support. All employees have access to a four-hour program, "Appreciative Inquiry and the New Partnership," and a process called "appreciative issues resolution" has replaced conflict resolution.

The positive orientation toward partnership is spilling over into relationships between the front-line and headquarters staffs. The company culture council, seeing the potential of appreciative inquiry to bridge differences and to help create a truly employee-centered culture, decided to use AI as the integrative philosophy and methodology for culture change. This led to the reinvention of the Zealots Program as the Positive Change Network, a virtual process for generating employee enthusiasm and capacity for positive change. And, most significant, stories are traveling through the company about the recent contract negotiations. They are being described as the smoothest negotiations in the history of the company's union relations. This is indeed a story worthy to be told.

FOUR POWERFUL LESSONS

As stated earlier, the lessons have been many. The GTE culture change initiative is a story of real-time, on-the-job learning. Each of us started with ideas about how appreciative inquiry could best serve GTE. We all began with models of how human systems change. Along the way all of us have been challenged to let go of what worked in the past and to create what was needed at the time. We did this with the Zealots Program, the union–management partnership, and a host of other appreciative inquiry applications in support of the culture change. Four lessons come forward from this work.

Lesson 1: The Power of Liberation

We have been repeatedly surprised by reports of actions taken by people who learned appreciative inquiry and decided to use it to make their workplace better. The surprise and the learning comes when we realize how much has been done and how little has been programmatically planned or prescribed by senior leadership—or anyone else, for that matter. Stories abound in the organization about people who, on their own initiative, created interview protocols and interviewed customers, brought AI to their team meetings, convinced their managers to conduct inquiries within their department or area, and solicited positive stories and sent recognition letters.

Appreciative inquiry is a change process that liberates the energy, enthusiasm, and commitment of people at all levels in an organization. It liberates people from the fear that they are wrong, at fault, or to blame, or that they might make a mistake if they try something different. It liberates them from the learned cynicism that makes creative, positive possibilities seem foolish. And it liberates them from the role of critic, a persona that creates distance between people, departments, and customers. It provides them with an approach toward work and work relationships that is fun, satisfying, and practical.

Holding a positive image of people and asking them to tell stories about when they are at their best enhances their willingness to participate and their sense of capacity to impact their work environment in a positive direction. When people are treated as if they do make a difference, they go out and make a difference. When people are treated as if they are the keys to successful customer relations and business development, they act as liaisons to customers and they care for the company's investments. When people are recognized as positive change agents and invited to use their capabilities to change the organization for the better, they do.

Lesson 2: The Power of the Positive Question

Over and over, we experienced the power of positive questions to create strength-based organizing and to render contentious stories irrelevant. When given opportunities to explore the organization's positive core—those factors that give life to the organization at its best—people drop the rhetoric of "ain't it awful" and enthusiastically engage in dialogue about possibilities for a better future. Deficit discourse is a learned habit of communication. Appreciative inquiry provides an alternative "habit of discourse." Appreciative inquiry as a form of organizational communication is more productive organizationally and healthier personally.

Moving an organization in a positive direction—toward greater levels of customer service, on-time performance, or teamwork—requires mastery of the art of the positive question. Embedded in every organization are situations of success, concealed by routine conversational habits of problem analysis and problem solving. Appreciative inquiry brings the organization's success to the foreground, creates a self-fulfilling learning environment, and inspires action. The unconditionally positive question may be leadership's best defense against low morale and high turnover. The power of the positive question brings people, learning, and the organization to life.

Organization change requires that people let go of their "givens": what they consider to be real, true, and certain. It requires a dislodgment of certainty, a journey into the unknown, and an openness to learn. Most change methodologies prompt resistance as they engage people in discussions of what doesn't work and why. Appreciative inquiry, on the other hand, helps organizations transcend contention and adversarial positioning through the power of the positive. Through the appreciative dislodgment of certainty, people become curious rather than contentious, listeners rather than insisters, and co-creators rather than naysayers.

Lesson 3: The Power of Discourse-Centered Change

As was described earlier, we worked from a narrative approach to change. In doing this we took the focus off of people and put it on stories and discourse. We put a spotlight on the narrative processes of the organization. The ways people relate and talk with one another became more prominent than the personality traits of people involved. The stories told about the organization became a central focus for inquiry and change.

Among the significant benefits of a discourse-centered approach to change is the capacity to transform cynical discourse into possibility discourse and to build positive morale among front-line employees. At GTE, appreciative inquiry was introduced to front-line facilitators as a method of facilitation to transform cynical discourse among front-line employees. We introduced the notion of discourse-centered facilitation as opposed to the more traditional person-centered discourse. We helped the facilitators focus on the discourse in the room—the stories participants were telling—and not on the personality traits or behaviors of their class participants.

Through this focus on discourse, participants learned the power of their communication to influence one another, customers, and the company as a whole. And they were given tools and information—appreciative inquiry, business strategies, and product knowledge—to positively contribute to the company. For the most part, they recognized the power of cynical stories to deplete the energy of a successful workforce, and the power of AI to build positive possibilities for themselves and for the organization.

Among the most powerful benefits of a narrative approach to change is the creation of a knowledge-rich work environment. It was an exciting adventure as we participated in the unfolding of the organization's learning capacity. As people learned about AI and began doing interviews, they became alive with new knowledge and insight. The organization's common knowledge increased significantly. Comments from participants in the process included the following:

"I now know so many people I didn't know before, and I understand what they do. I learned so much about other jobs in the company."

"I didn't really understand what went on in a call center until I interviewed my partner who works in a call center."

"I now know who to call at headquarters when I have a question."

The comments pointed out the many ways in which appreciative inquiry proves a knowledge boost to the people and organization involved.

Lesson 4: The Power of Focus on the Organization

A lesson we continue to learn as we engage hundreds and thousands of people in appreciative inquiry is one we first noted in our work with GTE. When people are asked to participate in a change effort targeted at changing behaviors—specifically, their behaviors—they are ambivalent at best. When people are asked to bring their best forward for the benefit of the organization, they do so with enthusiasm and pride.

Organizations are not the sum total of human behavior. They are concepts, images, ideals, and beliefs contained in the stories people tell about themselves and each other. Asking people to change behavior more often than not prompts resistance. Involving people in co-creating the future of their organization—their future—tends to evoke a spirit of cooperation and contribution. People want opportunities to use their gifts and talents, their creativity, and their ideas in acts of cooperative co-creation. AI provides a fertile forum for all stakeholders of an organization to actively engage in discovering, dreaming, and designing their own future. As one participant said of appreciative inquiry, "When I was interviewed I was asked to describe my wildest dream, and I described a workplace where everyone could be involved in designing the organization's future. And then, a few days later when I thought about the appreciative inquiry process, I realized I was living my wildest dream."

9

Creative Applications of Appreciative Inquiry in an Organization-Wide Culture Change Effort: The Hunter Douglas Experience

Amanda Trosten-Bloom

In early 1997, Hunter Douglas (HD) Window Fashions Division (WFD; a manufacturing company in Broomfield, Colorado) initiated a systemwide organizational transformation process. This effort, which engaged an entire system of nearly 1,000 people in all aspects of the AI 4D model, was one of the first interventions of its kind and a model initiative for its creative application of AI principles and practices. This chapter—written about eighteen months after the intervention began—describes some of the highlights of the effort, along with significant outcomes. It also discusses lessons learned about AI in general, and about AI as a vehicle for culture change.

THE COMPANY: "IN THE BEGINNING"

When the energy crisis of the 1970s set motorists gnashing their teeth at gasoline shortages, it also put into action some creative juices that resulted in the transformation of both a company and industry. On a wintry night in a big, drafty Victorian house in Massachusetts, a young inventor lay shivering in bed. As he contemplated what could be done to cover his windows—to keep the warm air in and the cold air out—he noticed that a double curtain on one of the windows had come together in a series of folds that trapped air between them. It was a honeycomb-like configuration that created a thermal insulating effect. The president of a small entrepreneurial company outside of Denver got wind of the idea and persuaded the inventor to work to develop a product. Soon Thermal Technology Corp. began manufacturing a pleated window shade in the shape of a honeycomb, called "Thermocell."

When the company ran short of resources, it approached several window covering manufacturers about a possible purchase of the product. Eventually, Hunter Douglas—the New Jersey–based company that had pioneered the first aluminum venetian blinds in the 1940s and 1950s—saw the unique shade and recognized its potential, not just as a functional product, but as an exciting new decorative window fashion.

A "STAR" IS BORN: THE BIRTH OF HUNTER DOUGLAS WINDOW FASHIONS

In 1985 Hunter Douglas purchased Thermal Technology and established the Hunter Douglas Window Fashions Division. The division manufactured and marketed Duette®, a unique variation of the honeycomb shade that came to be made with soft, durable fabric in a selection of colors. Duette Window Shades achieved unprecedented success and renewed consumer interest in window coverings, an industry that hadn't had a significant new product introduction in decades. Retail sales soared to an estimated $300 million by 1988. In 1997 the Duette honeycomb shade was still the single biggest brand in the entire custom window coverings market. Building on its core competencies of creativity, innovation, and marketing, the division developed another unique proprietary product with early and explosive sales: Silhouette® window shadings. Like Duette, this product garnered top national design awards and became the fastest-growing window fashion in North America and the leading revenue-producing division in the entire Hunter Douglas organization.

TRANSITION AND CHALLENGES

From 1994 to 1996, the Window Fashions Division underwent a significant upheaval in the leadership team that had so successfully led the organization to its position of market leadership. In 1995 the division's former vice president of finance assumed the position of general manager. He inherited an organization that had grown from

27 people in 1985, to 565 in 1995, to 687 in 1996. It had three separate product lines, four separate buildings, and plans to launch another new product within the next two years. Hunter Douglas Window Fashions Division had outgrown the speed, intimacy, and sense of community that had originally facilitated its success.

In an effort to regain some of the original "spirit" of the organization, the new leadership team elected to split the division into separate business units. Two business units were formed around products, while a third was dedicated to new product development. The goal was to develop separate cultures for product innovation and product manufacturing, and to spin off additional business units as additional product lines were created.

But all the change had finally taken its toll. The company worked hard to fill as many as possible of the newly created positions from within, but in the process the organization was "picked clean" of all of its experienced leadership. People who just two years before had been serving as front-line supervisors were now running business units. The behaviors that had initially made them successful—a "can do" attitude and a capacity to get things done—were in part preventing them from developing the leadership below them, in their new roles.

The change in the company's structure resulted in "silos," which were physically and emotionally disconnected. Leaders lost touch with the day-to-day aspects of the business, while production employees lost touch with everything outside their immediate functional or operational areas. Turnover increased at a time when the need for new recruits was at an all-time high. The workforce showed decreasing levels of motivation and initiative, resulting in decreasing levels of productivity. From top to bottom, people were over their heads in brand new water. They were confused about the organization's overall mission, vision, and direction.

IT'S NEVER TOO LATE FOR APPRECIATIVE INQUIRY

In the spring of 1996 the WFD conducted its annual employee opinion survey. For the first time ever, the survey showed downward trends in employees' experiences of Hunter Douglas. These data, combined with the issues already described, persuaded the division's leadership to commission a traditional OD intervention: one-to-one interviews with the general manager, all his direct reports, and all their direct reports.

Beginning in late 1996, a subteam of the leadership group (fondly dubbed the RATs, for Rapid Action Team) was assigned the task of analyzing the survey and interview data for trends. Following their survey, they were charged with recommending a plan to the larger Business Leadership Team (BLT), to correct negative perceptual trends in such areas as connection to the company's mission and vision, communication, and leadership.

While the RATs were engaged in their project, two of the team's members participated in a parallel organizational activity that involved the use of appreciative inquiry. These two RATs decided to apply what they'd learned. At the group's next gathering, they guided the RATs in writing modified "provocative propositions," clear statements of "what might be" in each of the areas of concern that had emerged from the surveys.

The results of this activity were extremely positive. Having seen the effect that their input had on the RATs' work, the same two team members decided to introduce the team to the principles behind their contribution. They invited the external AI consultant to present the approach to the entire group of RATs.

Based on a two-hour presentation of AI and its principles, the RATs recommended AI as the basis for an organization-wide intervention. The purpose of the intervention was to support Hunter Douglas in becoming the company it wished to be, one whose sense of humanity and community–global leadership would permeate all of its decisions and actions, and whose vision and strategy, culture, people, communications, customers, and business processes would be aligned and founded upon the best of what might be.

Despite the momentum that had already been built with regard to the traditional OD intervention, the leadership decided to "change trains" and follow the appreciative inquiry track. Following is a description of some of the high points or peak experiences, some of the more significant creative twists that this journey has taken along the way, and some of the lessons learned for future interventions.

GETTING LEADERSHIP ON BOARD: THE "ROAD SHOW"

Realizing that the BLT could only choose AI if it knew AI, the two external consultants who had previously facilitated different aspects of the OD intervention decided to partner and guide the entire BLT through a one-day introduction to appreciative inquiry. The session's goals were to do the following:

- Help the BLT experience AI as a tool for building trust, communication, and respect for differences within the division.
- Increase leadership's willingness to ask questions, trust nonleadership's opinions, and engage the workforce in decisions about the company and its future.

- Begin building trusting relationships within the team, as well as between leaders and nonleaders.
- Begin luring the organization as a whole into a high-participation process for cultural renewal.

The entire group of thirty-eight spent a full day off-site. The morning was dedicated to "discovery": discussion of the foundational principles, interviewing using the core questions, capturing common themes, and constructing appreciative questions. It was a warm and insightful session, the first "team-building" type of activity in which this group of thirty-eight had ever been engaged. But we still had to show what was different about appreciative inquiry. We had to show that both the process and product of an AI intervention would radically change the tone and direction of the Window Fashions organization, would build relationships that otherwise wouldn't exist, and would deliver a "no more business as usual" message to the entire workforce.

We conveyed that uniqueness with a bang. Right after lunch, we handed out additional copies of the core questions and herded the entire group onto a tour bus that carried them back to the HD staff and production facilities. Everybody was told they had to find someone to interview that met the following criteria:

- You've never met them.
- They're in a different business unit or functional area.
- They're a different gender.
- They have a different length of service than you (i.e., long-tenured if you're new, or vice versa).

It's important to note that the plant tour was a total surprise to everyone, including the supervisors and employees who were pulled from their normal activities to participate in the interviews. We'd considered the relative advantages and disadvantages of advance warning, and had decided that the surprise would substantially contribute to the "no more business and usual" effect that we were trying to create.

The Outcome

What did participants discover? They discovered, in thirty minutes, that the people on the floor shared many of the same hopes and dreams for the company as they did. As opposed to being incapable of envisioning a meaningful future for the company, nonleadership was able to enrich leadership's picture of what the organization could become.

- They discovered, in thirty minutes, that they could reach out across the artificial boundaries that had sprung up between the managers and the "hourlies," as production staff had been known in the past. This was, for example, the first time in eleven years that the head of marketing communication had set foot in one of the production facilities.
- They discovered, in thirty minutes, that they could make a human connection with people with whom they previously had no relationship. A head of operations shared the pride he'd felt when a printer from another business unit talked about the help she had received from fellow workers when her husband had gone through open heart surgery the year before.
- They discovered, in thirty minutes, that floor personnel's peak experiences—just like their own—had emerged as a result of "making a difference" in their workplace. For example, a maintenance technician had described his pride at being described as "Dr. Bob," the person who knew how to "fix anything."
- They discovered, in thirty minutes, that the hopes and dreams that they themselves had articulated in their morning session were mirrored essentially word for word, that, far from distracting from the content of the inquiry, the afternoon interviews had enriched their understanding and experience of the possibilities for the organization.
- Finally, they discovered in thirty minutes that the experience itself had the capacity to address a number of the issues that had been identified as needing attention: communication, respect, and alignment across business units and functions.

Feedback in the organization from that "road trip" was phenomenal. Within a day, the production facilities' grapevine filled with stories of the "suits" who had descended, and questions about what they were doing and why. Almost inadvertently, we had created great curiosity: a kind of anxious anticipation about the effort that was about to take place. By later weaving this surprise visit into our master communication plan, we paved the way for the work that began in earnest less than two months later.

As for the members of the leadership team who served as interviewers, the response was profound. An eleven-year veteran—formerly the executive assistant to the president—said it was her first time ever being inside of one of the production facilities. Someone else talked about being moved to tears during the interview. People shared their astonishment at the level of insight and wisdom they heard in the production staff that they interviewed. Others talked about feeling like they'd made new friends. For the first time ever, they saw a way to share the leadership of the organization with the people whom they were leading.

Based upon this experience and subsequent discussions, the BLT determined to embark upon a full-system culture change process, using appreciative inquiry as the vehicle. They committed to

- Interview every employee, using an employee-generated appreciative protocol.
- Contact customers, suppliers, and community members.
- Benchmark four to six "best in class" companies in the areas in which the division had committed to grow.

Their goals for the organization were as follows:

- To increase the company's overall sense of vision, purpose, and direction.
- To recreate the sense of ownership and purpose that had originally made the company successful.
- To rebuild vertical and horizontal intimacy, communication, and cooperation, both inside and outside the division.
- To teach through the act of doing, rather than exclusively through training classes.
- To become the "employer of choice" in the Boulder community by offering opportunities for personal and professional growth, both on and off the job.

Key Learnings

We learned many things about both AI and the team as a result of this session. The first and most important thing we learned was that it is never too late to introduce appreciative inquiry. When presented with an experience of the AI alternative, even people who are seemingly wedded to another course of action may choose to follow the positive path.

Second, we relearned the power of appreciative interviews to quickly and powerfully create relationships with the power to create reality, despite seemingly insurmountable obstacles.

Third, we learned that there are times when it is both appropriate and worthwhile to break cultural "rules" when introducing AI to an organization. Too often, as consultants, we soft-pedal and try to carefully match our intervention to the organization's existing norms. In so doing, we may imprint or reinforce the organization's self-imposed limitations, rather than providing our clients with graphic, generative alternatives that might serve them in the long run. Our introductory session worked, in part, because it shook participants up, and took them out of their comfort zones.

Fourth, this session reinforced the importance of experiential learning when introducing AI. The depth of possibilities offered by this way of working only become clear to people when they see it in action, when they experience an appreciative interview and the relationship and insight it evokes.

Last but not least, we learned not to rush the process of introducing AI. Our one-day session was a "teaser" and nothing else. Having gone through that, the BLT was receptive to discussing the long-range possibilities for AI in the organization. They could begin to imagine its applications and outcomes. This ultimately helped them to consider putting the significant time and resources into the effort that they ultimately approved.

It was nearly three months from the time of this session before we began any work with the organization at large. Despite our more-than-energetic beginning, there was a great deal of soul searching and "angst" that went into the decision to start over with a new OD model, and even greater concern over how we would proceed once we got past the discovery phase. Members of the BLT spent between eight and twelve hours together following the original training (with substantial activity in between sessions) before they were prepared to move forward with AI as the "intervention of choice."

SPREADING AI TO THE MASSES: KICK-OFF MEETINGS

Once the intervention was given a final "thumbs-up," the first order of business was to communicate enough to the general workforce to enable us to solicit volunteers to work on the design of internal and external protocols. An ad hoc subteam of the BLT formed to spearhead that communication through a series of kick-off meetings for all employees. Following is a description of the most unique and effective aspects of these meetings.

Employees as Customers

One of the company's "core competencies" had always been its attentiveness to quality and detail in its relationships with fabricators, dealers, and other customers during product launches and updates. We determined to turn that core competency inward, for the first time in the company's history.

We set aside the empty mezzanine in one of the production facilities. We used the staging that we had previously used only at trade shows and fabricator meetings and rented chairs for everyone, both of which were "firsts" for a company whose plant meetings had never lasted more than thirty minutes in the employee cafeteria.

We scheduled meetings on all three shifts, to meet people "where they lived." We sent out personalized invitations to every employee to the launch of "Focus 2000—Hunter Douglas's Bridge to the Next Millennium," and staggered attendance at different sessions to ensure that a cross-section of business units and functions would be present at every meeting. Members of the BLT served as check-in clerks and ushers, while others served coffee, tea, and dough-nuts or cookies as employees arrived.

At the end of each meeting we asked for people to both volunteer and nominate their peers to be part of a team of 100 people (nearly one-eighth of the workforce) that would design the protocols that would be used for internal and external interviews. We opened the process up to everyone, and selected only those who had been fre-quently nominated.

All of this sent a "no more business as usual" message to a staff that had previously become jaded on "programs-of-the-month" and traditional need-to-know and top-down communication.

Video as an Educational Tool

One of our greatest challenges was to give people an experience of appreciative inquiry in the very limited time frame that was avail-able (ninety minutes per session). Part of our answer was to *video-tape* appreciative interviews and show excerpts of the best during critical points in the presentation.

Weeks before the presentation, members of the marketing com-munication team descended upon all three shifts of the production plants with video crews in tow. They conducted ad hoc appreciative interviews with about fifty employees, using variations on the four core questions.

- "Tell me about your beginnings with Hunter Douglas. What were your most positive first impressions or excitements when you first came to work for the company?"
- "Tell me about a peak experience or high point in your time here at Hunter Douglas."
- "Without being humble, what do you most value about yourself, your team, Hunter Douglas as a whole?"
- "If you had a magic wand and could have three wishes granted to make Hunter Douglas the most alive, most rewarding, most fun workplace possible, what would those be?"

The raw tapes were edited into different segments of videotape, which were interspersed into the kick-off presentation. People had the opportunity to see themselves and their peers, and to hear about some of the most positive aspects of the organization and its people. They heard stories of people's first days at work, and of having been warmly invited to "join the fold." They heard stories of softball and bowling teams, and of company picnics. They heard stories of people's pride at making a great contribution to a really great product. They heard people's wishes for a "big sandwich day" and enhancements to their pay and benefit packages. (Over three years after the first interviews, "Show me the money!"—a quote from one of the machine operators who was interviewed on this first video—had become company shorthand for "let's get to the bottom line on this.) The videos created a sense of warmth, of honoring, and of valuing the past, which both educated people on the AI process and initiated the culture change even before the anticipated activities had begun.

Guest Speakers

Perhaps the most eventful decision we made for our kick-off meetings was to bring in guests from other organizations that had used appreciative inquiry to tell stories of their experiences and of the impact that appreciative inquiry had on them and their organizations. We worked hard to locate people with down-to-earth and easy presentation styles, people whose experience and manner would be compatible with the production workers who represented more than two-thirds of our workforce.

After a fairly extensive search, we found two speakers. One was a mechanic who had formerly been with ProCare (one of the earliest AI implementation sites); a second was from Nynex (one of the Baby Bells, at which AI had been used as an alternative to sexual harassment training). Though the industries that they had served were quite different from ours, their styles and their real-life experiences spoke clearly to our workforce.

The woman from Nynex shared the unique ways in which AI had been used as an alternative to sexual harassment training within her organization. She described how the team that was coordinating the intervention had put ads in the company newsletter, asking for volunteers to participate in a study of "positive cross-gender relationships" within the organization. She described the team's surprise when approximately 100 pairs of men and women—self-identified as having had an exceptionally positive working relationship—responded to their ad and agreed to take part in the interviews that ultimately resulted in a larger, organization-wide intervention. She also talked about some of the smaller steps their team had taken to build a positive sense of their workplace. For example, she described the posters that people put in their offices that said, "Catch someone doing something right."

The stories with the greatest impact for the lion's share of the Hunter Douglas workforce were told by the former automobile mechanic, who had taken his first-ever business trip to conduct customer interviews during his company's inquiry. Reflecting back on his experience with the ProCare inquiry, he described the "electricity" that had been generated as people began to dream of ways to make his car dealership the best it could possibly be. He also recalled his pride at having been sent out to conduct an external inquiry with a trucking company to inquire into their customer service practices and to bring them back to ProCare. He shared his pride at having been able to make such a significant contribution to his organization and his customers.

In the end, these presentations—along with the question-and-answer period that followed them—did more to "win over" the workforce. This was evident in employees' closing comments at the end of the meetings. In those last few minutes, people often commented that the most significant part of the gathering had been hearing about appreciative inquiry from people outside of Hunter Douglas, in particular the automobile mechanic, whom one person referred to as "a real person like me." These outside stories gave people both a picture of what was possible and enthusiasm for the process, conditions critical to their willingness to involve themselves in the design of the protocols.

The Outcome

As a result of the six kick-off meetings, nearly 300 people (out of a workforce that at that time numbered about 850) were nominated and/or volunteered to become part of the 100-person Protocol Design Team. One employee described herself as "skeptical, but willing to play," a significant leap in light of her reputation as someone with "an attitude." Another stood outside of the meeting room for the next two gatherings, lobbying people to nominate her to be on the Protocol Design Team. She was so enthusiastic about the process that she decided to "stack the deck" in favor of her involvement.

From the group of 300, the "top 20" (i.e., those who had received the most nominations and who had self-nominated) worked as a subteam to flesh out the balance of a team of 100, selected to represent a little more than 10 percent of the total employee population. We explained our criteria as follows:

- To create a true representative sampling of the workforce, taking into account differences in business unit, function, shift, gender, race, and "attitude."
- To involve as many self-nominees as possible in order to build upon people's inherent interest and energy.

Within two weeks, the final group of 100 had been identified and notified of their participation in the first off-site meeting. Their "job description" was to generate topics for a whole-company inquiry, and to create the internal and external interview guides for the Focus 2000 effort.

Clearly, the kick-off meeting's process accomplished its goal of building curiosity, enthusiasm, and momentum for the unfolding process. But one of the most striking outcomes of meetings was the one that was almost invisible. We found that the process of creating the videos—of asking the questions and disseminating the stories—was an education in and of itself. The three women who had conducted the interviews for the videos later described the impact that the process had had on them: "I felt so proud of my contribution to the process," shared one after the meeting was over.

These stories we collected—they really made a difference to the people in this Company. And being on the video really made a difference to the people we interviewed, too! Collecting those stories helped me get to know the people I talked to. Now, when I walk through the plant, I know people . . . I have friends! I've worked here for over ten years, and I've never had friends in the production buildings.

All three of the interviewers from the kick-off meeting became leaders in the Focus 2000 effort, working many hours of overtime to support the inquiry and to coordinate the division's communication of the stories and the magic. This reminded us, again, of AI's powerful capacity to unlock people's creativity and inspire them to engage their hearts and minds in service of the whole.

Key Learnings

Once again, as with the "road show" session, we learned the value of breaking cultural rules. Our decision not to treat this as "just another plant meeting" was one of the most important ones in the process. Our attention to the details of the experience had a significant payoff: Even the people who remained skeptical had to admit that this seemed different than anything they'd experienced before.

Our discovery of video as a vehicle for introducing the spirit of AI was one on which we built throughout the process. Both the filming itself and the presentation of the films significantly contributed to the initially positive inner dialogue that developed about the project and its intent. People began talking about—and therefore remembering—the company's higher qualities. They made relationships with the interviewers (as they were wandering through the plant) and with their coworkers (as they viewed the responses). It created a new kind of voice for the "masses."

Finally, we were reminded of the importance of storytelling in the reeducation of a company's mind and heart. First, this medium matched our message of AI. Next, our guest speakers' stories held more credibility for the masses at Hunter Douglas than any kind of stand-up presentation by even the most powerful "expert." Because of this format, our presentations were both easier to deliver and infinitely more powerful.

CONFLICT RESOLUTION USING AI: BUMPY BEGINNINGS

At our initial off-site meeting to design the interview protocols, two subteams were formed. The two teams simultaneously received training on the basics of appreciative inquiry. They then worked separately for the next two days to design the interview protocols for four different stakeholder groups.

The internal interview team dubbed itself "the Seventh Generation" in honor of the Iroquois Nation, which weighed all decisions of significance against their impact on the seventh generation to come. This team wanted to celebrate the impact that the Focus 2000 program would have on the seventh generation of Hunter Douglas employees and customers.

The external interview teams dubbed themselves "the Outsiders" in honor of the three "outside stakeholder" groups that they represented: customers, suppliers, and community members. From the beginning, the Outsiders were faced with more challenges than their internal counterparts.

First, the topics that were selected by the full group were more internally than externally focused. Therefore, the design of the external protocols was more challenging for these groups. Second, the team was split into three different smaller teams. They needed to continue working together for several weeks following the completion of the off-site retreat in order to complete their more complicated tasks. The mix of all three shifts made full-group meetings difficult, so subteams needed to form to create straw models and recommendations for the larger team to approve. Many team members couldn't be reached to discuss questions or plan future meetings, since nonprofessional staff was without phones, e-mail, or personal mailboxes. For all of these reasons, the group was challenged in the areas of bonding, collaboration, and communication. Third, the team contained a different mix of employees than the Seventh Generation. There was a larger percentage of professional and mid-level management staff than in the other team, and a more evident disparity of experience between people who regularly traveled for business and those who had never worked outside of the production facilities. Finally, the stakes were higher for the Outsiders as they conducted their interviews. There were greater travel and payroll costs associated with external interviews than with their internal counterparts. Also, a handful of the designated external interviewees had reputations for being "difficult," so the potential for "hard" interviews with a potentially negative impact on the employee and interviewee was somewhat greater than on the inside. In short, the circumstances of the task set this team up to reenact some of the company's core cultural issues, especially as they related to decision making, collaboration, and trust.

The Outsiders: Into the "Valley of Death"

Within a few weeks of their formation, the Outsiders began to experience significant distress. In some ways, the team began to live up to the darker side of its name, as it became more and more "outside" the mainstream of the AI process. Decisions would be made in meetings and then "unmade" by clusters of people (usually professional or managerial staff) outside of the meeting who became privy to additional insights or information.

The most notable example of this pattern was as follows. The full group decided, after a lengthy discussion of the pros and cons, that every member of the team should travel, if necessary, to conduct external interviews. After this large group meeting was over, a smaller group of professional and managerial staff started talking with one another separately. As they talked, they became increasingly concerned about two things (both of which had been discussed and dismissed in the larger meeting). First, they were worried about the costs that would be incurred with such a choice (these could be avoided by having interviews conducted by people who were already going to be at or near the identified site). Second, they were concerned about the risks involved with sending people who had little or no professional travel experience, and little or no experience working with professional- and managerial-level issues, to interview high-level managers at the identified sites. Following this off-line discussion, the professional and managerial subgroup came back with significant revisions to the original plan, and were seemingly surprised by the resentment and resistance that their proposed revisions met from the larger group.

Nonprofessional staff began to feel disrespected and excluded (a core theme that had initially led the organization down the AI path), and began complaining to their peers and filing grievances with the human resources function. Some of them were threatening to pull out of the process entirely, while others were meekly and quietly complying with the trend to have interviews conducted only by people who would be at the location anyway (i.e., professional and managerial staff).

The team looked as if it were about to implode. The company's leadership became concerned about the integrity of both the AI process and the precedent that this team's success (or failure) would set for the future. It appeared that the group was in desperate need of some support, but traditional team building (i.e., individual interviews, "venting," etc.) was contrary to the overall principles of the process.

Back on Flat Land

Between four and six weeks after the team was formed, we decided to address the group's issues through a six-hour team-building session founded upon the principles of AI. The session was mandatory for every participant in the Outsiders, and the general manager and facilitating consultant personally delivered invitations on all three shifts.

We began the session with one-on-one appreciative interviews, primarily between professional and nonprofessional staff. The protocols asked people to recall and describe their initial excitement when they were first asked to be involved with the team. They then were led to explore "peak" experiences—both in this and other teams—of effective decision making, collaboration, and trust.

Upon completion of the interviews, they identified common themes and developed a set of agreements or "ground rules" regarding how the team would self-manage in the future. These included agreements on how the group would make decisions, resolve differences of opinion, and manage conflict.

Through the lens of these ground rules, final decisions were made regarding protocols, interview assignments, and travel schedules. Despite their reservations, the general manager and professional staff agreed to endorse the larger group's decision to send nonprofessional staff out to conduct interviews. The die was cast.

The Outcome

Over the next three and a half weeks, thirty members of the Outsiders team conducted nearly eighty interviews. Production workers, professionals, and mid-level managers traveled in teams of two all around the country to interview a variety of customers, suppliers, and community members. Following are some of the best stories from their experiences:

- One line worker was assigned to interview one of the biggest "problem" customers, a man with a reputation throughout the company for complaining about everything and making unreasonable demands related to products, turnaround, and quality. At various points in his interview, "Jim Jones" (the customer) would begin to complain about something that was wrong with the Hunter Douglas product or operation. At each stage of the game, the interviewer would say, "Now Mr. Jones, I know this is very important—but that's not really the purpose of our interview. Let me write that down and have someone else get back to you to talk about your problem." At the end of the interview, Jones gave her a big hug and a tour of his production plant. Two months later, he participated in the first summit. He was a frequent, positive, and insightful contributor to the process. At the end of the third day, he asked for the microphone and shared, "In my mind, the Window Fashions Division has been engaged in one of the most powerful, positive activities I've known in my experience with the company. This is what will keep this company great in the future."

- Another production employee traveled to Omaha to interview one of the company's biggest distributors. He heard a story in his interview of that company's program to employ homeless people. In this program, the owner of the facility provided up-front repayable stipends to homeless people, allowing them to purchase basic clothing and make a down payment on an apartment, in exchange for coming to work at the company. He boasted of the results: measurable reduction in turnover, partnered with the satisfaction of having helped people lift themselves up out of desperate poverty. A month or so after returning from his interview, "John" (the interviewer) asked permission to make a presentation to the president of the division's parent company during his next visit. He came to the meeting with a detailed proposal for piloting a similar program as a way of simultaneously filling vacant positions and providing a significant community service.

- Several people returned from interviews filled with appreciation for Hunter Douglas and its work environment. One man returned saying, "The employees at that other company couldn't believe that they'd send a machine operator like me out to do this kind of interview! They said I must be working for the best company in the world, and I began to think that might be true." Another woman reflected, "I never knew how good we had it here, till I saw some of the working conditions at those other plants, and heard about their pay and benefits. The people here need to know what they have. They need to know what a good place this is to work." Having personally seen alternatives and received feedback from their interviews, both employees more fully recognized the excellence of the Hunter Douglas work environment and the level of responsibility they had been given through the Focus 2000 program.

Members of the Outsiders team documented their discoveries in a binder and on videotape. The written results were included in a feedback report section called "The Newspaper" and were incorporated in the benchmarking findings. The best and most powerful stories were condensed onto continuous-loop videotape, which ran in the employee cafeterias for nearly a month after the interviews were complete.

Managers and professionals on the team—even those who were initially concerned about sending production employees out—almost universally agreed that nonprofessional involvement in external interviews was one of the most important elements of the Focus 2000 process. Nine months later, the general manager reported this as having been "the most significant and positive decision we made" in the entire Focus 2000 process. "I can't believe we almost didn't let them go. It was a 'moment of truth,' and thank goodness we made the right decision."

Key Learnings

This was just one of several episodes that threatened to derail the positive energy of the AI effort. In fact, as we proceeded deeper and deeper into the intervention—as safety and trust began to increase—more and more of the company's habitual patterns came up for inspection and repatterning. We learned first from this episode (and then from subsequent episodes that followed in other parts of the organization) the importance of "walking the talk," of believing in AI as a viable tool and using it in even the most "dysfunctional" of situations. We learned that it is important to "bless" the upsets, to look at them as signs of the organization's self-correction, and to use them as opportunities to do things differently, one episode at a time. Finally, we were reminded of the importance of the generative metaphor—the one visible experience of success—as a tool for retraining and reeducating large groups of people (see also Chapter 5). Had the Outsiders "gone under" (as it briefly seemed that they might), their failure would have been proof (on the grapevine) that "nothing can ever change within the Window Fashions Division." Because the team succeeded instead, in such a stellar way, they proved the opposite: that line employees and leaders could, indeed, work out differences and collaborate effectively to accomplish great things for the organization.

THE INSTITUTIONALIZATION OF INSPIRED ACTION: A SUMMIT FOR POSITIVE ACTION

Within three months of the Protocol Design Team session, nearly 500 internal and external interviews were conducted. A team of thirty from all shifts, functions, and levels of the WFD then gathered to identify the highlights, themes, hopes, and dreams from the stories collected. The mid-term report they would produce became the foundation and pre-reading for a three-day "dreaming" summit that would take place about one month later.

On the last afternoon of the summit we held a three-hour "open space" session. During this session, participants were encouraged to convene meetings on topics about which they were passionate, and which were related to the implementation of the seven provocative propositions we had written over the past two days. A list of thirty-eight proposed topics was multivoted down to the top fourteen, and forty-five-minute initial meetings were convened.

At the conclusion of the summit, the fourteen "conveners," as they came to be known, gathered again to create an ongoing process and protocol for ongoing inspired action within the Window Fashions Division. They developed the concept of "Action Groups": cross-functional clusters of volunteers who would develop and support the implementation of proposals for organizational improvements related to the company's overall mission and vision. The first fourteen Action Groups were formed around the "open space" topics that had emerged at the summit.

The concept was for Action Groups always to be initiated by a convener, someone with a passionate interest in (but not necessarily line responsibility for) the topic at hand. The convener would initiate an Action Group by writing a purpose statement for presentation to the AI Advisory Team. That team would prioritize the proposed topics, based upon the provocative propositions, and maintain a continuous flow of fourteen "active" groups at any given time. Once a group was established as "active," conveners would recruit two "co-champions," identify which functions in the organization should be represented in the group, and solicit volunteer participants.

The Infrastructure That Made It Happen

The co-champion's job was to attend meetings and provide coaching, support, and guidance regarding objectives, membership, and resources.

Each group also had access to trained facilitators, people who had training and skill in general meeting management and group facilitation, with particular expertise in the practical applications of appreciative inquiry. Initially, the first fourteen conveners were trained as facilitators. Later in the process, the organization trained a group of "master facilitators" who could be called upon either to do the actual facilitation or to train new facilitators as they emerged.

The AI Advisory Team (consisting of twelve representatives from throughout the organization) served as the funnel through which Action Groups were formed and disbanded. They prioritized the Action Groups in terms of "active" and "inactive" status. They kept track of the activities of all of the groups, to help eliminate duplication and combine resources, as necessary. They also reviewed the final proposals and authorized action related to their ongoing implementation.

The Outcome

Having gone into and out of an initial period of confusion (trying to determine the groups' scope and authority, membership, and so forth), eleven out of the original fourteen Action Groups took off like gangbusters. Of the other three, one merged with another group and two were deferred for later action. About ten months after their initial implementation, the following actions were initiated on behalf of the organization.

Fostering Creativity in the Workplace

This group conducted an international search and identified a training program out of Europe that provides a concrete skill set and process for helping people think "out of the box." They have proposed to make this training mandatory for every employee in the company. In addition, they have proposed creation of an administrative or advisory team to facilitate implementation of structural and organizational changes that would help to foster innovation and creativity at every level of the organization.

New Hire Orientation

A standardized, twenty-one-module new-hire orientation has been created and implemented. Every employee hired prior to its implementation will eventually go through this program as a way of building a sense of unity across the company and educating people on the business as a whole.

Recognition

The first-ever Employee Recognition Dinner took place, honoring the "heroes and heroines" of the Focus 2000 effort. Each person who attended the dinner was there by peer nomination. Five people who received multiple peer nominations were given larger awards.

This has now become a regular, semiannual event that is tied to the general business, rather than strictly to the Focus 2000 effort.

In addition, a values-based recognition program has been initiated, which allows peers to recognize and tell stories about peers for behaviors that exemplify company values. As people attain the highest level of recognition in this regard, they will be eligible for gifts as significant as paid sabbaticals.

Fun in the Workplace

This group essentially became a standing committee, initiating monthly all-company activities whose purpose is to have a good time and enhance morale. Their activities have included "theme days" for dress (including "Dress Your Supervisor Day," "Tie-Dye Day," "Clashing Day," etc.), and a "Blast from the Past" celebration, to which people brought photographs or mementos of themselves at a younger age (an opportunity for people to see their coworkers through a different lens, and to learn of common bonds that they hadn't known existed).

Mentorship

A formal mentorship program has been initiated, offering both "mini-mentorships" (for people interested in exploring particular career tracks) and "full mentorships" (for people who want up to half-time training in a field outside their area of training and expertise.

Promoting the AI Philosophy and Experience

A process has been initiated for introducing the principles of AI (without naming them as such) to the harder-to-reach members of the workforce. This harder-to-reach group includes all those people who, because of language or cultural barriers or a natural skepticism, have been unable or unwilling to participate fully in the Focus 2000 process.

Career Paths

Two years after the inquiry, a career planning function was added to the human resources staff. The career resource center came to contain current job descriptions and organization charts for every position in the company. Eventually, it will also provide links to the existing tuition reimbursement program, in addition to providing one-on-one career counseling, resumé-writing assistance, and general career-related training and development.

Voluntary Overtime and Flexible Scheduling

At the time of the first summit, the number-one presenting issue was mandatory overtime for the workforce. This issue drove many of the Action Groups and activities that flowed from that conference, including cross-training and strategic planning. Eight months after the first summit, mandatory overtime had been virtually eliminated, through improved planning and communication. A year after that, one of the business units instituted a new shift schedule, which allowed people to work four days on and three days off. Now, three years later, many people in staff functions have the choice to telecommute, while production employees are experimenting with job sharing.

Hunter Douglas University

Within six months of the summit, steps were taken toward formation of a Hunter Douglas Virtual University, a central source for professional and personal development for HD employees, customers, and other stakeholders. Two years later, the division broke ground on a Corporate Learning Center. In 1999 Hunter Douglas University was officially opened, complete with a computer laboratory, a lending library (including career resource center), multiple conference rooms, and a dividable classroom wired for audiovisual and sound and capable of seating up to 150 people. This facility has allowed the company to build upon what's become a core capability of periodically hosting large, cross-functional, cross-level conferences that facilitate learning, relationship, and connection to the company's larger mission and vision.

Creating a Shared Vision

Over and over in the interviews people's "three wishes" had included a desire for greater clarity of vision within the company, a clearer, more compelling sense of "where we're going" that would allow people to allocate time and resources in a more methodical fashion. One year after the original Focus 2000 protocols were designed, the company launched its first-ever strategic planning conference. In that conference, nearly seventy-five people—ranging from senior leadership to hourly employees—worked to establish the company's strategic vision and strategies for the next three to five years. As a result of the interviews, synthesis, and conversations that took place at the conference—which was the company's second summit—the company made the revolutionary commitment to a strategic vision that included movement beyond the world of "window fashions" to include a global (versus national) market.

Cross-Training

About nine months after the first summit, a formal cross-training program was introduced to the workforce. The intention was to pilot the program with "high-potential" line workers from each of the business units, and then to expand the program and make it available to the general workforce. In addition to creating more of a "renaissance" workforce, it was imagined that this program would be seen as the first step toward developing a formal succession-planning and leadership-development process. One of the women who participated in developing this program describes what happened when it was about to be implemented:

I came away from that Summit clear that cross-training was very, very important. I talked to my co-workers, and they all said, "Yeah, yeah—they'll never support this or let it happen. Sure we need it, but it won't go through." . . . Well, I joined an Action Group and worked hard. We were given the responsibility and authority to act on our vision. We designed a great program, proposed it to the Advisory Team, and got the go-ahead to test it. Then . . . nobody signed up!!! . . . Once we got over trying to "drive" it through, we stepped back and thought about it. We realized, finally, that there was a loud, clear message trying to be heard. "They" weren't the problem—it was the organization. The organization didn't really have a passion for cross training. . . . When our cross-training program died, I was disappointed but OK. In the end, the only thing I really accomplished was getting an answer—but that was a big thing. It meant that I had the power to get an answer.

Initially, people had hoped that the Action Groups would provide a forum for anyone in the organization to take the initiative to make things happen. People were excited about the possibilities for interdisciplinary input on issues related to the overall good of the organization. Finally, they were excited to have their voices heard, and to see the potential for action to be taken in areas that they have previously hoped and dreamed. As they evolved, these groups significantly furthered the agenda of the general workforce and the organization as a whole. Some of the programs that were implemented by these groups had been in process for years before this, without meaningful conclusion. Equally important, the groups provided a forum through which people could make a difference on things that mattered to them. They reeducated people about their power and influence in the organization. "We had always had support to take action on behalf of the organization," said one employee, "but this time—suddenly—people were making resources available and paying attention to what we were doing. They backed us up, and made it possible for us to follow through on—and finally do— the things that we knew needed to be done."

Though the Action Groups eventually completed their work and disbanded, their spirit remains in the organization three years after they were first formed. Employees continue to band together around topics of mutual concern, and frequently present solutions to problems that managers have lacked time, energy, or insight to correct. For example, in early 2000 a cross-functional cross-shift employee group in one of the business units identified a way to significantly reduce "vane jams," which had consistently resulted in thousands of dollars in losses and returned goods, not to mention the hardship and irritation of related rework.

Key Learnings

Years after the initial inquiry, with action having been taken in most of the originally identified critical areas, we're faced with new and exciting challenges that were nonissues in the past. For example

- How do we capture and celebrate those successes? We continue to use "time lapse photography" as part of our now-annual strategic planning process, and are contemplating other ways to get the stories back into the system on a more universal basis.
- What is an appropriate organization structure to ensure that resources and time are made available to the people who step up to the plate and convene action groups in the future? Our first round of conveners spearheaded action groups in addition to their regular responsibilities. This became a source of frustration and stress for some of those people; it was also a disincentive for other people to take on such responsibilities in the future.
- How many employee-sponsored groups (Action Groups or otherwise) can we operate at any given time? In retrospect, fourteen company-sponsored groups were too many, particularly given the fact that these ran parallel to the primary activities of the business.

As a consultant, I continue to ponder over these Action Groups' birth and development, and I find myself with more questions than answers. Without a doubt, they had a challenging, if not difficult, beginning. Many of them floundered for months, trying to figure out what they were trying to accomplish and how they would know if they got there. For some time it appeared that many of the groups were dying, and then "magically," at about six months, nearly all of them came out of incubation with detailed, professional proposals that had a significant impact on the organization and its employees over an extended period of time.

I wonder whether their rocky start needed to have been so rocky, or whether there might have been a smoother, more systematic way in which they could have gotten on their feet. Some days I believe that the lesson is to trust that the necessary people and structures will emerge. Other days I believe that some initial sense of boundaries and structure would help similar groups to get up and running more quickly, and with less frustration. What we do know is that an "incubation" period is something that's to be expected and planned for. We also know that having people of passion is critical, but that having access to skilled facilitation and resources is equally important. Finally, we know that a commitment to continuous learning and continuous improvement is critical if an organization is to create an effective, viable Action Group system of this kind. Our answers (which were developed, in some cases, with great pain) have worked for us. For example, we eventually established a "buddy" system to help new conveners and Action Groups get on their feet. We began to document the things that earlier groups did that helped them get going, and are offering those things as "tips" for newcomers. As the Action Groups eventually gave way to "process teams" (employee-formed and run vehicles for making a difference in the work and the workplace), we developed a formalized "chartering" structure that enhanced communication between champions and teams and ensured that resources were available to implement.

IMPORTANT CROSSROADS IN THE JOURNEY

Topic Choice Is Fateful

When the initial protocols were designed, we tried to involve as many nonleaders as possible in order to expand the sense of vision, community, and ownership to the entire workforce. We also tried to ride the energy of people's interest and enthusiasm, and as much as possible involve volunteers (rather than people who needed to be coerced). Though our logic had great merit, the result was that a group that was skewed about three to one in favor of nonleadership selected our inquiry topics. As a result, we ended up with all people-related, "touchy-feely" topics—the topics that were of most meaning to the average member of the workforce given the downward turn morale had taken over the last twelve to twenty-four months:

People

Education

Quality of Work Life

Morale and Recognition
Communication

The good news about these topics is that the actions that flowed from them during our "delivery" phase were of clear, immediate interest and concern to the general workforce. They evolved activities and programs that had an enormous impact on people's day-to-day quality of life, particularly for employees at the hourly and production level. The bad news was that these topics had less impact on the bottom-line aspects of the business than they might have, had we engaged more leaders in the selection and topics or explored things with a more immediate connection to the "business of the business."

We dealt with bad news about these topics by "bending" the second half of our interview data during the synthesis process for our second summit. The focus of this second summit was on strategic planning. Rather than simply working with best stories, best insights, and so on, we asked a series of questions concerning "culture as strategic advantage," "best in class," and "creative business opportunities," asking people to scan the interview notes for information related to these key topics. The result was a detailed description of the company's core capabilities, strategic advantages, and strategic opportunities, including the opportunity to attract and retain the highest caliber of employees out there by becoming "one of the top 100 employers in the United States." Just as we were taught early on in the intervention that it's never too late for appreciative inquiry, we learned from this closing wave of synthesis that it's never too late to expand the implications of a topic.

Designing the Social Architecture

Another significant choice was made at our first summit, when we constructed our provocative propositions (which we called "design statements"). This was our time to recreate the "social and technical architecture" of our organization to reflect and respond to our most positive past experiences and highest future aspirations (as reflected through the initial Focus 2000 interviews). It was an opportunity to weave insights about our original people-related topics into the fabric of the organization.

Of course, our original topic choice had already had a "fateful" impact on the data we had received during the discovery phase. People's hopes, dreams, wishes, and peak experiences were almost all related to the original, people-related topics. We didn't understand at the time how to take these data and make them real in such areas as financial and operating systems, products and customers, or physical environment. It was time to make choices about where we would spend our time and resources. Instead, we wrote compelling but for the most part general and ungrounded "dream" statements.

To the company's credit, the actions that flowed out of these design statements were very grounded and powerful, and, again, had a significant impact on the organization in areas that were of immediate concern to the general workforce. But when the groups first formed, most of them seemed to be dealing with issues that, like the proverbial "elephant," could only be eaten one bite at a time. I've wondered if some of their early struggles around mission and scope were the result of the design statements' overly "global" construction.

AN OPEN QUESTION:
WITHIN OR BEYOND THE EXISTING STRUCTURE?

Our decision to stick with volunteers throughout the Focus 2000 effort (rather than mandating participation) worked both for and against us. It worked for us in that it allowed the people with the most energy for Focus 2000 to contribute their energy in ways that were really helpful to the effort. It worked against us in that it created some "push-back" from people who were left behind (from off-sites and interviews) to keep the business going during others' absences. Over time, some of the more active participants experienced anywhere from low to moderate levels of frustration and resistance from their leaders and peers alike.

Different members of our advisory team hold very different opinions about the merit of the approach we took. Based on benchmarking he has done with other organizations that have undergone significant culture change efforts, the general manager in particular feels strongly that our effort would have been even more successful if we had worked within—rather than alongside—the existing organizational structure. He feels that had we worked harder to bring the mid-level folks along (i.e., through earlier training and/or direct involvement in the interview process), they would have supported the process more completely with the people who reported to them. It's a question we have asked, and it has no clear answer.

PROGRESS REPORT

The appreciative inquiry process at Hunter Douglas Window Fashions Division exceeded most leaders' and employees' expectations, both in the first nine months of its life (from initiation through summit) and in the three years that have since passed. Here are some of the results that we use to measure an increase in employee motivation, vision, and commitment.

Four years after the culture change process was first initiated, the general manager and vice president of human resources reflected on just a few of the more striking changes they'd experienced:

Within the first year, our production and productivity both improved—largely as a result of people's increased participation in "problem-solving" and decision-making activities. Our operations improvement suggestions were up over 100 percent. This, in turn, has had a big impact on both our quality and our internal customer service. Last but not least, today's employee retention is the best it's ever been—despite years of record low national and local unemployment. The division is simply a different place than it was when we began our efforts.

In addition, the human resources function marked increased participation in tuition assistance, especially among hourly employees. They now regularly host two Toastmasters chapters (the first was formed by participants in the Focus 2000 effort). Participation in Dale Carnegie seminars regularly hovers at thirty-five to forty people, a more than 100-percent increase in average participation prior to Focus 2000.

On-site research by a master's candidate from Pepperdine University showed positive changes in each of the areas he measured as a result of the Focus 2000 efforts (Chandler, 1998). In particular, his research indicated that since the implementation of appreciative inquiry there have been improvements in

- Employees' understanding of organizational goals.
- Employees' understanding of how their work fits with the organization's goals.
- Employee commitment to the organization's goals.
- Employees' sense of ownership for their work.
- Employees' motivation to be productive, innovative, and creative.

All of these quantitative findings were supported by qualitative employee comments gathered during on-site focus groups.

Perhaps most telling were the results of an unplanned series of "Employee on the Street" interviews conducted about nine months into the Focus 2000 effort. Of the employees who were polled, 75 percent had been only tangentially involved in the Focus 2000 program. Most of these employees described Hunter Douglas as a kinder, gentler, more open place to work than it had been prior to the introduction of Focus 2000.

WHY THE PROCESS WORKED

As the stories of the company's beginnings show, Hunter Douglas and its people share a number of core competencies:

- Their phenomenal success in the marketplace was partly the result of their capacities to imagine, create, and market innovative, forward-looking products. They know how to formulate a vision and to communicate and "sell" that vision to a relatively conservative marketplace. This translated into a willingness and capacity to see the value of the AI process, which, at the time, had been relatively untested in the corporate and for-profit sectors.

- They know how to solicit, listen to, and respond to people's "crazy" hopes and dreams. Some of their most innovative products had emerged from offhand comments made in focus groups or on the phone with customer support representatives. This meant that discovery—so integral to the AI process—was a process that made intuitive sense to them, even though the context was somewhat unfamiliar.

- They are a company of "doers." They take personal responsibility for getting things done, and they recognize and reward that same behavior in others. They have a "sense of urgency," and they easily and happily juggle lots of balls at the same time. This meant that they could not only handle—but on some level they enjoyed—the intensity and confusion that was created when a project of this magnitude was initiated and implemented in such a brief time frame (only six months from BLT training through the first summit).

In the past, the company had only directed these skills in the areas of marketing and product development. As a tool, appreciative inquiry allowed Hunter Douglas to harness these skills in the service of a larger vision and audience. It allowed

- the entire workforce to learn from the wisdom and insights of the "founding fathers."
- the company to build upon what had worked in the past, and to infect the entire workforce with the contagious energy, ingenuity, enthusiasm, and accountability that had made the company so successful.
- everyone in the organization the opportunity to share responsibility for the future of the Window Fashions Division.

Finally, AI provided a consistent approach and process for building, dreaming, planning, and decision making, something everyone from the custodian to the general manager could understand, participate in, and support. In its early days, Hunter Douglas Window Fashions Division was a large family with a compelling purpose. Today, it is recreating itself in that image through the use of appreciative inquiry.

PART IV

Building Community:
Transforming for the Global Good

10

The Appreciative Summit: The Birth of the United Religions Initiative

Gurudev S. Khalsa

This chapter tells the inspiring case story of the first Appreciative Summit designed for the purpose of launching a global effort called the United Religions Initiative (URI). Its founding intention was the hope that people and their religions might cooperate across the boundaries of faith to end violence in the name of religion and collectively light the way to a better world in the new millennium.

After setting the context of the challenge we faced, I explain how we approached developing the first global summit for the URI. The design of the summit is presented in detail, along with stories, quotes, and example outputs to give you a sense of what we did, why, and how it worked. Then, in the last two sections of the chapter, I share what happened as a result of the summit, where it has led, and the lessons I've drawn from this first experiment and some of the subsequent follow-up.

The "we" that I refer to throughout this chapter is a team from the Social Innovations in Global Management (SIGMA) Program in the department of organizational behavior at Case Western Reserve University's Weatherhead School of Management. For this summit, the team consisted of SIGMA's chair, Dr. David Cooperrider, Kathryn Kaczmarski, and myself, with many other colleagues providing counsel. I want to thank both David and Kathryn for their colleagueship on this multilayered adventure of discovery toward a destiny still being shaped.

EMBRACING THE CHALLENGE:
GLOBAL ORGANIZING ACROSS FAITHS

The United Religions Initiative was conceived in 1993 during a sleepless night for the Rt. Rev. William E. Swing, the Episcopal bishop of California. Earlier that day he had taken a call from the United Nations asking him to organize an interfaith service to celebrate the United Nation's fiftieth anniversary at Grace Cathedral in San Francisco, where the U.N. charter had been signed. He would bring together the religious leaders, they would invite the diplomats and political leaders, and it would be a grand service and celebration. What bothered him that night wasn't the logistics of organizing a one-hour interfaith service two years down the road, but a nagging question that would not go away: "If the nations of the world have struggled together toward global good for nearly 50 years, why not the religions?" The call became a calling, as Bishop Swing, in answer to the larger question he heard, committed the rest of his life to the possibility that the religions, too, might be "moral enough" to come together in a permanent daily assembly, a sort of spiritual United Nations, to work for peace and other global priorities.

Upon returning from a worldwide pilgrimage in spring 1996, Bishop Swing summed up his encounters by saying he was even more convinced that a United Religions would happen, and even less clear how. Being called to bold action to match his bold vision, Bishop Swing had by that time not only floated the idea, but also launched a raft that might carry it: the United Religions Initiative. Its goal was to bring the United Religions into being by the year 2000. In July 1995 a group of local interfaith people in San Francisco began meeting to pursue the vision and create a nonprofit organization (the URI) to carry it forward. An idea was suggested to host a conference during the last week of June (coinciding with the next U.N. anniversary) that would bring together religious leaders interested in creating a plan for the development of a United Religions. By the time Bishop Swing returned from his world pilgrimage, the proposed conference was little more than two months away. Though many informal invitations had been made and a hosting committee had been formed, an agenda for the conference and a plan for how to run it had yet to be created.

This was the situation when a group of us from SIGMA were asked to help design the URI's first global summit. Why were we excited and what was the challenge we faced? Imagine what a spiritual partner of the United Nations might offer to the next millennium. Imagine what could happen if the world's religions found a way to work together for peace, rather than foment war. As organizational scholar activists, we found the URI to be the most ambitious and visionary transboundary cooperative global venture we had encountered. Its potential to actualize the spiritual core of life toward greater global cooperation was awe inspiring. At the same time, the challenge of overcoming the boundaries created by our religious institutions (both within and between faiths) seemed enormous. It was as scary an opportunity as it was exciting. All we could do was offer our best, and bring our courage with us.

OUR APPROACH: TOWARD AN APPRECIATIVE SUMMIT

In March, we had the chance to meet the man who would later become the URI's executive director, the Reverend Charles Gibbs, and after returning from his worldwide pilgrimage, Bishop Swing met with us in April. From both of them we learned not only of the extraordinary nature of the venture, but of the exceptional character of the people who led it. That this was an organization truly led by spirit became apparent. Confident but unassuming, they demonstrated both a remarkable clarity about the timely potential of a UR and a refreshing innocence that didn't claim to know how to achieve such a vision. In that environment, we fit right in, because we certainly didn't know either. But we sensed that here were partners ready to pursue their vision in the spirit of inquiry, with an openness to discover and a readiness to work with many stakeholders, which seemed to us the only way such a big idea could achieve the breadth and depth of ownership required to launch it.

When we gathered with the host committee in May, we focused on three questions: (1) What are the values we want this conference to exemplify? (2) What is the central task of this conference? and (3) Who are the stakeholders needed to achieve that task? We did not go into the meetings with a clear design in mind, but wanted whatever we created to build upon the answers to these three questions. We had shared with Bishop Swing and Reverend Gibbs some ideas and experiences from our work with appreciative inquiry, but we had also talked about drawing upon other large-group processes to custom design something appropriate to this situation. The vision of an appreciative summit emerged.

After much dialogue, the central task and title chosen for the summit was "A Time for Action: Discovering the Steps for a United Religions Charter." The lengthy discussion was essential to being clear about what this gathering was really for and thereby to design a conference that suited that purpose. The following list summarizes the key messages that the conference title was intended to convey and the guiding values or principles that the host committee wanted the summit to reflect:

What's in a Name?

- The purpose of this conference was not itself to create the United Religions or its charter, but to create a process leading toward a United Religions charter.

- None of the organizers claimed knowledge of the steps to bring a UR into being, but asserted that if a collection of concerned stakeholders was brought together, collectively they could discover what these steps were.

- This conference would go beyond the stage of envisioning the possibilities of a United Religions to focus on the action necessary to make it happen.

The Guiding Intentions

- To create a spirit of hospitality and openness.

- To share at a personal level from the very beginning and throughout.

- To honor each person for who they are and what they bring.

- To have this be a time of retreat and renewal as well as fulfilling productivity.

- To ensure equal opportunity for everyone's participation.

- To make space for storytelling, both one-on-one and in community.

- To avoid, as much as possible, the making of speeches as a conference norm.

- To reserve time for silence, pausing to reconnect.

- To incorporate a spiritual dimension explicitly, with sensitivity and optional participation, drawing from the diverse resources in the room.

- To move from the silent center to the personal to the organizational.

The next day, after a long evening of design work, we shared the 4D model of AI and began laying out a block diagram for the conference week. Within this context of a vision of the whole week, we together made many refinements to fully capture the intentions already expressed. And we also talked at length about who else needed to be invited (on short notice) to truly bring the "whole system" into the room. In addition to the obvious need for a variety of religious and interfaith leaders, the group decided to include a few corporate and NGO executives, philanthropy and communication specialists, and scholars in the fields of religious and organizational studies, each for the unique expertise they would bring to this task. What would tie them loosely together as stakeholders was a vital interest in the possibility that a United Religions organization could make a significant contribution to our world. By the time the day was done, we had the outlines of a design that seemed to do justice to the host committee's goals and values, and a good mix of stakeholder invitees with which to launch this initiative into the world. Now all that remained, in the last month before the conference, was to ensure that a close approximation of our desired mix of people would get there, that the design outline would get translated into an agenda and detailed plan of activities, and that all of the logistical arrangements for the conference would be in order—no small agenda.

A letter was sent out ahead of time explaining to participants the unique nature of the conference. One paragraph explained what we referred to as an "Appreciative Future Search":

This conference will be a space for us all to discover our calling to this initiative and the resources we bring, to find our common ground together, and to mobilize ourselves toward actions that can bring our dreams into reality. It is appreciative in that we will consciously value the personal experiences and trends in interfaith work supporting this initiative now, and it is a future search in the sense that none of us can know now what the United Religions will be or how it might come into being until we engage in the process of creating it.

Our vision was that the use of appreciative inquiry would enable the stakeholders of the URI to grow the plans for creating a UR out of deeply held values and their best experiences of interfaith cooperation and/or organizing across boundaries. Basic, one-on-one interviews would help evoke and create an immediate sense of connection among the participants as they came together for the first time, and enable them, by virtue of their sharing, to familiarize themselves both with the topical content of the conference as well as its novel style—completely void of speeches and monologues. Building on the foundations of the AI interviews, the interweaving of Future Search (FS; Weisbord & Janoff, 1995) approaches was intended to aid in the development of creatively formed shared dreams for the URI, supported by the committed, self-organized actions that are a hallmark of this OD method.

THE DESIGN: HOW THE SUMMIT WORKED

The summit began with a welcome from Charles Gibbs and a shared minute of silence, a practice that would become routine by the end of the conference. Then Charles offered a poem after which Bishop Swing said a few words to set the tone of the week. His concluding words are illustrative:

At the first of this century, there was a time when human beings knew in their bones that we should fly. So all kinds of people glued feathers to their arms, climbed to the top of the barn, began flapping, and jumped off. And sure enough, right around there, we learned to fly. I don't mind standing in front of you today smelling of feathers and sticking with glue. I'll tell you right now, I'm jumping.

This Summit comes down to one invitation to you around the creation of a United Religions. "Come, let's fly!"

The facilitating team followed by introducing the process of the conference. We invited participants to consider themselves on a pilgrimage toward the possibilities of a United Religions and to join in making the conference a space of deep listening, generative sharing, and unconditional presence for each other. We also offered the provocative proposition that all of us can bring the transformative vision of the UR into being only if we ourselves are willing to be changed in the process.

Figure 10.1 shows the flow of the conference week, using the AI 4D model of discovery, dream, design, and destiny. What follows will acquaint you with the activities in each segment of the conference, as well as illustrations of some of the participants' perspectives and key outputs.

Discovery

This first phase of the summit comprised a set of four activities over the first day and a half intended to support participants in discovering the rich diversity of their own resources and experiences, their collective sense of history relevant to this initiative, and their combined perspectives on all the factors bearing on the launching of the URI now. It included (1) a "holographic" AI interview process, (2) the co-creation of three giant timelines, (3) a group mind map and institutional group reflections, and (4) a sharing of personal artifacts.

Holographic AI Interviews

One of the innovations of the Appreciative Summit is the use of a holographic AI process to initiate the conference. It is holographic in this sense: Everyone, within the first morning, had a chance to experience a mini-whole of the conference, both listening to and expressing their most heartfelt views on the full range of subjects on the agenda.

Participants began by pairing with one other person at their table, spending an hour and a half interviewing each other. The AI proto-

Figure 10.1
Summit Design

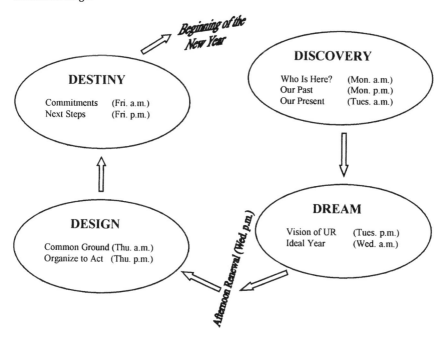

col invited participants to share stories of certain high points in their lives, of the strengths they brought to this conference, what they valued most about their religion or faith, their hopes for a United Religions, and preliminary ideas on what would be required over the next years to bring such an organization into being. Next they introduced each other to the others at their table (assignments for which had been predesigned to maximize diversity) and reflected on some of their interview highlights. After lunch one spokesperson from each of the six tables introduced his or her group to the entire conference.

The following are some exemplary "discoveries" from the holographic AI introductions:

- "If you want to live in a good world, it has to be good for all." (Rita Semel, Jewish interfaith leader)
- "No one has to die for God anymore." (Ravi Perumon, Hindu journalist)
- "Dag Hammarsjøld and U Thant were my spiritual teachers at the United Nations; they influenced me to bring spirituality into the dialogue of the U.N." (Former U.N. Secretariat official)

- "I have struggled with the tension between God's love of all people and the assumed superiority of Catholicism; with the tension of being taught about humility from a personal posture, contrasted with the triumphalism of the Church." (Ecumenical Officer for the Catholic Diocese of Honolulu)

- "I just returned from an audience with Khomeini and Rafsanjani; it is big news when Zoroastrians are greeted by Iran's political leaders in the homeland of Zoroastrianism." (Rohinton Rivetna, Zoroastrian leader and Founding Trustee, Council for the Parliament of World Religions)

- "We must begin by asking forgiveness of each other; we must listen if we want to be listened to. I have not found this journey of interfaith as diminishing my commitment to my faith, but rather as an enrichment of it through contact with others." (Anglican officer in World Congress of Faiths and International Interfaith Center, United Kingdom)

- "The demonization of Muslims has inspired me to give myself to interfaith work, where the calling is to give voice to the deeply rooted values of all the world's religions." (Iftekhar Hai, Director, United Muslims of America)

- "My inner city ministry brought me to an ecumenical and interreligious inclusiveness that brought out a 'pioneer' instinct to work where the need is manifest." (Sister Joan Kirby, Roman Catholic, Executive Director of the Temple of Understanding)

- "The most precious gift is the awareness of being a soul, a sparkling child of God, and of recognizing the soul, the essence of life, in each of us." (Sister Jayanti, Brahma Kumaris European Director)

The holographic AI process serves several purposes:

1. It gives everyone equal voice from the beginning.
2. It establishes a model of both sharing and listening in a deeply focused, intimate way.
3. It offers every participant a chance to explore his or her own thinking in the relative safety of a one-on-one dialogue.
4. It quickly generates a deep sense of connection among participants.
5. It draws out the appreciative foundations of our work together, both in the rich content of what gets shared and in the relational grounding it provides.

Timelines

The next task, taken from the Future Search model, was the generation of a set of three timelines representing the group's collective sense of relevant history in three dimensions. The time span chosen was roughly 100 years, dating back to 1893, when the first

Parliament of World Religions was held, widely considered to be the beginning of global interfaith efforts. Long rolls of butcher paper covered three different walls as participants were asked to record (in words and pictures) memorable events, notable milestones, and turning points in three arenas:

- global or world events.
- events in one's own religion or community of faith.
- interfaith efforts.

Afterward, people returned to their now-established "home" groups to take on the task of making sense of the timeline data. Each group was assigned a timeline and asked to interpret it, identifying themes and patterns that have shaped the environment for interfaith efforts. Examples of the highlights reported include the following:

- Since the dialogues of the first World Parliament (which was dominantly Christian, but introduced Eastern faiths to the West), a long period of conflict and growing global awareness has led to a flurry of interfaith dialogue in the last few years.
- There is an increasing fragmentation of religions and at the same time an increasing awareness of interdependence, leading to a greater participation in noninstitutional and nondogmatic forms of religious practice.
- There is a rise of meditative–contemplative traditions across faiths, and a new openness to indigenous faiths.
- A new paradigm of religion is gradually being born, shifting from ideological preeminence toward a more experiential foundation.
- The power behind bottom-up decision making is manifested in the democratization of the world; this is not about capitalism, but about encouraging every voice to express itself and be respected.

By the end of this activity there was in the room, now colorfully decorated with our own rendering of history, a rich sense of where we have traveled these past 100 years and who has been called to be here in this room at this moment.

Mind Map

The next morning began, as did each morning and afternoon session of the conference, with an invocation by one of the conference participants, either preceded or followed by a minute of collective silence. Though many of the offerings featured different religious traditions, there was no requirement that these inspirational offerings be religious ones. Indeed, we believe that similar openings could be well applied in summits of any sort. Both the inspiration and the silence served to ground us anew each time we came together.

The task in front of us was the creation of a collective mind map of all the factors and trends impacting upon our present focus, the creation of a United Religions organization. Adopted from Future Search, this is an exercise in group brainstorming, where anyone can add their opinion to the colorful mapping of factors impacting this initiative. What results is an eight-by-twelve-foot diagram of local and global trends, both hopeful and challenging, that make up the ground from which a UR would emerge.

Following a whole-group sharing of reflections on the completed mind map, participants used colored dots to informally vote for the most important trends affecting the URI. Interestingly, the major trends identified were largely positive, supporting the development of the URI now. The one most significant challenge identified was how to have interfaith gatherings of leaders ultimately make a difference "in the pews," or, more broadly, among the grassroots faithful around the world. Based on the experience of the many interfaith veterans in the room, this recognition may have been the seed of one of the most important conclusions of the summit: To be successful, the URI could not afford to enroll only the top echelons of religious leaders, but must become an instrument of grassroots organizing.

The following are some of the most important trends identified as affecting the URI now:

- The trend toward a sense of global spirituality.
- The growing recognition of common values at the heart of every religion.
- The increasing leadership role of women (and women's style).
- More positive collaboration among religions.
- The ongoing challenge of translating what happens in leadership circles and meetings like this one to have relevance for the grassroots.

After a break, participants were asked to regroup themselves according to tables arranged by institutional affiliation. The following groupings were used in this case: international interfaith organizations, local religious organizations, private-sector (profit and nonprofit) organizations, and universities. Each group discussed what it was most proud of and sorry about in respect to their institutional group's contribution to the stated trends. Highlights from each group were then shared with the community. The purpose of this exercise, also used in Future Search, is to enable people to effectively connect with their own institution's role in creating the situation as is, including admissions of shortcomings. Partially because the people at this conference came from such a diversity of organizational affiliations, this exercise did not seem to generate any breakthrough insights or "confessions," although a prominent member of the international interfaith community mused at lunch that perhaps he (and that institutional group) had missed an opportunity to be more forthcoming with each other.

Sharing of Personal Artifacts

The final step of the discovery phase was designed as a bridge from the global but abstract big picture of the last couple of exercises to the touchstone of the individual's motivation and vision. In order to animate the upcoming dream phase, we felt it was important to support everyone in getting back in touch with why they personally were drawn to be here. So we had asked them, in their advance preparation for the conference, to bring with them an artifact or story that symbolized what called them to join this interfaith journey toward a United Religions. The sharing was powerful, as everyone leaned in to hear some heartrending tales. The URI's executive director told and showed photos of his brother with Down's syndrome, from whom he first learned about differences and compassion. Other participants shared meaningful symbols (everything from paintings to pendants) from their religions, explaining their deeper meaning in the context of interfaith. Some had collected rocks, shells, or water from all over the world. The founder of the Temple of Understanding, shared her story of presenting her dream of a spiritual United Nations to Eleanor Roosevelt at a White House tea party. All the personal keepsakes were later displayed on a common table for all to enjoy and ask about. It proved to be excellent preparation to launch the collective group dreaming.

Dream

Tuesday afternoon was largely devoted to the home groups' consideration of a set of questions designed to extend their inquiry from the rich data of the past toward the possibilities for the future. After thoroughly discussing questions that had them imagine the future UR in the year 2026 and the journey taken to get there, each group presented their dream in a variety of creative formats: poems, radio dramas, metaphors, artistic images, interviews, stories, and so on.

This exercise was a blend of the appreciative inquiry and future search approaches to enable dreaming and visioning. On the one hand, it drew upon the extensive discovery process preceding, including the AI into people's best experiences of interfaith and transboundary organizing. These were built upon in the questions that had the group discussing visions of the year 2026. Although no provocative propositions were explicitly developed, they were implicitly foundational in the dreams, and recordings of important points from the discussion were kept by the groups. On the other hand, the creative presentation of the dreams, consistent with the FS approach, allowed everyone to capsulize their images in a more holistic form than simply verbal report-outs, and to share their visions as an entire group with effect and in forms congruent with their imaginings. For most, this became a real peak moment where people could really feel that the UR was possible.

The following are some dreams, metaphors, and images of a United Religions:

- A decentralized, inclusive network. The UR embraces all types of religious and spiritual beliefs and traditions, with a special eye to the education and involvement of youth. The UR is a nonhierarchical network with "UR Centers" around the world, and there is equality in leadership, represented by a "revolving leadership circle" and advisory "council of elders."
- A wheel, where all the different religions are different spokes of the wheel, in different colors, yet with a common center.
- A spiritual web or internet. The UR is a worldwide spiritual web of interactions, placing people into tight relationship with each other at international, national, and local levels, through spiritual links. Through high-tech "virtual holography," we are able to communicate interactively and multidimensionally in an ongoing dialogue.
- Three concentric circles, where the inner circle (the heart) is the activities and dialogues of local interfaith groups, the middle circle symbolizes international interfaith groups, and the outermost circle represents all the religious groups. All points on and within each circle connect to each other through the common center of the UR. Individuals and groups coming together inside provide the seeds for individual religions to flower and form fragrant bouquets with one another.
- A "spiritual United Nations," a sacred space of prayer and worship, where the center is a place of quiet, empty in itself, but providing the common linkage to all indigenous and religious traditions. Here we find mutual understanding and the freedom to express ourselves and our traditions, honoring the voice of each tradition. It is a neutral ground and sanctuary for world leaders.
- A garden large enough for all plants. The inception, evolution, and ongoing operation of the UR involves people of all faiths from all parts of the planet, as a democratic, grassroots movement.
- The heart of a body. With the body as a metaphor, the heart is the UR, pumping out life to all its interconnected parts, which inspired the following poem:

I am the UR
I am a heart beat
I am a little thing just now
that points to God's call to everyone.
  I am not an idol.
  Breathing as one
  holding the center
  open for all to enter.

I am silence
I am strength
In silence at the center.
  I am the UR
I pump acts that sustain life throughout
I stand as a visible permanent heart for all.

A wide variety of metaphors and images of a future United Religions were presented. To illustrate the richness of these presentations, let me offer a segment of the first and the last. In the opening dream, Ravi Perumon, a real-life radio talk-show host, posed as a correspondent for Global Awareness Network in the year 2026. After interviewing members of his group, who presented major achievements of the UR, such as its "Bill of Spiritual Rights," its "Five Basic Harmonies," and its rooting in indigenous family wisdom ("If you know how to lead a family, you will know how to lead the world"), Ravi offered these closing remarks:

But before we go, allow me to share some personal reflections, taken from my journal of 30 years ago . . .

I dreamed of a day when no one was killed in the name of God. That day is now.

I dreamed of a day when selfless giving and the practice of tithing, the concept of God's Money, was the norm. That day is now.

I dreamed of a day when ahimsa, non-violence, non-hurtfulness in thought, word, and deed had become the norm. That day is now.

Iva Goldman dreamed of a day when rock stars and movie stars and athletes would lose their luster and teachers and nurses and mothers would become the objects of adoration and the role models of our children. That day is now.

Jim Lord dreamed of a day when children had grandparents and parents they could ask for advice, and would, and would heed that advice, and of a day when the children would become the agents of inquiry among their elders. That day is now.

Mary Garner dreamed of a day when the human ego would be harnessed and all aggression would be channeled into constructive energy—that we would remember that we are spiritual beings of light, love and harmony in physical form—and that the power of that light would spread throughout the world creating heaven on earth. That day is now.

And Dr. Robert Muller dreamed of a day when every time one eats, one thinks and thanks first, and of a day when all people meditate upon awakening, and when church bells greeted each new day. That day is now.

And I prayed for all of us to recognize that somewhere, in some space, this United Religions was already perfect, already created, and that divine guidance in implementing God's perfect design was already at work within us and through us, and by knowing He sometimes speaks in whispers, that we only needed to be quiet enough on the inside to hear His gentle voice.

That day is now.

I'm Ravi Perumon, thanking you for being here, on the Global Awareness Network.

The last dream presentation was an unscheduled one, and a fitting grand finale. It came from ten-year-old Walter Gray, the son of a conference participant whose day-care arrangements had (fortunately) gone awry. As everyone else presented, he sat, listening, while also playing with the oragami paper he had brought. Then, at the end, he stood up and said he had something he wanted to share. So while he folded a colorful piece of paper in front of our eyes, only revealing its form with a final twist at the end, he told this story: "Once the religions of the world were far apart, but I figure in the near future, they'll be coming closer and closer. And when they get closer and understand each other, there will be something more than anyone thought was there—a STAR! And a beautiful star it was, with a different color of the rainbow for each ray, each representing a different religion." So powerful was this final offering, and so charming and innocent its source, that the multicolored star has become the symbol for the United Religions Initiative. In June 1998, at the third URI Global Summit, Walter Gray, then twelve years old, made a guest appearance to show everyone who wanted how to fold that star.

The dreamers were not only idealists, however. One of the questions posed to all the groups asked them to identify the barriers that had to be overcome in attaining their vision. The following is a sampling of these:

- Most organizational structures in churches, religions, and institutions are currently top-down. This model won't work for the UR; a new model of organizing must be used.
- The proposed title (United Religions) is a barrier; the easy analogy with the United Nations is helpful for some and problematic for others.
- There are many, many delicate questions of membership, representation, and decision making.
- Funding, funding, funding.
- Fear, ignorance, old habits, and reluctance to change.
- The tendency of organizations (including religions and interfaith organizations) to create turf boundaries that must be honored and transcended in this initiative.

- The possibility some will see the UR as superfluous in relation to existing interfaith initiatives.
- Since the UR can't be built around blame or "enemies," its design must be different, inclusive.
- The challenge of crossing government boundaries, issues of sovereignty, barriers to cooperation.
- The concept of "great" or "authentic" religions, the danger of excluding others, the tyranny of the "One Truth."

The last step in the dream phase (from the AI 4-D model) allowed everyone to get more down to earth by imagining the ideal year, beginning now, that would launch the URI's work toward a UR. This was excellent preparation for the next phase: design. With everyone having expressed via their group's report their own sense of the whole of what needed to be done, the formation of self-organized groups in the next phase was holistically grounded.

Renewal

After two and a half days of hard work, Wednesday afternoon was a time to consolidate, integrate, rest, and relax, renewing energy for the final phases of design and destiny. As one participant later expressed it, crossing the "river of renewal" between dream and design allowed a washing away of personal agendas and suppositions (his own included), so that, purged of dross, design could be done with clarity.

The renewal activities included a picnic at the Presidio, a walk through the wonderful natural environment of this former military installation, and a service at the Interfaith Center at the Presidio. Titled "A Service to Celebrate the Possibility of a United Religions," the service included wisdom offerings from the sacred traditions of eleven different faiths and inspiring music sung from the heart of a sister of the Brahma Kumaris (a Hindu sect with all women leaders who now have over 3,000 centers around the world). But the most moving part of the ceremony was also the simplest. Imagine being given a flower as you enter this simple chapel, and carrying it down the center aisle to anywhere you choose to sit, holding the flower until, at service end, you again enter the center aisle, and place your unique flower into a gigantic vase that soon holds the most magnificent arrangement you have ever seen, all created in the moment by all the diverse hands of this gathering. As you placed your flower, you received in return a vial of sacred water, gathered and mixed from over twenty sacred sites on all six inhabited continents, and you now stand around the periphery of the chapel, with only the flowers in the center, and only the world's most sacred water in your hands, ready to return to wherever home is for you. Perhaps more than any other event of the week, this simple service revealed the spiritual heart that moves this initiative forward.

Design

When we gathered Thursday morning, we began by trying to identify and review the common ground that seemed to have emerged during the past three days in four domains: images of organization, purpose, principles and values, and action agenda areas. Based on individual reflection and small-group discussion, as a community we created a large diagram of these four areas, each containing the themes that seemed to reflect common ground.

Following this review, we moved to creating self-organized groups ready to tackle elements of the agenda for the next year. Based on the principles of Harrison Owen's (1991) "open space," any participant could propose a topic or agenda item for which he or she was willing to be the convenor. After about a half hour of such topic announcements, we had filled an agenda for twenty-four open space meetings, eight happening simultaneously in three different time slots. Everyone could then choose which meeting(s) they wished to be a part of, and with whoever showed up, the meetings began. Twenty-three action plans resulted from these meetings, each with people identified to carry the work forward. The products and action plans included the following:

- A draft purpose statement to be further refined.
- Plans for regional conferences in various parts of the world.
- Funding strategies.
- Clarifying areas of focus among international interfaith organizations.
- Building strategic alliances.
- Preparing and distributing a United Religions newsletter.
- Revisiting the name of the nascent organization.
- Conceptualizing a "Spiritual Bill of Rights."
- Launching a communication and endorsement campaign.
- Creating a collection of guiding principles for writing the UR Charter.
- Planning a 1997 global summit, "Toward a United Religions Charter."
- Setting up a staffed office in San Francisco.

Subsequent to the summit, these plans were organized into a more coherent form, with six action areas containing related action initiatives, each with its own designated communication coordinator: (1) charter-writing process, (2) organization, (3) regional gatherings and enrollment, (4) communications, (5) funding, and (6) action.

There was a tremendous sense of energy, well nurtured by the first half of the conference, now released into these action initiatives. Though the results of the action planning groups would not be shared until the following morning, Thursday evening was a time to celebrate. In honor of launching this initiative for a United Religions in the same place that the United Nations had begun fifty-one years earlier, we celebrated with a special dinner Thursday evening in the very room of the Fairmont Hotel where the U.N. Charter had been signed. We celebrated, told stories, and shared both a meal and a sense of history in the making. The celebration was important in acknowledging how far we had come in four short days in establishing the beginnings of a global community committed to this initiative.

Destiny

The next and final day of the summit continued the galvanizing of people around initiatives as each of the action plans was presented to the total group, each participant reflected on his or her individual commitments, and reflections were offered on the process of the week. People expressed, aloud and in writing, profound feelings of being moved by the personal sharing and process of the week to a new sense of what is possible when a group gathers as we had done this week. The following are a few illustrative comments:

- "I'm delighted to know there are technologies for arriving at a common mind as we have done this week. Bless you all!!! My love to all of you—and my deepest commitment."
- "I have been most deeply affected by the personal sharing we experienced and the presence of spiritual power behind this undertaking."
- "I have gone from being an observer of this initiative, who felt slightly embarrassed by its grand designs to being a participant 'believer' who will spread the word about it."
- The conference "peeled away layers of the onion, day by day, which enabled a deeper look into the UR concepts without having to agree. By the end, some decisions and actions became possible without having to destroy the organic, progressive evolution of possibilities."
- "I see the reality of the initiative of UR in a more concrete and realizable form."
- "There have been very deep personal bonds formed with individuals from diverse spiritual or religious backgrounds. These are profound and will continue."

• "This world religions initiative and the people who came together has been an experience of the Ultimate. We have experienced the light and love of God within each person. Each one of us holds precious the context from which 'our spirituality' has come. We transmuted the mere tolerance of other faiths to a deep acceptance. The unseen dimension at work here has brought about an experience coming from our spiritual heart. We became a community of spirit and oneness in action."

RESULTS: BOUNDLESS ENERGY FOR POSITIVE ACTION

Immediately after the summit, an office for the United Religions Initiative was opened with the hiring of an initial staff of three. The Rev. Charles Gibbs was officially named the URI's executive director. A total of twenty-three action plans were initiated by the self-organized working groups from the conference, each with an identified leader or convenor to guide the continuing work over the next year. These groups were, in turn, organized into six action areas, each with a communication coordinator based in San Francisco. From wherever their home was, conference participants began acting not only on the formal initiatives they had launched at the summit, but also on other spontaneous efforts related to the URI, such as creating local meetings, contacting funding sources, attending other interfaith gatherings as a URI "representative," and so forth.

Several key documents resulted from the summit. A comprehensive conference summary (Khalsa & Kaczmarski, 1996) was produced, documenting the process and outcomes of the summit. A working draft of a URI Declaration of Vision and Purpose was developed from the start made by a working group at the summit, continued afterward via e-mail dialogue among a number of conference participants. A mission statement for the URI was put forward, along with a strategic plan encompassing four key goals for the coming twelve months. In addition, a proposed four-year timeline was proposed, with key milestones for each year, leading up to a worldwide charter signing for the United Religions on June 26, 2000.

That timeline specified that in June 1998 a first draft of a proposed charter for the United Religions would be produced by a charter-writing conference attended by a diverse group of leaders. Indeed, such was the outcome of the Third Global Summit of the URI in June, attended by over 200 delegates coming from five continents, thirty-eight countries, thirty-two faith traditions, and fourteen indigenous communities. This benchmark draft charter was then to be circulated around the world through the networks of these delegates and beyond. The action plans called for convening regional "vision gatherings" around the world to build momentum toward the UR charter-writing summit. By September 1998, six regional conferences had been held (and more are being planned) based on the model of the Appreciative Summit. Each conference has had a similar impact to the one in San Francisco, that of launching a set of participant-led initiatives that give the URI a presence and a calling in each locale, with a network of enthusiasts spread over the globe. A summit-inspired workbook on envisioning the United Religions in smaller groups was initiated in 1996 and used by many to seed local efforts in 1996 and 1997. A subsequent outgrowth was a full-blown "home gathering" strategy, complete with supporting materials that were developed and tried out in 1997–1998 and distributed at the most recent global summit. Similarly, a URI newsletter launched in 1996 by one of the conference participants is still being regularly produced, and a full-fledged URI Journal, with reflective, in-depth articles, has been added.

As an early experiment in marrying appreciative inquiry with Future Search, the first URI summit provided an excellent foundation for the development of what we are now calling the Appreciative Summit. More than simply combining some of the best elements of both, it took the visionary spirit of AI and merged it with the powerful action orientation of Future Search. The result, in the case of the URI, was the emergence of a nascent organization rich with visions of possibility and rooted in relationships among a diverse group of people committed to enacting plans toward those visions.

LESSONS: FOUNDATIONS FOR FURTHER EXPERIMENTATION

Our own experiments with the summit process have continued in our ongoing work with the URI, including providing design and facilitation leadership for each of the succeeding global summits and all six of the regional summits. In each case, we have built on the model of the Appreciative Summit, modifying as appropriate to suit the particular focus of the gathering, its cultural setting, the input of its hosts, and the desired outcomes of the conference. What follows are some of the lessons from this ongoing work, as well as what we gleaned from the 1996 summit.

Holographic AI Start

Devoting most of the first morning to the AI interview and introduction process is a powerful way to begin. It sets the stage for everything that follows, and emphasizes from the start that this is not "business as usual." Nearly everyone feels valued and well connected by the experience, but just as important, the actual content of what has been shared informs, directly and indirectly, the conversations and visioning to follow. I believe that feedback such as "transmuted the mere tolerance of other faiths to deep acceptance" is attributable to the spirit of inquiry and relationship that AI established. In addition, the holographic quality of the interviews was important in enabling everyone to have, at first, an egalitarian sense of the whole and of the ground we would cover together.

It may well be that this beginning is especially important in a conference where diversity is high and many of the people are meeting for the first time. The relative safety of the interview makes for a powerful way of being introduced to others, first in the small group and then the community. Unlike the fairly superficial ice-breaker approach (where pairs introduce each other after only a brief conversation), these introductions are characterized by real insight into what is truly important to each person and what they bring to the conference.

Another indication of the impact from the AI interviews is my observation (both at this summit and later ones) of conference participants who arrive late, and therefore miss the interview and introduction process. These folks seem to have a harder time integrating into the conference flow and understanding the appreciative spirit that pervades the group after only a few hours together. They tend to be less personally drawn in (or not as easily), and if there are going to be any vocal critics of the conference process, they tend to come from among these ranks (see the next section on conflict and critique). It's definitely one of those instances where explaining what was done is a poor substitute for the experience. We've tried doing "catch-up" interviews, but they are often hard to schedule and do not have as much force as everyone doing it simultaneously.

Overturning the Conflict Paradigm and Critical Bias

One of the reviewers of a draft of this chapter commented on the counterintuitive lack of signs of tension, of conflict. Indeed, this dominant reality was one of our greatest surprises as well. David Cooperrider has often remarked how he entered this summit with more trepidation and concern that it might blow up than any prior experience. And the amazing discovery was that this conference turned out, instead, to be one of the easiest and smoothest rides ever. Often when I've presented this case, I've raised this puzzle: Was the apparent absence of conflict a problem, an indication of less than genuine engagement?

First, I should clarify that tension was not completely absent, but it didn't show up in typical ways. Ironically, the biggest sense of controversy was generated not within the room, but by a media report from a press conference held midday Tuesday. After what conference attendees experienced as an excellent presentation of the United Religions idea from the perspective of three of its strongest advocates, we were all shocked Wednesday morning to read the *San Francisco Chronicle*'s ridicule of us as idealistic brainstormers discovering rampant conflict in our midst. The article's lead ran, "Bishop William Swing, who wants 5 billion people to get along, found out yesterday how tough it is to persuade two other people" (Rubenstein, 1996). From an open sharing of perspectives on where in the world the UR might locate itself to the acknowledged need for greater geographic and religious balance in the group's composition, this reporter constructed a dominant story of disagreement, and misquoted a former U.N. Secretariat official as saying that he "thought the whole thing might not even work." Anyone who has ever met this effusively optimistic official will know that such words would never leave his mouth—about anything—let alone an idea he cares passionately about. In the midst of our devastation and open-mouthed disbelief, Robert walked in and we asked him his reaction. With his usual ebullience and ever-present wit, he put it all in perspective: "It's incredible! But I'm not disappointed. It's just like Schopenauer says: Great ideas always go through three stages. First, they are ridiculized [*sic*]. Then they are violently opposed. And finally they are accepted as common sense. And I'm so delighted that we're already at stage II." Later that day he wrote a letter to the editor, which was never published, inviting the reporter to keep his letter and the article as a souvenir for the day when the URI is "accepted as common sense."

Perhaps this experience of having conflict projected onto us galvanized us against an "outside enemy" who would critique anything we said. But it also mirrored a larger reality of the dominant deficit discourse against which this initiative was consciously intended as a ray of hope. Indeed, during the "prouds and sorries" exercise of the previous day, the gathering of academics bemoaned the bias toward critique that is the hallmark of their profession. What the *Chronicle* article demonstrated to us was that an institution (the media) bent on seeing the world conflictually can socially construct that reality out of even the most meager scraps.

On reflection, what I observed among the conference participants was not an avoidance of conflict or a lack of authentic engagement, but an owning of the tensions as internally experienced. When people are openly sharing their personal struggles (e.g., from the AI introductions, with the presumption of supremacy one is indoctrinated within one's own faith), it becomes unnecessary to project evil onto the other and infinitely easier to engage across differences with compassion.

The relative absence of negativity was nowhere more striking than in the mind map. During a typical Future Search, it is common for the balance of trends reported to be overwhelmingly problem focused and depressingly negative. Weisbord and Janoff's (1995) guide to conducting Future Search even has a diagram of the emotional roller coaster to expect, with its nadir at the end of day one, just after the mind map has been created. They refer to it as the valley of "despair" resulting from the overwhelming complexity of the "mess" that the mind map typically portrays. They state, and I agree, that the confronting of this mess, and the anxiety that accompanies it, can be beneficial in teaching us to "live with" confusion. But I also wonder whether it is really the best way to prepare for the step of visioning, when our creativity needs to be "out of the box" of problem solving and into a realm of consciousness beyond where we were when we created the mess.

We were curious whether the use of a mind map in the midst of an Appreciative Summit would lead to any different results. At first we toyed with the possibility of putting an affirmative topic in the center of the mind map circle (something like "all the forces supporting the development of a UR now"). But we rejected this because we did, in fact, want to surface perceived obstacles and challenges as well as find the supportive factors (it was more the ratio that we were concerned about). To our delight, as the branches of the mind map filled up, there was indeed a greater weight of positive trends than negative, and those that were negative were often couched as part of the call for a UR, not just preventive forces. This greater bent toward hopefulness, without diminution of "reality checks," reflected the spirit of optimism pervading the conversation in the room.

On subsequent occasions we have put more emphasis on the open discussion following the mind map's creation. As members gathered around the map are invited to comment on what they observe (ideally after a break), there is a natural inclination to bring deeper and more critical reasoning to bear, but now it can be done by linking it to the shared creation of the group, rather than an individual voice. Based on later successes (the first regional URI conference in Oxford, England, for example), I believe having ample time for unrushed commentary on the mind map is crucial to making the exercise a powerfully substantive success. I've also learned this on the flip side, from situations where we were rushed and some indigestion was the result.

The Personal Artifacts Bridge

One challenge that the Appreciative Summit faced that was different from the standard Future Search schedule was moving directly from the mind map and interpretation activity into visioning (or, in our lexicon, dreaming) without an overnight to digest. What we designed, and what seemed to work well, was to use this point in the agenda as a time for participants to share with each other the personal artifacts they had brought from home (by advance request) symbolizing why they were called to be here. Shared at their home tables, the artifacts gave each person a chance to bring the focus of the conference back down to a very personal level. People reported this sharing to be very touching and energizing, and in line with the point of the previous section, it allowed everyone to bring whatever tension they had back within themselves, from which source the motivation to pursue the radical idea of a United Religions stemmed. Later, when the artifacts were displayed on a common table, they visually and viscerally offered a powerful sense of the group as a whole and led to the informal telling of more stories across groups.

The Pause That Refreshes

I have heard fellow practitioners describe typical Future Search conferences as a bit frenetic. In this case, I have rarely seen a group more committed to sustained hard work throughout a packed agenda of four an a half days. Even with a half hour to go until the afternoon break on Wednesday, I remember people digging into a new task with a vigor that surprised me. Many participants reported a feeling of spaciousness about the week that they found refreshing. Indeed, there was a relaxed sense of urgency, a paradoxically meditative spirit in the midst of many intense conversations. What could account for this?

I think this sense of refreshment comes from a set of practices that allow not just minds to meet but spirits as well. At the 1996 summit the factors contributing to spaciousness, and to our spirits meeting, seemed to include the following:

- One afternoon out of the four and a half day agenda was devoted to renewal. Our lunch and hike in the Presidio refreshed us even as we continued the conversation, and the afternoon's conclusion with an interfaith service was one of the high points of our gathering.
- The inclusion of regular moments of silence and inspirational offerings throughout the five days. Resetting our consciousness before each morning and afternoon round helped to provide a spiritual rhythm to the day.

- An (optional) group meditation practice for a half-hour each morning, led each day by someone from a different tradition.
- The invoking of spirit from the very beginning by Charles Gibbs, Bishop Swing, and ourselves as we introduced the week. This, together with the caring service provided by all of the conference staff, provided a sense of being valued and a norm of mutual hospitality. Since then, hospitality has played an increasingly important role in URI summits.
- The tone set by the appreciative interviews on the first morning. Energetically and spiritually, these encounters modeled a meeting of spirits that was built upon over the rest of the week.

One question that arises is how much of this would be possible in a conference not explicitly about faith and not dominantly attended by religious and spiritual people. There is certainly no guarantee that spirit will be emphasized just because religions gather. To break out of normal conference mode, where one person is speaking at length while many listen, is unusual, even in interfaith conferences. And while inspiration is certainly possible in this mode (call it the preacher model, if you will), it by no means guarantees everyone will feel included in the encounter. Many veterans of the international interfaith circuit told us how special the quality of meeting was at the summit, even among people who already knew each other, because of the relational root of the summit.

I have no doubt that each of these items could be adapted for use in almost any AI summit, regardless of the project or the client system. By its nature, AI already pulls for the spiritual dimension, where our values and our valuing are rooted. Experimenting with regular and diverse offerings of inspiration, periods of silence, walks in nature, and even meditative practices are becoming increasingly familiar to people. While still a break from typical corporate culture, it is a break (or a pause) that refreshes.

Self-Organized Action Groups

The lack of clearly defined stakeholder groups or functional groups in the URI meant that there were no preexisting structures available to fall back on when it came time for action planning. Rather, it was an ideal opportunity for truly self-organized action. Recall that what we did to lay the ground for this aspect of the design phase was to invite everyone, via their "home groups" to identify perceived common ground in four key areas: images of organization, purpose, principles and values, and action domains of the future United Religions. This, plus the earlier dream work on the ideal next twelve months, provided a good stimulation for people to organize for action.

The use of Harrison Owen's (1991) "open space" approach at this point in the conference matched our shared belief in the importance of truly participant-led initiatives arising from the common ground of our earlier conference work. Rather than imposing any order on the mix of dreams and designs already developed, the open space became a way for each participant to get in touch with his or her own calling to serve this initiative in the coming year. As individuals came forward to announce proposed topics, it soon became apparent that the diversity of needs for this budding initiative were being well spoken for, from funding and communications to enrollment and regional conferences. Even though time was short by this point in the conference, most of the action plans generated took root and yielded fruit.

Affirmation of Destiny

As with the opening to the Appreciative Summit, I believe that the closing is an equally important and underacknowledged element of a good conference design. Just as openings are often treated as mere ice breakers, without discovering their potential for depth, sometimes closings are regarded as nearly dispensable, something that can be accomplished very quickly within a standard form. From a Gestalt psychology point of view, closings are understood to be an essential element of the "cycle of experience" that our society is particularly prone to overlook. Good closure, for any significant experience, is the key to ending in a way that values what has been accomplished and frees up the energy of that experience to be available for the next activity—in this case, heading home and the subsequent initiation of action in the year ahead. A powerful ending can make a huge difference to how we remember an event and what feelings we leave it with.

At this URI summit, and at subsequent ones, a simple evaluation process and documentation of personal commitments have been standard fare. While these provide an important outlet for expressiveness looking back and looking forward, it is really the ritual that follows them that gives significant energy and meaning to the closure. And every one of these has been unique. In one of the regional gatherings, for instance, people lit individual candles from the central candle that had burned during the week, offering their commitment aloud as they carried the light out to the surrounding circle. The large central candle was, in turn, offered as a gift to the next regional URI summit, to be carried there by the executive director.

When we stop to honor our parting in this way, just as we deeply honor our meeting, there is clarity that our gathering has not been merely mundane, but sacred. Again, while the modality may differ with other types of groups, I believe that any Appreciative Summit should have a closing that helps members reconnect with the "big picture" and experience themselves as valuable contributors to the work yet to come.

Valuing People, Not Roles:
Letting Go of the Prouds and Sorries

In our first experiment with the Appreciative Summit, the weakest element of the design was probably the prouds and sorries exercise that followed the mind map. In Future Searches, it is intended to be a time when people move into a more affective mode of expression, saying how they truly feel about their own stakeholder group's contribution and taking responsibility for the shortcomings in their efforts. In an Appreciative Summit, the atmosphere is imbued with affect from the beginning, so that is not in short supply. As for reanchoring the work in one's own stake (following the mind map experience), the artifacts exercise seemed better suited to this. One reason prouds and sorries may not have clicked is the lack of stakeholder groups with clearly defined boundaries in this conference: Though we asked participants to divide themselves institutionally among local interfaith, international interfaith, religious organizations, business, nonprofit, and academia, many could fit in more than one group, and the cohesion of any group around a uniform perspective or behavior was not strong. Consequently, a group-based prouds and sorries made little sense. But even in a more typical case of an organizational summit, the deep appreciative orientation enables participants to build on their expressed successes to envision better ways of working together without rehashing all that hasn't worked. When we used Appreciative Summits for the regional conferences of the URI, we did not use the prouds and sorries exercise and didn't feel we missed it.

EPILOGUE: THE BIRTH OF THE
UNITED RELIGIONS INITIATIVE

The formal birth of the United Religions Initiative as a globally chartered organization occurred on June 26, 2000.[1] The charter signing ceremony took place in Carnegie Music Hall in Pittsburgh, Pennsylvania. With the largest number of bridges of any U.S. city (over 700), it was a fitting environment for an organization whose first principle states, "We are a bridge-building organization, not a religion." The charter signing was part of the fifth annual global summit. It marked the end of a four-year, inclusive process of designing and building the organizational, spiritual, and financial foundation of this unique global institution. Over 300 people attended the 2000 summit, representing seventy-five founding "cooperation circles" or chapters located on all six inhabited continents. Delegates came from forty-four countries, while the thousands signing the charter remotely via mail, fax, and the Internet came from sixty-five countries and sixty-four different religions.

Depending on your point of view, four years may seem a long time or a very short time for such an ambitious vision to be actualized as a globally chartered organization with roots in every land mass and an enviable balance sheet for such a youthful nonprofit. But what evolved out of the organizational process that began with the summit described in this chapter has been a miracle of self-organizing. It has been a testament to the power of the "chaordic" model (Hock, 1999) as well, where the dance of order and chaos found in nature was emulated to create a nonhierarchical, highly principled, but ultimately self-evolving structure, of which the charter is the penultimate touchstone. As the charter went through many iterations of drafts based on input and living experiments with it around the world, so too did the appreciative summits that constituted the model for our annual gatherings. From the fifty-five people who gathered at the Fairmont Hotel in 1996 facilitated by three OD professionals from SIGMA, we grew to a global team of thirty mostly nonprofessional conference designers and leaders, whose planning took place almost entirely electronically over several months, with our first face-to-face meeting the day before each summit began. Throughout it all, the sense of mutual trust and appreciation has been a huge factor in creating an organization that everyone feels ownership in. We all also share a hope that, in time, what was born can mature into a global force for the purpose we labored so long to put into words and to live into with our hearts:

The purpose of the United Religions Initiative is to promote enduring, daily interfaith cooperation, to end religiously motivated violence and to create cultures of peace, justice and healing for the Earth and all living beings.

NOTE

1. Information about the URI, its charter, and worldwide activities (including video clips of the charter signing) can be found at www.uri.org, or by writing to office@uri.org or P.O. Box 29242, San Francisco, CA 94129 (415–561–2300).

Appreciative Storytelling: A Narrative Approach to Organization Development and Change

James D. Ludema

As organizational scholars and practitioners become increasingly aware of the socially constructed nature of organizational life, linguistic strategies for organization development and change that focus on altering conversational patterns within organizations are gaining increased attention (Boje, 1991). This chapter offers a narrative view of organization transformation in which organizations are seen as following certain dominant storylines that support or inhibit certain patterns of behavior. Appreciative storytelling is offered as a means of helping organizations to "rewrite" the dominant storylines that guide their perceptions and behavior, thereby opening up new possibilities for action. The emergence and growth of Vision Chicago—a multiorganizational, cross-sectoral alliance dedicated to the redevelopment of the city of Chicago—is used as an illustration to show how the appreciative storytelling process can be used to promote positive organization change.

VISION CHICAGO BACKGROUND

Vision Chicago began as a joint venture partnership between Seattle-based World Vision, Inc., and the Chicago-based Mid-

America Leadership Foundation (MLF). World Vision is one of the largest private voluntary international relief and development organizations operating in the world today. Founded in the early 1950s to ease the plight of Korean War orphans, World Vision has grown to serve over 32 million people in ninety-one countries through 6,400 relief, child care, and sustainable-development projects.

The Mid-America Leadership Foundation, established in 1986, is a citywide organization that equips and empowers neighborhood leaders and local community-based groups to provide assistance to families and children in low-income Chicago communities. Through a three-year incubation process, the foundation helps visionary leaders and fledgling nonprofits translate their vision into reality through consultation, technical assistance, and leadership development. The foundation also helps communities assess their needs, marshal resources, and identify solutions.

After working side by side in Chicago for many years, on October 21, 1992, World Vision and MLF drafted and signed a joint-venture agreement, formally establishing Vision Chicago. According to the agreement, Vision Chicago was to function as a "bridging organization" (Brown, 1991). It would serve as a facilitating agency to form a broad, multiorganizational, cross-sectoral, collaborative alliance dedicated to the revitalization of the city of Chicago.

Despite its admirable aspirations, in the early stages Vision Chicago enjoyed little support within World Vision or within the Chicago community. At World Vision, many senior executives thought that Vision Chicago was an "economic and programmatic sinkhole." They doubted that Vision Chicago could make much of an impact on the social problems in Chicago, and they saw it as distracting World Vision personnel from focusing on their primary mission of generating resources for overseas programs. Similarly, in Chicago, local leaders, community groups, and even the members of MLF's board were suspicious that World Vision's interest in Vision Chicago was primarily self-serving. They feared that World Vision would use Vision Chicago as a vehicle to gain increased access to Chicago's financial base and then take money from Chicago to invest in projects in other cities and countries around the world. Thus, when Vision Chicago began, the prevailing "story" in which it was embedded was one of utter impossibility, that the redevelopment of the city of Chicago was hopeless and that Vision Chicago was doomed to failure. This story was told over and over by many people close to Vision Chicago, both within the Vision Chicago structure and within the greater Chicago community.

There was, however, a small group of leaders from World Vision, MLF, and the city of Chicago who were more optimistic. They thought that the Vision Chicago concept could work and that it held strong potential for making a difference in the lives of the rich and the poor in the city. In pursuit of their dream, they used a process of appreciative storytelling to work with their respective constituencies to rewrite the dominant storyline that surrounded Vision Chicago. As the appreciative storytelling process gained momentum, people began to listen to each other in new ways across traditional boundaries. They discovered that they shared a common love for the city and had common hopes for its future. They began to dream about what they could accomplish if they combined their respective resources and strengths, and they started to sketch out what a Vision Chicago might look like if it were to conform to their highest hopes and aspirations. Steadily, the Vision Chicago storyline shifted from one of hopelessness and despair to one of possibility and excitement about the future.

Perhaps more important, action followed story. During the period of our involvement with Vision Chicago (twenty months, from April 1993 to December 1994), the initiative mobilized a collaborative network of over seventy organizations, resulting in over $5 million of direct aid, gifts-in-kind, and professional services. In June 1994 Vision Chicago was recognized by the Council of Foundations as one of eight "Models of Hope" for its pioneering work in rebuilding America's cities.

Today, Vision Chicago's impact continues to grow, both in Chicago and beyond. In Chicago, it has become a self-sustaining and expanding set of over 500 organizations dedicated to long-term change and holistic response to the needs of children and their families. In other cities around the United States, "Vision Cities" modeled after the Vision Chicago initiative have emerged and are experiencing similar success in promoting social, spiritual, and economic revitalization. Similarly, aspects of the Vision Chicago model and the appreciative process used to create it have influenced World Vision's operations in locations around the world, such as Africa, Asia, Latin America, and the Middle East. Finally, Vision Chicago and other Vision Cities have played a major role in reshaping the strategic direction and organizational structure of World Vision's U.S. operations. World Vision is currently "regionalizing" its structure to more fluidly and effectively promote the emergence and growth of Vision Cities around the country. The remainder of this chapter tells the story of this remarkable process of transformation. After briefly exploring the narrative character of organizational life, the chapter shows how the appreciative storytelling process was used to shift the dominant conversation about Vision Chicago. It concludes with some generative propositions about the use of appreciative storytelling as a tool for organization change and transformation.

ORGANIZATIONS AS STORIES

Organizational life can be seen as "narrative" in two important ways (Gergen, 1994). First, organizations make themselves (their identities, priorities, values, and directions) understandable to their members and to other organizations by means of the stories they tell about themselves and the stories others tell about them. In the case of Vision Chicago, for example, MLF was known in the city as an entrepreneurial organization, a trustworthy partner, a pioneer in effective community development approaches, and an unyielding advocate for urban concerns. A host of stories circulated through the city that supported these views. Likewise, in the suburbs, World Vision's identity was bolstered by many stories that depicted it as a large and powerful organization with a high level of integrity, an excellent international reputation, and strong connections to Chicago's resource base.

At the same time, organizational life is largely carried out in narrative form. Organizations follow certain storylines that have been created and sustained within our particular culture. Although both MLF and World Vision were supported by positive stories in certain communities, they also floated in a stream of cultural stories that were less sympathetic. For example, one of the most difficult barriers for World Vision to cross in the city was the perception by local residents that it would siphon off resources from Chicago and use them in other cities. This perception was primarily a product of the cultural storyline that says that national organizations do not respect local voices, a storyline that, based on experience, has significant believability for city residents throughout the United States. Another storyline that shaped the context of Vision Chicago early on was that "collaborative alliances don't work." For a variety of reasons, some theoretical and some experiential, this story was accepted and repeated by many important influence makers surrounding the Vision Chicago initiative.

Thus, at the outset, the dominant storyline that many people were telling about Chicago and the possibility of a Vision Chicago was one of hopelessness and despair. For example, a vice president at World Vision said about Vision Chicago, "It's impossible . . . totally unworkable. The last thing we need is to get entangled in a bunch of relationships in Chicago that suck resources from the bottom line rather than add to them." A resident of the Chicago community said, "We don't need a Vision Chicago here. There have been too many 'Vision Chicagos,' and they're always getting excited about something but never doing anything about it." By trying to establish the joint-venture partnership and attempting to form a broad-based collaborative alliance, Vision Chicago members faced the challenge of shifting the dominant storyline in which they were embedded to be more understanding and supportive of their desired direction. To do this they would have to engage a wide variety of people, both in Chicago and at World Vision headquarters, in appreciating and blending their respective individual stories to become credible to each other and to the broader communities in which they were embedded. In Gergen's (1994) terms, they faced the formidable task of weaving together a host of micronarratives (local, personal, and organizational stories) into a set of macronarratives of common intelligibility that would lead to collective action.

AN APPRECIATIVE STORY-IN-THE-TELLING

To build a shared macronarrative, the author, along with a small design team of leaders from World Vision, MLF, and the Chicago community, turned to appreciative inquiry. On nine separate occasions during a twenty-month period, participants came together in small- and large-group meetings to talk with each other about Vision Chicago. The purpose of these meetings was to involve people from a variety of backgrounds, communities, organizations, and sectors in designing the emerging organization. These sessions were crucial to the growth and development of Vision Chicago. It was here that the negative and pessimistic stories about the hopelessness of the city of Chicago and the impossibility of Vision Chicago were transformed into hopeful stories based on the heroic real-life experiences of the participants. Following is an example from one of the large-group sessions. It begins with a brief description of the setting of the meeting, moves to an exploration of the positive questions that were used to guide the storytelling process, and concludes with excerpts from the meeting. It illustrates how the appreciative storytelling process can be used to weave multiple micronarratives (as told by the participants themselves) into shared macronarratives that guide action.

The Setting: Mt. Sinai Hospital, Chicago

The meeting was convened by the Vision Chicago Design Team and held in an elegantly adorned banquet room of the Mt. Sinai Hospital in South Lawndale, a near-west suburb of Chicago. The purpose of the meeting was to take the next step in the "creative evolution" of Vision Chicago. Participants included thirty-eight members of the North and South Lawndale communities (including politicians, businesspersons, nonprofit organization members, church members, and community leaders), five MLF staff, three World Vision staff, and the author. Community member Rita Morales, an executive at Mt. Sinai, arranged the meeting space, and she spared no comfort. Round tables of eight filled the room, covered with linen table cloths, set with full place settings, and decorated with brilliant bouquets of red, orange, and yellow flowers. As participants arrived, those that knew each other greeted one another with hugs, kisses, pats on the back, and handshakes.

When it looked as if most participants had arrived, community member Noel Quisneros read a passage from the Bible, offered a prayer, and invited everyone to sit down to breakfast. A breakfast of eggs, sausage, bacon, pancakes, toast, orange juice, and coffee was served and enjoyed amidst vibrant conversation. After the dishes had been cleared away, Noel called the meeting to order. Again he turned to the Bible and read excerpts from the book of Nehemiah. In that book, Nehemiah, who had been living away for many years, returns to rebuild the city of Jerusalem, which had been destroyed by the Babylonians. Noel issued an impassioned call to the members of Vision Chicago to follow the example of Nehemiah: to bring together rich and poor; urban and suburban; black, white, and brown; government, business, and the church; and to assume the leadership to renew, revitalize, and rebuild the communities of North and South Lawndale.

The Positive Questions

After a brief round of introductions, participants were invited to conduct one-on-one interviews with each other using an appreciative inquiry protocol. The interviews lasted two hours (one hour each way) and covered four basic questions (see the appendix to this chapter for the full interview protocol):

1. What is it that gives "life" to your community? That is, what do you love most about your community and what has contributed most to its vitality over the years?
2. What is it that gives "life" to Vision Chicago? That is, what are the forces and factors that make Vision Chicago possible?
3. What are your hopes for your community? What are its positive possibilities, and what needs to happen to translate them into reality?

4. What are your hopes for Vision Chicago? What are the project's positive possibilities, and what needs to happen to translate them into reality?

These questions were designed to invite dialogue about the most positive, life-giving, life-sustaining aspects of both the Vision Chicago initiative and the Chicago community from the perspective of their members. To invite storytelling, interviewees were encouraged to think of specific examples and tell specific stories to illustrate the experiences from their past. For example, for the basic questions 1 and 2, interviewees were prompted with the following questions (among others):

Looking at your entire experience with your community (or organization), can you recall a time when you felt most alive, most involved, or most excited about your involvement? What made it an exciting experience? Who were the significant others and why were they significant? What did you do? What did others do? What were the most important organizational factors that made it a peak experience?

Similarly, when focusing on the future, interviewees were invited to engage in a form of futuristic storytelling to describe and explore their hopes. For example, for questions 3 and 4, participants were prompted as follows:

Create in your mind an image of this community (or Vision Chicago) 20 years from now. What do you see? Be guided by your hopes and not your fears. What's it like? Describe it in the most vivid detail that you can. Who's involved and who's doing what (community citizens, young people, families, government, churches, universities, businesses, other organizations, etc.)? What do you see?

Now, imagine that you are standing in this community twenty years from now and you're looking back over the last 20 years to the present. What were the most significant things that were done to transform your community? What did you do? What did others do? How was it accomplished? What role did Vision Chicago play?

As participants shared stories with each other the rise in energy in the room was palpable. The sharing of positive stories allowed organizational and community members to get to know each other and to begin to "see" and understand their community and Vision Chicago in a new way. Instead of focusing on all of the deficits and deficiencies, they began to (re)discover the strengths and potentials that, over time, had been obscured from view. The stories from these interviews would serve throughout the day as an energizing force for envisioning and designing the future of Vision Chicago.

Storytelling Circles

After the one-on-one interviews and a short break, participants gathered back around their tables of eight and began to share their stories. As they did so, they began to discover the many experiences, hopes, and dreams for their community that they held in common. They also began to learn more and more about the "positive core" (Cooperrider & Whitney, 1999) of strengths, assets, capacities, capabilities, traditions, best practices, and so on that sustained the life of their community. They began to see the importance and potential of a Vision Chicago that would work in their interest to enhance the vitality of the community they loved. These storytelling circles allowed the positive stories that were generated in the interviews to begin circulating through a larger audience. As they circulated, they were enriched and augmented by the stories of others, and they created an ever-expanding sense of possibility about the future. Each group chose one of the stories told by its members to share with the large group. They were asked to share the story that they felt most powerfully communicated the forces and factors that gave life to their community and to Vision Chicago. They were invited to use any creative approach (prop, visual aid, skit, song, dance, etc.) they wished to present the story. Then we broke for lunch.

Large-Group Dialogue

After lunch and a brief period of preparation, the presentations began. As the stories were told in the large group, those listening were asked to interpret the stories by asking themselves, "What gives life to Vision Chicago? What are the key forces and factors that have contributed most to its health and vitality?" After all the stories had been told, we took time to share insights via roving microphone, and to capture on flipcharts the "forces and factors that give life to Vision Chicago." Later, in the afternoon, we used these forces and factors as a springboard for looking to the future to create an "image of the possible" for designing Vision Chicago.

Following are four narrative segments that demonstrate how individual stories (micronarratives) were interpreted and intertwined by the participants into collective stories (macronarratives) that reflected their aspirations for Vision Chicago. The first three segments—Rita's Story, Tom's Story, and Leonard's Story—are condensed and slightly edited versions of actual stories recorded verbatim during the session (all names have been change to respect confidentiality). They are three stories of many that were told that day. The fourth segment, "An Emerging Macronarrative," reflects insights made by participants during the large-group dialogue. The insights were captured on flipcharts by volunteer participants. Many themes from the micronarratives can be found embedded in the emerging macronarrative, but additional themes also appear. This is to be expected. The appreciative storytelling process is never stagnant. By nature, it remains fluid as new voices are incorporated and fresh ideas are generated through dialogue.

Micronarrative 1: Rita's Story (a resident of the South Lawndale community)

I've got a story that has to do with my kids' school. My kids were small and in elementary school and I wanted to know more about their school, what was going on. I wanted to meet their teachers, I wanted to make sure they were getting the best education possible, I wanted them to know that I was interested in their school. So I began visiting their school and talking to their teachers and talking to their principal. It was really interesting because in doing so I could meet parents outside the school that take their children to school and pick them up. I didn't see too many parents inside and I wondered about this. . . . So I started talking to some of the parents outside and asked them, "How come you're not inside the building? Why aren't you talking more to teachers or the principal?" "Well the principal really doesn't want us in there because we don't speak English." And I said, "You're kidding!" And they said, "No. She won't allow us in there. She doesn't like us speaking Spanish inside the school." So I really got upset. I called some people to come to my home and we talked about it some more. Then I thought, "This is an issue for the community to really deal with." And so I organized a group of parents and I took down and documented their statements, and we requested a meeting with the principal. We presented these concerns to her. She totally denied them. But more parents started coming forward once the word was out. We met with the principal, assistant principal, area superintendent, Board of Education board members, and, finally, with the President. They all told us the same thing. We said we would like her transferred and we reserved the right to interview other individuals for that position. They told us we couldn't do that. There were unions. . . . We kept pushing for it. After meeting all their criteria and going their route we just boycotted the school. And we literally took over until we had something in writing that she would be transferred. We said we're not disputing that she's a bad principal, but she's not right for this school or this area. Finally she was transferred and we were able to select our own principal. It was a first for this community. These are the kinds of things we are doing when our community is at its best. We were taking the responsibility for making change, needed change, not just sitting back and complaining about it or being afraid. These are the kind of projects that Vision Chicago should support . . . projects that make a difference in the lives of people right here in our community.

Micronarrative 2: Tom's Story (a World Vision executive)

My story is about what it has taken to keep Vision Chicago alive so far. Vision Chicago has been a struggle since the beginning, but it is a struggle that is being won by the courage and passion of people like you and me. In the very early going, our challenge was to create a coherent identity for Vision Chicago, otherwise World Vision, MLF, and others wouldn't support it. We had to develop a clear picture in our minds of what it was that we were trying to manage, and everyone had to be brought into that picture.

The first thing we did was to form a Community Ministry Council, a bunch of church and community leaders from around Chicago who could tell us what to do. We wanted the first voice heard to be that of the community that would have to live with the results of our efforts. We selected a group of people who were representative of the racial, gender, and religious diversity of Chicago. Then we had a series of about six meetings to determine where we should work, what we should do, and how we should do it. Those six meetings were like graduate school for me. I learned so much about Chicago, its history, its politics, its challenges and resources. I also met some people who were genuinely dedicated to the transformation of the city—good people. These were people who's primary concerns were those of justice, compassion, and the well-being of the community.

Once the Community Ministry Council gave us our marching orders, we had to launch Vision Chicago. We had to give it some visibility, etch it into the hearts and minds of the Chicago and World Vision communities. The best way to give a new program visibility is to get the heavy hitters involved. So I called up World Vision's President and asked him to come to Chicago with all the team resources typically seen in fundraising efforts for international programs. He agreed. We planned his visit for March 1993.

The third thing we did was begin to package the program in an inviting way that people could look at and say, "Oh! So this is Vision Chicago. Makes sense. I like it. I'll fund it, or I'll volunteer, or I'll contribute in some other way." And, oddly enough, it was around the packaging of Vision Chicago that the collaboration between the different divisions at World Vision and the collaboration between World Vision, MLF, and the Community Ministry Council really began to work. We still didn't have an official contract, but things were happening. We were beginning to actually do the collaboration that we're so fond of talking about.

It was at this point that I decided that if Vision Chicago were going to reach its potential, it would be because of people's passion. I remember getting off the phone to Angela Williams sometime in August and saying to myself, "Now that woman has passion, and it's passion that's going to make this thing happen!" And so I decided that from then on I was going to look at the whole Vision Chicago thing as a romance. It's all about love and romance! It's about me loving and romancing MLF, World Vision, the Community Ministry Council, the Chicago foundations, and about them romancing me and each other. Like I said only moments ago . . . it's going to be courage and passion that make this thing fly.

Micronarrative 3: Leonard's Story (an MLF executive)

I'd like to tell a story that I think captures the spirit of what we're trying to do when we say Vision Chicago is a "bridging institution." Rev. Gregory Thorton's Calvary Church and Ministry Center in Lawndale was one of our early grantees. He got a few thousand bucks and the help of an accountant and plumber from Meadow Brook Church to build a fish store, a project that would provide good food for the community and employment for some of the guys in the Calvary transitional shelter. But after the grant was given, the fish store was still not up and running. The guys from Meadow Brook were getting frustrated—too much talk and not enough action. So I sat down with Rev. Thorton and told him of the potential that could be lost if he didn't get the project on track. He agreed to meet with me and the guys from Meadow Brook to work things out.

Once we started to meet together I began to realize that the two parties were seeing reality through two completely different lenses, and because of that they distrusted each other. Rev. Thorton had used some of the fish store funds to respond to higher priorities in the shelter—they needed a bunch of new plumbing because their pipes kept bursting. Furthermore Rev. Thorton kept hitting the Meadow Brook guys up for more money and gifts, but it was premature; the relationship was not there yet. From Thorton's perspective, the Meadow Brook people lacked breadth of vision and commitment to the city. All they cared about was completing the fish store on an accelerated time frame for their own satisfaction. Yet this whole situation was a misunderstanding, simply a [vast] difference in perspective. Rev. Thorton was looking at the whole thing through the lens of survival, whereas the folks at Meadow Brook were beginning to see it as trickery. Both parties were feeling taken advantage of.

So we met a number of times until we could get to the point of understanding and reconciliation, and then Rev. Thorton began to open up and share his broader vision with us; he began to disclose his ideas for his ministries in a very transparent and genuine way. When he did that the folks from Meadow Brook began to understand why the fish store had become a low priority, they began to connect with his vision, and they began to get so excited that they got other people from their church involved—architects, contractors. Then we got a task force together—consisting of Tom and I, Rev. Thorton and a couple of people from his board, some of the folks from Meadow Brook, and a couple of others I brought in—and we created a common vision for developing the ministry center, wrote up a plan, and brought it to the city for funding.

We were hoping for $300,000; we got $500,000! And now the task force has the renovation of the whole block in view. But for me the most exciting part is how the task force is collaborating together. They are working with each other across cultural, economic, and geographical barriers that were previously uncrossable. Only a few months ago they were accusing each other of trickery, dishonesty, and lack of commitment and integrity! This never would have come together without an organization like Vision Chicago to serve as a bridge of understanding between the two [now three] groups.

An Emerging Macronarrative

After each storytelling circle told their story, the large group discussed what they had heard. Together they identified seven key forces and factors at work when Vision Chicago is at its best:

1. Vision Chicago is much bigger than any one person's plan. This requires an act of faith, a confident belief that something above the individual and even above the whole carries the thing along.

2. A willingness to "give ourselves away" to be in service of this much greater good. We just plant the seeds of relationship, water them, cultivate them, and watch them grow.

3. Success depends on gathering a team of people who provide each other strength. This team must consist of people from all of the different groups that are part of the "whole."

4. A commitment to stay at the table, to keep our eyes and hearts focused on the bigger picture, the broader goal when we feel we are getting jerked around or when the way isn't clear or the road is rough.

5. The fifth element is continuity. If we're going to do Vision Chicago right, we need to make a good fifteen-year commitment to developing the city. We have to remember that the transformation of people, both rich and poor, and the transformation of the city itself is our ultimate goal. This requires a long-term commitment.

6. We need to build relationships of trust. In cross-value, cross-cultural relationships, open communication, trust, and understanding take time and expertise to develop. Vision Chicago can serve as a "translator" (linker, bridge, facilitator, convener) between cultures, value systems, and knowledge bases. "Vision Chicago builds new healthy relationships where previously they did not exist." In this light it is crucial to have staff that are bicultural and can bridge different cultures, languages, and so on.

7. Strategies, programs, and plans have to be based on the local situation. The status quo includes boundaries that separate; Vision Chicago involves bringing people together across those boundaries to work together. This is especially relevant when you consider the boundaries between the inner city and the suburbs, those between races, and those between inner-city churches and organizations and the foundation and business communities. A critical role of Vision Chicago is to shift people's attention from boundaries that separate (ethnic, cultural, socioeconomic, geographical, and theological) to bridges that connect. This is also true within World Vision. Vision Chicago permits us to focus on what people bring (their strengths), what connects us rather than separates us.

These excerpts illustrate how in the appreciative storytelling process the micronarratives emanating from the one-on-one interviews and the storytelling circles become intertwined with each other to create the beginnings of a new jointly held macronarrative. In the large-group dialogue sessions, participants shared their own stories with enthusiasm, listened with empathy to the stories of others, and then collaborated to find "higher ground" (Whitney & Cooperrider, 1998) that adequately incorporated their multiple voices. For example, the seven key forces and factors identified by this group incorporated ideas and images from each of the three stories (among others). Rita's suggestion that Vision Chicago is at its best when it helps local residents address troublesome local issues can be seen in points 4 ("staying at the table"), 6 ("long-term commitment"), and 7 ("based on the local situation"). Traces of Tom's idea that passion matters can be found in points 1 ("requires an act of faith"), 2 ("willingness to give ourselves away"), and 3 ("depends on gathering a team of people who provide each other strength").

Leonard's image of Vision Chicago as a "bridging institution" is embodied in points 3 ("people from all the different groups"), 6 ("Vision Chicago as a translator"), and 7 ("focus on what connects rather than separates us"). Because the emerging macronarrative included multiple voices and was grounded in superlative examples from the past, it created a powerful image of possibility that was greater than the sum of its parts and yet inclusive of each participant.

Weaving a New Story of Possibility

After the large-group dialogue, we took a break. Upon returning, participants were invited to share their "stories of the future" for Vision Chicago at their tables. These stories were intended to bridge the best of "what is" with participants' speculation or intuition of "what could and should be." Their aim was to help the group envision a collectively desired future, and begin to move toward that future in ways that successfully translated story into reality. After about seventy-five minutes of discussion at their tables, participants shared their images of the future with the large group via roving microphone. The images were captured on flipchart paper by volunteers. The following images of the future are a composite of the many different images offered by participants of the meeting as they built upon each other's stories. Together they represent a new story of possibility for Vision Chicago. Although the new story is written about the future, according to the conventions of appreciative inquiry, it is written in the affirmative mode as though it were already true in the present:

Vision Chicago is a collaborative alliance that includes a whole host of partners beyond World Vision and MLF. World Vision and MLF remain the managing partners, but there are many other associate partners. There are three Community Ministry Councils, one on the West Side, one on the South Side, and one on the North Side. The Community Ministry Councils are doing the planning, along with World Vision and MLF, to ensure appropriate and effective programming.

We are working in six major communities, with two collaboratives in each, all supporting a wide range of programs. Our programs are developed collaboratively and focused in the arena of human need, particularly housing, education, and economic development (employment and small businesses). As a result of the work there are better community services, safety, and healthy families. We also become an advocate for justice through community mobilization.

The collaboratives have developed the local capacity for self-sufficiency and are being supported by multiple churches, individuals, foundations, and businesses—this was intentionally structured in from the very beginning. In partnership with Vision Chicago, around the city there are 20 independent "mega-churches" like Meadow Brook, 10 denominations with their respective congregations, 180 city churches (i.e., 30 in each of the six collaboratives), 20 corporations and/or banks (such as Amoco or Sears), and a smattering of politicians. Rather than being a funding agent, Vision Chicago is a funding catalyst.

Vision Chicago is catalyst, agent, facilitator of the inception of "sister" programs in other cities where the program develops it's own unique design, but also retains a common purpose, thereby translating learnings and assimilating new experiences that continue to enhance the effectiveness and impact for all participants. As these "sister" programs multiply, they become a dynamic source of learning for other sites, and there is a sense of heritage that comes out of what is here.

OUTCOMES: TRANSLATING STORIES INTO REALITY

The dialogue session just described was one of many that took place as Vision Chicago emerged. In each session, stories of the best of the past and hopes for the future were shared, interpreted, and amplified. Bit by bit a common yet fluid set of macronarratives of Vision Chicago began to form that included the voices of members from World Vision, MLF, other organizations in Chicago, and members of the urban and suburban Chicago communities. As people came together across the boundaries of faith, race, class, and sector to share with one another their profound, sincere, and often uncommonly courageous stories, they began to realize that they held in common many deeply held values, a love for their city, and a desire to work with each other to strengthen their communities. They also began to realize that their diversity, rather than being a barrier, was a strength that would allow them to accomplish much more together than any of them could accomplish alone.

Through this appreciative storytelling process, the dominant story surrounding Vision Chicago slowly began to shift. For example, the same vice president at World Vision who had characterized Vision Chicago as impossible, after sharing stories with members of the Chicago community, became an enthusiastic supporter. In one meeting he said, "We've got to start by bringing together the sleeping giant of the suburbs with the vibrant change agents of the inner city. But we don't approach them on the take. We approach them with a vision for a transformed Chicago and we invite them to partner with us to refine the vision and to help make it come to fruition."

Similarly, after months of dialogue the resident of Chicago who previously had said, "We don't need a Vision Chicago here," became one of its primary promoters. In a meeting to introduce Vision Chicago to a group of local business entrepreneurs, when she encountered a line of skeptical questioning, she said, "Vision Chicago will help to transform this community because it's focused on the right things. Nobody here wants to gain political power or control a certain territory. Our sole purpose is to minister to the community."

Action followed story in a way that far exceeded initial expectations. The outcomes of the appreciative storytelling process with Vision Chicago can be seen in three key areas: (1) the rapid financial growth of Vision Chicago through a new relational approach to fundraising, (2) the local impact of new initiatives and collaborative partnerships begun by Vision Chicago, and (3) the changes in World Vision as an organization.

Financial Growth of Vision Chicago

Vision Chicago has gone beyond traditional approaches to fundraising to establish cooperative strategies. Instead of "asking donors for money," Vision Chicago focuses on establishing direct, long-term, multiparty relationships between itself, donors, and local organizations and programs. This approach has proven highly successful, in terms of both financial growth and program development. In terms of financial growth, from 1993 to 1998, locally generated income channeled through Vision Chicago for local projects rose over 500 percent. In addition, Vision Chicago significantly diversified its financial base. In fiscal year 1993, 90 percent of all Vision Chicago income came from individual donors, and 10 percent came from local churches. In fiscal year 1998, 34 percent came from individuals, 22 percent from churches, 15 percent from storehouse fees, 12 percent from foundations, 12 percent from government, and 5 percent from businesses.

New Initiatives and Projects

Programmatically, Vision Chicago has moved World Vision and MLF from grant-making agencies to partnering agencies that establish joint-venture relationships with a variety of existing organizations in the local context. Many new initiatives benefiting the Chicago metropolitan area have grown out of these partnerships. CityLINC, Vision Chicago's volunteer resource program, is one example. From 1994 to 1998, more than 16,000 volunteers provided 133,000 community service hours (valued at more than $1.5 million) to 250 community-based organizations working in Chicago neighborhoods. Volunteers provide a range of services, including painting, cleaning, and repairing houses; serving on boards of local organizations; and providing trade and professional consultation. But perhaps CityLINC's most important service is that it brings into relationship people from diverse backgrounds who traditionally have been kept apart by ignorance and fear.

Vision Chicago has also become deeply involved in Chicago's public schools through its Super Saturday and Kids 'N Need programs. Super Saturday links urban and suburban churches and businesses with struggling West Side schools by providing volunteers who give five hours a month to tutor students on math and reading skills. In collaboration with the School and Home Office Products Association's (SHOPA) Foundation for Education Excellence and Brother to Brother International, Vision Chicago's Kids 'N Need program provides free school supplies to schools in low-income communities. In 1997 nearly 90,000 items, including everything from construction paper to three-ring binders to globes, were offered free to 6,000 students from twelve West Side schools.

A third new initiative started by Vision Chicago is the Storehouse, a warehouse on Chicago's West Side that provides quality building supplies at a generous discount to local nonprofit organizations that develop affordable housing. The Storehouse also provides a valuable service to donating corporations through tax benefits and reductions in operating costs. In 1997 more than 120 construction companies provided the Storehouse with $1.5 million worth of building materials. As a result, 442 churches and community organizations and 47 individual members were able to refurbish their low-cost housing units and other buildings in Chicago.

Changes at World Vision

Vision Chicago has spurred change at World Vision headquarters that has affected its domestic strategy, corporate identity, and organizational structure. World Vision has applied the concepts discovered in Vision Chicago to six major cities around the United States: Seattle, Los Angeles, Minneapolis–St. Paul, New York, and Washington, D.C. It has chosen the Vision Cities strategy as its predominant model for action within the United States. This shift has caused World Vision to rethink its organizational purpose and priorities away from being strictly a fundraising arm for the World Vision international partnership to being a bridging organization that establishes close productive relationships between a wide variety of individuals and organizations committed to social, spiritual, and economic transformation, both locally and globally. To support this shift in strategy and identity, World Vision has initiated a major structural change to enhance collaboration between its various divisions and provide flexible, responsive support to its Vision Cities.

These outcomes—financial, programmatic, organizational, and interorganizational—provide an illustration of what is possible in terms of organization development and change when dominant organizational narratives begin to shift from stories of dejection and despair to stories of possibility and hope. The story of positive possibility becomes the image of the future toward which individual and organizational action is mobilized.

LESSONS LEARNED

I have engaged in appreciative storytelling processes with many organizations in the corporate, government, and nonprofit sectors over the last few years. Reflecting on these experiences and the ones presented in this chapter so far, the following factors emerge as essential to success.

Beginning with Friendship

Begin with one-on-one interviews. As the "positive principle" of appreciative inquiry suggests (see Chapter 1), momentum for organizational change requires large amounts of positive affect and social bonding, things like hope, inspiration, and the joy of creating with one another (Bushe & Coetzer, 1995). Appreciative interviews promote strong social bonding in two important ways. First, they encourage friendship. Each person has a unique constellation of accumulated stories in their life: stories about our childhoods, families, schools, jobs, friends, communities, hopes, and aspirations. These stories provide a sense of identity, meaning, and history. When we share these stories in a mutual exchange, they provide entrée into one another's lives in a direct and personal way that goes beyond traditional roles that often separate. They open up the opportunity for us to approach one another with interest, empathy, and understanding. This is particularly true when the stories we invite focus intentionally on those aspects of our lives and our accomplishments that we are most proud of. When I look for the things you prize, esteem, and cherish most in yourself, I'm sending a strong message that I value you for who you are. When you do the same for me, you are sending the same message. This creates an immediate sense of mutuality and acceptance in our relationship and increases the potential for trust and cooperation.

Relational Improvisation

The second phase of appreciative storytelling involves dialogue in small groups. These storytelling circles have the feel of sitting around a kitchen table with esteemed friends or family members reminiscing about the people, events, and experiences that have shaped our lives. In many ways they create a space in which participants can build a strong sense of community, solidarity, and hope for the future. First, they allow participants to discover the things they hold in common. Invariably, participants are amazed by the experiences, values, hopes, and aspirations that connect them at a deep human level despite apparent differences.

This provides a sense of social connectedness through which participants begin to see themselves as part of a community in which they have an important place. As Freire (1994) puts it, this kind of dialogue is "the opportunity available to me to open up to the thinking of others, and thereby not wither away in isolation" (p. 119). Second, storytelling circles allow participants to connect with each other affectively. As people share positive stories, a spirit of fun, joy, laughter, and gratitude very quickly begins to emerge. Shortly, as participants discover one another's strengths and establish relational connections, they develop an emerging sense of group identity that connects them to each other and to their common future.

It may well be that the kind of community building that occurs in appreciative storytelling is the very definition of collaborative organizing. The ends and the means, the process and the product, are isomorphic. Appreciative inquiry's principle of simultaneity suggests that inquiry and change are not truly separate moments, but are simultaneous. Inquiry is intervention. When our knowledge about how to organize is generated by a positive process of storytelling that facilitates social relation and promotes cooperative action, in itself it becomes a generative act of organizing. Unlike traditional approaches, such as organizational diagnosis, process reengineering, or top-down strategic planning that separate the "knowing" from the "doing," appreciative storytelling links them together in mutually reinforcing ways. Conversation and cooperation, inquiry and innovation, appreciation and action become concurrent activities in a dynamic process of what Barrett (1998) terms, "relational improvisation."

Perspective of Wholeness

Involve the "whole system" in the process. Appreciative inquiry's constructionist principle suggests that social knowledge and organizational destiny are tightly intertwined. To be effective, executives, leaders, and change agents must be adept at understanding, reading, and analyzing organizations as living, human constructions. From this perspective, having the whole system literally "in the room" is essential for four reasons. First, this is the only way to hear one another's stories directly. When you hear another's story directly, it creates a relational connection that does not occur through other modes of communication. This relational connection is essential for building a deep level of understanding and for uncovering new possibilities that previously lay dormant or undiscovered. Second, bringing the whole system together provides immediate and broad access to information and innovation. In any organization, knowledge and information are widely distributed, and the people "closest to the ground" often have the knowledge most critical to organizational success. By involving a broad spectrum of people, the appreciative storytelling process provides access to a wide range of ideas and information that enrich organizational learning and spur innovation throughout the system. Including the whole system is also important, because, as Weisbord (1987) says, people will support what they help to create. When everyone is involved in shaping the new emerging macronarrative, everyone can find a place in it, and it is enacted with more commitment and enthusiasm. Finally, having the whole system in the room is quicker and more effective than traditional methods, because it directly engages the entire organizational system in envisioning, designing, and implementing the change.

The Power of the Positive Question

Asking unconditional positive questions—that is, questions that explore, no matter what the situation, no matter what the circumstances, that which gives and sustains life in our human communities—stands at the heart of the appreciative storytelling process (Ludema, Cooperrider, & Barrett, 2000). This is based on appreciative inquiry's poetic principle, which suggests that organizations are an "open book." We can study virtually any topic related to human experience in any human system or organization, and what we study anticipates what we "find," "discover," and help to create. Many organizations cripple themselves by telling the same negative stories over and over again until these stories come to define reality. Appreciative storytelling invites organizations to establish new relationships with their pasts. It invites them to learn from the empowering elements of their histories that have been overshadowed by prevailing negative stories. By doing this, it provides organizational members with new insights about what gives health and vitality to the organization. Positive questions do not change the past; they promote generative learning by calling attention to aspects of the past that have been ignored, forgotten, or left out of the dominant storyline. This releases an outpouring of new constructive conversations that refocus an organization's attention away from problems and toward hopeful, energizing possibilities.

CONCLUSION

In organizations, the questions we ask determine the stories we tell, and these stories, in turn, directly and significantly influence our levels of optimism and energy to engage in constructive action. When we inquire into alienation versus joy, conflict versus cooperation, deception versus trust, stress versus creativity, stagnation versus innovation, the stories we tell become increasingly bleak and discouraging, and our energy for action becomes diminished. On the flip side, when our inquiry focuses on the best of the past and the most promising potentials for the future, our stories become increasingly inviting and encouraging, and our energy for action expands. In the case of Vision Chicago, our storytelling was intentionally framed in an appreciative way. The questions we asked were selectively designed to search for the positive, life-giving aspects of the Vision Chicago project. Even though some people suggested that the project was "impossible," "unworkable," or "dead in the water," the inquiry began with the assumption that the emergence and growth of Vision Chicago was indeed a possibility and that the most valuable role we could play as inquirers and organizational practitioners was to study and encourage the forces and factors that supported Vision Chicago's existence. This process allowed the participants to begin relating to each other in new constructive ways, to discover an empowering "reservoir of strengths" that previously had remained shielded from view, and to craft a story of hope and positive possibility to guide action. Over time, this story of hope, as it evolved in a dynamic yet coherent way, became the vision and energizing force that compelled positive action.

Thus it is essential, even in situations where it seems as though there is little to appreciate, that the questions we ask steer our stories in the direction of the most life-giving, most empowering, most hopeful directions possible. The more we share stories of positive possibilities, the more adept we will become at translating those possibilities into reality.

APPENDIX

Interview Protocol: An Appreciative Look at Lawndale

1. To start, I'd like to learn about you and your organization.
   - What attracted you to your organization? What was your initial excitement/impression when you joined?
   - Looking at your entire experience with your organization, can you recall a time when you felt most alive, most involved, or most excited about your involvement? What made it an exciting experience? Who were the significant others and why were they significant? What did you do? What were the most important organizational factors that made it a peak experience?

2. Let's talk a moment about some things you value deeply. Specifically, what do you value most about yourself . . . your work . . . and your organization?

3. Now let's talk a bit about your community.
   - Looking at your entire experience with your community, can you recall a time when you felt most alive, most involved, or most excited about your involvement? What made it an exciting experience? Who were the significant others and why were they significant? What did you do? What did others do? What were the most important organizational factors that made it a peak experience?
   - Can you tell about a time when you felt especially proud to be a member of this community? What made you proud?
   - Why do you work here in this community? What draws and compels you to do what you do?

4. Now I'd like to invite you to sit back, relax, and create in your mind an image of this community twenty years from now. Be guided by your hopes. What's it like? Describe it in the most vivid detail that you can.
   - Who's involved and who's doing what (community citizens, young people, families, government, churches, universities, businesses, other organizations, etc.)?
   - Now imagine that you are standing in this community twenty years from now and you're looking back over the last twenty years to the present. What were the most significant things that were done to transform your community? What did you do? What did Vision Chicago do? What did others do?

5. Let's move on and talk specifically about Vision Chicago. Why are you involved in the Vision Chicago partnership? What excites you most?
   - What is the unique contribution that your organization brings to Vision Chicago?

6. When Vision Chicago is functioning at its best, what are the key factors (leadership, structures, values, relationships, coordinating mecha-

nisms, etc.) most associated with the project?

7. What are the benefits of collaboration from your point of view?

8. Take a moment and imagine Vision Chicago five years from now. What's it like? Describe it in graphic detail.

   - What are the key factors (leadership, structures, values, relationships, coordinating mechanisms, etc.) most associated with the project?
   - What could it be and should it be like?

9. If you had a magic wand and could do three things to heighten the overall health and vitality of Vision Chicago, what would those three things be?

10. If you were a consultant to a group of organizations in New York or Los Angeles who wanted to create a Vision New York or Vision Los Angeles, what would you tell them to do . . .

    - more of?
    - less of?
    - completely different?

12

Conclusion: Rethinking What Gives Life to Positive Change

Ronald Fry and Frank Barrett

> If we are going to bring out the human potential at its best, we must first believe in its existence and its presence.
> Victor Frankl (1978, p. 29)

In this chapter, we wish to address the call by Cooperrider (in the Foreword) for "an epidemic of positive change." More specifically, the fateful question to be considered is what the most powerful and generative lessons are from the application of AI in the field—lessons that can empower our personal and collective capacities to enact futures we desire. It is important to appreciatively inquire into the theory and practice of AI. We hope in this chapter to contribute to that conversation and stimulate further inquiry. We begin with a look at implications for the individual practitioner (anyone) who seeks to be a catalyst for positive change and the lessons from the application of AI about the kind of declarative stance such a person needs to embrace and enact in order to foster positive change by others. Then we address an emerging "model" or blueprint for a contagion of positive change and how it is distinctive from the more commonplace theories of planned change.

Conventional theories of planned change, capitalizing on a portion of Kurt Lewin's seminal theories, focus on overcoming resistance in order to make change happen. This notion of resistance as a predictable, strong, natural force that must be overcome, carries with it other assumptions about human nature that curtail innovative potentials. In this view, we organize for change by mobilizing against resistance. In fact, textbooks on planned change contain elaborate vocabulary of human deficit (conflict, sabotage, passivity, etc.), causes of resistance (threat to security, lack of trust, fear of failure, uncertainty, etc.), and techniques to overcome resistance (participation, education, facilitation, coercion, etc.). This elaborate vocabulary has some unintended consequences: Ultimately we find, and act upon, the very factors that our elaborate vocabulary has prepared us to notice. Managers anticipate frustration and are encouraged to take preventive action to minimize or overcome resistant behaviors. Worse, the very act of anticipating antagonism and opposition subtly breeds a hopelessness in human potential that can deteriorate into cynicism. We propose a bold alternative to this notion of managed or planned change—a view to unleashing or aligning with a positive change force or direction that is already there, needing only to be discovered and liberated. Finally, we end with an overall summary of implications for how to think about and view the opportunity to bring about positive change in organizations. First, we turn to a basic proposition concerning how anyone can "be the positive change they wish for" and become a catalyst in the process.

OPPORTUNITY FOR AN APPRECIATIVE
DECLARATION OF FAITH

Positive change is fostered through an appreciative declaration of faith in the universal goodness of human groups and organizations. In the early part of the twentieth century, philosopherand psychologist William James felt that people, by nature, long to keep an ideal uppermost in mind—that humans welcome the opportunity to direct attention toward higher purposes. Almost four decades later, in his classic work *The Human Side of Enterprise* Douglas McGregor (1960) was seen as a revolutionary when he posited an appreciative set of assumptions one could apply to the underlying causes of individual behavior. This list of assumptions, labeled "Theory Y," held that people basically want to work hard and do what is best and that they are capable of innovative and responsible actions. Theory Y directly countered the prevailing, in-use beliefs about people as problems, inherently resistant to work and change. McGregor's message, and enduring contribution to the organizational sciences, was simply, "What you see is very often what you get." If leaders, managers, supervisors, teachers, parents, and so on see others as lazy, those others tend to appear lazy in the environments created for them. If, on the other hand, we view the other as inherently able to learn, willing to pursue a goal that has meaning for them, and the like, that is indeed the way they tend to act.

Like those of James and McGregor, appreciative inquiry's assumptions are generous: experiences with AI signals the power of holding affirmative beliefs about human systems. Our work with, and our colleagues reports of, appreciative interventions has led us to believe that humans have rich reservoirs of courage and the freedom to sustain belief in the profound goodness of human nature, the nurturing potential of relationships, the creative power of collective action. The practice of appreciative inquiry calls us to seriously stand in, and act from, a space where we believe in the ultimate goodness and beauty of humanity—a universal *humanitas*. AI is inviting practitioners to hold out positive assumptions about groups, groups of groups, and whole systems or communities. Work in the field suggests the following affirmative declarations as a starting point:

- Communities and organizations welcome the opportunity to tell stories about positive experiences, to share their memories of past successes. The customary belief that we learn best or most powerfully from our mistakes is not the whole picture. As recent cases utilizing AI presented in this volume attest, every time members are given the opportunity to share best past stories and experiences, there appears a collective willingness, if not excitement, to build from the lessons embedded in these stories.

Through storytelling societies and families communicate the moral backbone, the sense of what is good and worth upholding, the moral themes that create a sense of identity. Telling positive stories about successes, ideals, values, and vital concerns is formative and welcome: Both speaker and listener are transformed. Through sharing stories of positive experiences and past successes, characters are exhibited, self-efficacy is reinforced, virtues are celebrated, situations and environments become animated. This reliving of virtuous deeds and compelling actions unleashes hope in the direction of vital concerns; literally stimulating vitality. When members tell one another positive stories, they keep hope alive in the system. They remind one another that humans can grow and develop toward the highest ideals, that they can initiate bold actions beyond previously imagined constraints, that they are capable at any moment of fresh response to old stimuli and able to create novel solutions that defy old habit patterns. Furthermore, these stories foster a collective hope that the group or organization can contribute to the ultimate good, to further human compassion, dignity, respect, cooperation, joy, peace, solidarity, justice, creativity, and nobility.

- *When invited to participate in dialogue, people welcome the opportunity to share what they like and value about their work.* The popular notion that groups will always want to vent their complaints first or that groups will always regress to the least positive point of view simply does not fit the experiences documented when the appreciative inquiry process is embraced. Even in systems under unusual stress or decline (see Part II of this volume), groups engaged in an AI process will either tire of endless complaining and self-organize (coconstruct) a new, more positive story, or look on their own for positive experiences. AI taps into peoples' deepest moral instincts for what constitutes a full, meaningful life—a life that makes a meaningful contribution to larger purposes. Just as media images depict the world as a more violent place than it really is, our everyday discourse in organizations sometimes dwells on images that breed what some have called "routine cynicism." When cynical discourse becomes routine, when images of the future are enfeebled or clipped, people sense that something vital is missing. People long for the opportunity to entertain what Charles Taylor called "the incomparably higher" positive imagery that offers glimpses of hopeful, possible futures. They welcome the opportunity to tell a different kind of story that explores successful experiences. Conversation that is sustained through positive affect that impels people to want to continue to engage with each other is pursuit of more understanding and continued relatedness (Homans, 1950). It is not enough, however, to merely think positively or speak positively. Experience with AI suggests it is the interaction—the guided conversations and interviews, the presence of a committed listener, the group reflection on inspiring stories—that results in an experience of positive affect that leads people to want to continue that dialogue with themselves and initiate new dialogues with others. Relating in appreciative ways becomes contagious.

- *Through surfacing and sharing past best experiences, groups are unequivocally compelled to contribute to realizing higher ideals, to create a desired future.* Conversations that focus on past successes are persistent and discerning steps in an ongoing venture. Stories that celebrate what people value about themselves and others when they are operating at their best displace frozen habit and create an openness to discovery— an innocence and playful willingness to be "surprised by joy" (to paraphrase C. S. Lewis' reverent phrase). These stories generate a powerful affective bond, a sense of the implicit continuity and connection with one another, with one's organizational predecessors. Sharing positive stories leads participants into a state of discovery, a quest for new images, a desire to seek a new perspective that accommodates both the profound and the commonplace in paradoxical syntheses. What begins to take form is a "collective consciousness of common purpose." Historical recounting of what group members value most in their personal experiences reveals underlying, shared beliefs and values about cooperation and collective effort. Relationships are transformed: Members develop a language that creates a common ground around higher purpose. The specific probes to "peak moment" stories that ask people to describe what, in their stories, they valued most about themselves, others, and the situation are on the surface a "metastory" of connectedness, relatedness, and interdependence. In the subsequent reflection on what factors cause or give life to these moments, or what anyone would wish to keep doing no matter what else may change, people experience renewed hope and confidence. From this shared sense of hope springs a shift in responsibility wherein members, valuing their connectedness, share accountability for the past and express the desire to be responsible for a more ideal future. Notably, there is no call for a logical SWOT (strengths, weaknesses, opportunities, and threats) analysis or a ranking of highs versus lows to determine readiness or feasibility for change. Once the collective consciousness—shared valuing—about relatedness and connectedness is brought to the surface and linked to an individual member's experiences, the only wish is to move in the direction of more peak experiences—more possibilities for success, goodness, and health. After numerous experiences in a vast array of social and organizational systems, we conclude with confidence that people value the opportunity to imagine positive futures.

Appreciative stories are almost magical constructions that call people to reflect upon the meaning of friendship, courage, wisdom, justice, and innovation. But they move people beyond reflection. Because appreciative narratives are about actions that took place in time, they also trigger people to consider ways that they too can bring higher ideals and values to life through actions. Just as observers of beautiful art work are inspired to see new dimensions in a familiar landscape and readers of classic stories such as *Les Miserables* or *A Tale of Two Cities* are inspired by the courage, resilience, and nobility of the human spirit, organizational participants in appreciative story telling are no less impacted. People naturally welcome stories that hold out the promise of a fulfilling and meaningful organizational life. Appreciative stories of peoples' peak experiences offer this glimpses of future worlds that invite participation and commitment.

- *All social systems have experiences of effectiveness, creativity, justice, social responsibility, compassion, accountability, and the like in their history.* Groups are never without something positive in their history to revisit or explore anew. No social system is immune to success, goodness, and health. The idea that outside expertise is necessary to persuade or logically convince groups to change or to take new action, is not supported by the reports from the field using AI. Rather, when helped to examine their shared histories, groups are always able to identify positively with some aspect of the topic or issue under question. This assumption is important, because in its absence we assume or take for granted a story of history that is couched in problems, crises, confrontations, difficult decisions, and dependencies. In the field of international development, for example, those in developed nations, as well as "underdeveloped," have colluded in a history that defines certain communities and cultures as deficient, uncivilized, needy, and dependent upon the expertise, money, and altruism of the others. A study of fifteen capacity-building projects using AI revealed that the reframing of antecedent conditions was both necessary and possible in all cases (Srikantia and Fry, 2000). Whether it be the cessation of U.S. funds to eleven NGOs in Ghana or decades of underperforming primary schools in the Bronx, New York, the collective discovery and articulation of local resources, strengths, and moments of excellence preceded documented capacity or performance improvements. The point here is not to eschew outside expertise but rather to engage with it from a position of self-confidence, efficacy, and desire to learn—not from a position of dependence and lack of ownership.

- *All cultures and communities wish to create a better world for the next generation.* The importance of generational continuity and desire to do good for the future well-being of our children is a common, human agenda. The AI process often exposes shared values regarding ways of relating and working together that serve the goal of sustaining jobs, customer relations, group cohesiveness, mutual respect, and so on in order to achieve a system or organization outcome that benefits the next generation. Whether it be thousands from different faiths coming together to create the United Religions for Sustained Peace (see Chapter 10) or the author's work with Teamsters union members at Roadway Express, who cooperate alongside management in appreciative summits to improve throughput so that their younger brethren in the union will have a good place to work for generations to come, the motivating force of generational connectedness is unmistakable. This is noteworthy in the face of the more commonplace belief that each is out for his or her self-interest or, at best, the interests of his or her immediate family or reference group. It is as if an "integrity of community" is necessary as an antecedent to change; a shared experience of the importance or value placed on "we-ness" over time.

These are simply starting points—new or different assumptions about groups and human systems that have been evidenced by work in the field with AI. Be it a group of five to seven or a summit with hundreds, people engaged in AI processes have behaved as if these assumptions were true. We began this section with a subtitle calling for a "declaration of faith." This term is borrowed from another classic work, Chester Barnard's *The Functions of the Executive* (1968). In summarizing his thick, rational, and prescriptive discourse on how executives bring value to the enterprise, he ends with an affirmative assumption, reminiscent of Victor Frankl's assertion, quoted at the beginning of this chapter, that the key to this "story," how to organize and lead well, is an act of faith; a belief—often without proof—in the power of people with free will to strive to cooperate. AI reveals that organizational capacities are enhanced as members are brought together with such a declaration of faith as a guiding principle. Acting from faith in the goodness and cooperative potential of human systems, AI practitioners put in motion appreciative processes that create the very cooperative outcomes they assume.

WHAT GIVES LIFE TO POSITIVE CHANGE?

We turn now to the process of positive change: how it comes about and what factors most contribute to enabling it to occur and be sustained. With this declaration of faith in mind—and heart—the following propositions emerge from use of AI in the field.

Positive Change Begins with an Appreciative Dislodgement of Certainty

Experiences with AI suggest a modification to Lewin's (1951) classic "unfreezing—change—refreezing" model of the change process. As edified by Edgar Schein (1973), unfreezing, or the experience of disconfirmation, is critical to initiating behavioral change. Termed by others as discovering the "pressing need" or sensing problematic urgency, this stage of seeing what is wrong, not sustainable, in the current state is necessary if people are to behave in new ways. Indeed, a glance at today's popular models of organization change reveals that they begin with the importance of a shared sense of urgency that something must be altered in the current state to avoid dire consequences (cf. Kotter, 1995). Such a disconfirmation process described by Schein assumes the need for outside expertise to logically argue that the current state is not effective, that it is wrong, or to induce guilt, creating a negative feeling of anxiety or lack of integrity. Kotter finds this type of unfreezing extends to the point of leaders actually manufacturing crises.

There are often unintended consequences to this approach to change: When leaders continually create a sense of threat and looming scenarios, imaginations shrivel. Under conditions of crisis and urgency, self-efficacy and collective efficacy are undermined as people become pessimistic about what they can do to change circumstances. Such scenarios trigger downward spirals that are dizzying in their momentum: When we live in a world that is fraught with urgent crises, we often surrender our creative powers in hopes that some knowledge specialists will design elegant, technological solutions which, like the incomprehensible, persistent problems, are too difficult for us to grasp. A continual sense of crisis cripples the social imagination: Hope is clipped as people learn to assume that another crisis is looming, even when conditions "appear" stable, leading to a kind of "routine cynicism." Under the influence of such scripts, no wonder we think we need experts to save us.

Contrary to conventional models of planned change, appreciative inquiry begins with the assumption that disconfirmation by itself does not stimulate the social imagination to expand and play with new possibilities. AI offers an alternate view of what needs to be unfrozen, or dislodged, so change can occur. In appreciative conversations of best past experiences—the interviews and guided conversations that highlight moments of vitality, creativity, and exceptional moments of efficacy—the hammerlock on the status quo is loosened; the "common sense" about what is or is not possible in the current state is disrupted. Taken-for-granted scripts like "it could never happen here," "we've all heard this before," or "that problem will never go away" are actually displaced, at least temporarily. Good stories, like parables and fables, create openings. When participants recall, reflect upon, and transmit stories of exceptional positive moments, expansive possibilities open, the improbable becomes imaginable, and dreams expand. AI creates a space for people to notice their own creativity and resilience in the face of past challenges, to play with ideas, to become absorbed in positive images of future possibilities. It is interesting to note that this affirmative dislodgement of certainty can also occur in a situation where everything might already be viewed "as good as it can be." Advocates for establishing a sense of urgency at the outset of a change project do so because they often believe that so-called resistors are in denial about the need to do anything different: Overall, things are pretty good so why change? This line of thinking is often a rejoinder to AI enthusiasts from those who assert that "reality testing" is necessary to unfreeze attitudes that things need not be better or different than they are. Yet, in the appreciative, best past conversations, the realization that truly best moments are just that—exceptional and momentary—suggests that something beyond the norm (positive or negative) is possible. The view that everything is as healthy or excellent as it can be is subtly displaced in favor of an idea that something even better might be possible.

Elaboration of the Group's or System's "Cooperative Core" Creates a Holding Environment That Encourages Experimentation and Enables Further Exploration of the Unknown

The outcome of affirmative dislodgement of certainty is a curiosity, wonderment, and awe in the state of affairs—a renewed questioning about what can be accomplished. This is necessary but insufficient to mobilize people to engage beyond general, abstract exchanges. A sense of psychological safety is required to truly inquire into unknown possibilities—to really dream the ultimate desired state—without it being treated as some intellectual exercise or game. Schein (1973, p. 245) notes the creation of this sense of safety as an important part of the unfreezing or readying process. He describes it as the reduction of threat or removal of barriers accompanying the lack of confirmation or guilt induction. In contrast, as AI encourages people to coinquire into their stories in terms of what factors most accounted for those peak experiences, the cooperative capacity of the group or system is unveiled. It is impossible to relate a best past story and not find something to value in another, or others (even adversaries), or in the situational structures, that helped make that moment possible. The stories are rich with interrelatedness: occurrences of working together to accomplish something meaningful. Memories of excellence in cooperation are given a surface and collectively acknowledged. As groups are encouraged to share these observations and analyze the common factors that gave life to a certain category of experience (teamwork, high margins, premium service, speedy throughput, amazing arrival experiences, etc.), a shared sense of the group's ability to relate and cooperate is affirmed (versus lack of confirmation). A confidence that expressed ideals might be possible to achieve through cooperative acts is heightened.

Positive conversations, particularly rich metaphors and generative stories, facilitate spirited action that support higher expectations and ideals; these hopes and expectations open up new vistas and alternative activities that support inspiring stories. For example, unleashing a conversation about a cooperative achievement in high commitment work teams might inspire more experiments in cooperation, which in turn might seed more stories, theories, networks of language about what supports cooperation. The nineteenth-century poet and critic Matthew Arnold, perhaps in a perplexed moment of isolation, reflected the downward spiral of routine cynicism when he wrote of "wandering between two worlds, one dead, the other powerless to be born." The two worlds—past patterns of social action and imagined futures—interact, stimulate, and rely upon one another: Shrunken images of the future stimulate recall of routine; vibrant stories of past vitality trigger grand anticipations. When members engage in appreciative interviews about vital life experiences, they too are wandering between two worlds, one animated and inspirational, the other surging to erupt.

The intentional articulation of these life-giving factors by the group or system involved in AI establishes a continuity to connect future ideals with past abilities. Because this technique prepares for change not by shocking or threatening someone into it but by acknowledging the shared ability to work together, it enables people to consider complex challenges previously unimagined. This explains why AI efforts do not stop at simply replicating, or copying best past experiences. The rediscovery of a collective ability to cooperate, along with images of something at its best, allows for imagining new possibilities above and beyond those past experiences. Positive change is thus experienced as continuity with change, not the disconfirmation of continuity, to prepare for change. Other studies have voiced the importance of considering continuity in change. Collins and Porras (1994) have concluded that "preserving the core" must accompany stimulating growth. Srivastva and Fry (1992) have established continuity as a fundamental life-giving force in organizational life. By surfacing and collectively verifying what a system is already capable of doing cooperatively and asking the question, "Which of these core factors do we want to continue doing, no matter what else may change?" AI establishes a "cooperative core" as the source of continuity between past and future. This enables members to engage confidently and enthusiastically in conversations about what else could be done in the future and to avoid searching for an outside expert or idea to rescue them or to depend upon in order to consider changing.

Synchronous Experiences of Positive Affect
Generate Interest in Shared Possibilities

In Lewin's (1951) model, people, once unfrozen, change by identifying with a model to follow or emulate or by scanning multiple sources for examples of new ways of behaving. Schein (1973, pp. 252–254) identifies both positive and negative ways in which this identification takes place. In either instance, the importance of another is critical, be it a charismatic figure, a change agent, a superior, or a colleague. Some degree of dependence (at least initially) upon this other person with a better or more correct way is essential. It is through this identification process that individuals come to experiment with new behaviors and evidence of changing. Schein notes that scanning appears to be the most typical path toward changing their behavior, given the absence of a strong emotional relationship with a change role model in many instances. It is just this positive emotional relationship that impels people toward positive change in AI efforts.

From the onset, AI is an interactive, relational process that invites people in pairs, groups and ultimately in large town-hall or summit collections to interrelate with one another about what they value most in their past and what they hope for most in the future: best past experiences, cooperative abilities in the system, images of the desired future, and ways to move toward those images. The experience of these choreographed conversations—in the moment—creates a strong positive affect in most participants. This collective experience of positive emotions, involving many people in the same time and place, results in people wishing to engage further. It is not only the content people are sharing and coming up with in analyzing commonality in their stories that leads to a willingness to experiment or try out new ideas. More, it is arguably the feelings of hope, joy, respect, confidence, importance, and common fate that create a contagious process of engaging to explore what is possible.

To put it another way, if one group were to analyze stories of best past events and delegate the results to another group to design future changes and then pass that design on to another group to implement, the synchronous effect of a crescendo of positive affect—in the moment—would be difficult to achieve, and the likelihood of sustaining any change would be less. Hence the difficulty with "managed" processes of change, even with the best intentions to involve and empower the change targets. Organizations are too often prone to work in linear, sequential patterns (handoffs) than in simultaneous patterns that would allow this synchronicity of positive affect to ignite and fuel the change process. The documented value of future searches, summits, town-hall meetings, and the like has been to interrupt the inherent segmental and sequential habits of problem and opportunity management in favor of larger, collective endeavors. Experiences with AI help us to observe why these contagious events succeed when they do. Relationships are formed, renewed, and sustained upon a foundation of positive affect that is often missing in the day-to-day workplace surrounding these events. Under these circumstances, the true nature of human groups is revealed; people cannot help wishing to continue and build upon these interactions based in positive affect (Homans, 1950). They self-initiate, commit to, and invite further engagements beyond the synchronous experience without needing authorization or permission from traditional leadership.

There is a vital rhythm to the building of appreciative learning cultures. Passionate stories about peak experiences have the potential to intensify action; people feel drawn to explore them further and to experiment with scenarios of better worlds, energized by the possibility that they can build the kind of world they want to live in. People experience an open orientation for the better, much as creative artists do: They move beyond constraints, transcend contradictions, integrate disturbing eruptions, and build ever more creative constructions.

Engaged in an appreciative search for continuity, relationships flourish under conditions of hope and caring. When one begins to care about an idea (or a person), one naturally wants to know more, to explore what is conducive to its growth. The hopefulness that springs forth in appreciative learning cultures seems to be a reference to the future but is really a caring that enlarges the significance of the present. Hope is an expression of the present, alive with possibilities rather than a "waiting for something good to happen." Hope activates energies and powers to act in present contexts and, in this sense, is related to courage—courage to take risks and go beyond the safety, predictability, and security of the routine.

Acts of Positive Change Are Spread and Sustained through Centrifugal Processes of Attunement

When people evoke images of possible futures, they nourish a spirit of restless, ongoing inquiry and wonderment and relational connections. An underlying theme in this chapter is that change is inherent in human and organizational dynamics; it is something to be connected with, or discovered, rather than something to be added on, forced (against resistance), or manufactured. Keeping with the metaphor of theme, change could be understood as being more like jazz improvisation. As Barrett (2000) describes, players strive for *"attunemen"* by listening, anticipating, and responding to each other. They continuously engage in streams of iterative turn-taking, creating, and idea sharing, while others support, complement, and anticipate new opportunities to blend, encourage, and augment the emerging art form. When a "groove" is struck, players successfully negotiate a shared sense of the beat, and the music takes on a life of its own. So it can be with organizational transformation. At GTE, for instance, Whitney et al. (Chapter 8 of this volume) report how a self-proclaimed group of AI zealots stimulated organizational transformation by improvising numerous applications of AI in operations, corporate communications, service centers, and supervisory training. Never with a corporately mandated strategy, but successfully negotiating support all along the way, the positive change efforts of these "attuned" change agents are depicted just as Barrett found in the jazz context:

Players enter this undulating flow, constantly interpreting the musical material before them, merging their own ideas with others, attempting to create a coherent statement. They are constantly anticipating one another's intentions, making guesses and predictions. Players are committed to stay engaged with one another, to listen to emerging ideas and to pay attention to cues that can point to an unexpected trajectory. (2000, p. 240)

In the case of the United Religions Initiative, hundreds from different faiths found the "common chord"—religions cooperating for the purpose of peace for future generations—to be the flow that sustained negotiations, innovations, and initiatives for more than three years to finally launch a global organization, the form and purpose of which we have not seen before. As Khalsa reports in vivid detail (see Chapter 10), through a series of global and regional summits members established relationships wherein they experienced deep connections to shared values and meaningful images of the future that they could only describe in sacred terms. Again, the similarity with the dynamics of attunement in musical improvisation is noteworthy:

Attunement suggests that when members are richly connected they are able to respond to one another's utterances. Such a context may provide a "holding environment," a safe context allowing one another to explore, develop, grow. Musicians often refer to this as a "groove." . . . Players talk about these moments in sacred terms, as if they are experiencing something out of ordinary time. (Barrett, 2000, p. 240)

So positive change results from a connectedness or relatedness embedded in a search for attunement. The attunement achieved pulls the participants to new heights, beyond their capacity, evoking positive descriptions that relay a sense of joy and ecstasy.

Attunement is not static. It can last, but not indefinitely or to a planned timetable. In this sense we view positive change as sustainable for a period, but not something that "refreezes" as in Lewin's (1953) change model. Indeed, the goal is not to produce a new stasis that will remain at some level but to continue the search for attunements that result in innovation, new knowledge, expanded skill, and widened horizons. Evidence from the field suggests that enduring positive change, in terms of organizations in transition, is associated with widening circles of inquiry and dialogue around possibilities for change. In a study of fifteen capacity-building efforts using the AI approach, Srikantia and Fry (2000) found that success was frequently related to the setting in motion of a centrifugal pattern of conversations, an ever increasing agenda to involve more and more voices in the search for attunement. For example:

- A community development project in a rural West Virginia county begins with an AI training program for small teams from ten nonprofit agencies and expands to include children interviewing 2,500 households . . .

- In an effort to transform the future images of a village in Russia, a journalist conducts AI interviews with a number of residents. This evolves over time into an intentional sampling of children, artists, and senior citizens in a collective process of inquiry and dialogue about new, positive images of the community. This results in a "best practice" adopted by other villages and cities, leading to efforts today to facilitate such an inquiry on a national scale.

The use of the word "centrifugal" here is to imply an intentional process that fosters inclusion; it may be introduced by an individual or small group; but it rapidly expands, inviting and engaging more and more people in the process of inquiry and dialogue.

The flow or momentum is from the center out, not from the top down, as more traditional managed change processes appear. At the center is not a special group, the top team, or a charismatic leader. The center is the experienced attunement of best past success factors, realization of a cooperative capacity, shared images of the future, and attractive plans for action, all encompassed in relationships characterized by positive affect. This may begin with just two individuals, but it rapidly spreads to others, almost by necessity, as if by centrifugal force pushing outward from a center. In each new conversation, a new attunement is possible, initiating its own centrifugal pattern of engagements.

CONCLUSION

In embracing the image of an "epidemic of positive change" we have posited some alternative propositions about the dynamics of organizational transformation that differ in many ways from those of the mainstream, with its commonly followed models of change. The following list, with the left column adapted from Kotter (1995), highlights some of these distinctions:

Managing Transformation	Unleashing Positive Change
Unfreezing	*Affirmative Disruption*
Establishing a sense of urgency	Voicing best past moments of exceptions to practice
Forming a powerful coalition to guide the change	
	Elaborating the Cooperative Core
	Collective articulation of how exceptional moments have been achieved in the past

Changing

Creating a vision

Communicating the vision

Empowering others to act

Experience of continuity

Plan for and create short-term successes

Refreezing

Consolidate improvements and remove system, policies, and people that don't fit the vision

Reinvigorate the process with new projects, themes and change agents

Institutionalize new approaches

Valuing of what practices to keep, no matter what else may change

Experience of continuity

Synchronous Experience of Positive Affect

Collective imaging of an ideal state

Self-organizing around most attractive possibilities

System affirmation and celebration of plans and initiatives

Centrifugal Processes of Attunement

Ever-expanding conversations to align values, cooperative capacity and ideals, resulting in improvisations for positive change

Positive change, as viewed here and evidenced through experience with appreciative inquiry methods, is not the consequence of managed tasks or phases of a master plan stemming from a vision created by an elite, dominant leader or cadre.

- It is more a matter of choreographing conversations: finding the fateful questions to pose, prompting to unveil cooperative capacity, engaging in ways to free up imaginative abilities, and helping to listen with an ear toward attunement.
- It is more about story collecting and telling than it is about projects and timetables.
- It is more about designing spaces for improvisation than for mastery of a score.
- It is more about synchronized expression of positive emotions of hope, joy, fulfillment, and so forth than sequential meetings to exchange knowledge and make decisions.
- It is more about centrifugal connections than hierarchal communications.
- It is more about impromptu, emergent action than about approved plans.
- It is, at the core, all about faith in an unconditional positive regard for humanity and its organized entities, not about caution, urgency, pragmatism, and protective stances.

It is important to note that the listing of propositions about positive change in this chapter is a necessity of this written form of communication. It is difficult to avoid making associations to ordering or phasing in the dynamics we have discussed. Indeed, most of the models of change one can access in the literature today are linear representations, at least in part. We believe that an epidemic of positive change does start with a declaration of faith and an affirmative dislodgement of certainty. Beyond that, however, the paths to attunement are varied in time, rhythm, tempo, and intensity. At some point, positive affect must be jointly experienced in the moment. At some point, a sense of continuity creates a safe haven for risking an idea or opinion, or volunteering to act. At some point, someone steps out of the choreographed dialogue and, with support, initiates new action. At some point, it appears of utmost importance to approach others not in the room, not for buy-in, but from curiosity and hope that they have more to add to the emerging, collective art form that is the organization. To cling to the need to control or predict when these moments will or should occur is to try to make a change happen. The epidemic we support and are inviting the reader to embrace requires that we all open to changing, to improvising, to attuning, to appreciating, and so on. The more we commit to making something happen, for us or for others, the more we deny the cooperative capacity of humanity to create and innovate together.

In this chapter we have tried to stimulate a new conversation about why and how human systems change. We believe the time is ripe for rethinking the nature of positive change. Without denying that change can occur from a paradigm of command and control, or momentum against resistance, we see that positive and sustainable change can also result from a fundamentally different stance. For decades we have conducted and studied organizational change through a problematic lens: There is always human resistance and scarcity of resources to contend with. The growing documentation of experiences with AI in the field, suggesting the propositions presented here, show promise for an approach and view toward change that requires no more or less than faith in the goodness in human nature and the willingness to engage in good conversation, interaction devoted to appreciative inquiry, and the wonder of organizing.

References

Anderson, C. A., Lepper, M., & Ross, L. (1980). Perseverance of social theories: The role of explanation in persistence of discredited information. *Journal of Personality and Social Psychology, 39*, 1037–1049.

Barnard, C. (1968) *The functions of the executive.* Cambridge: Harvard University Press.

Barrett, F. J. (1998). Creativity in improvisation in jazz and organizations: Implications for organizational learning. *Organizational Science, 9*, 605–622.

Barrett, F. J. (2000). Cultivating an aesthetic of unfolding: Jazz improvisation as a self-organizing system. In S. Linstead & H. J. Hopfl (Eds.), *The aesthetics of organizations* (pp. 237–255). London: Sage.

Boje D. (1991). The storytelling organization: A study of story performance in an office supply firm. *Administrative Science Quarterly, 36*, 106–121.

Boyce, M. (1995). Collective centering and collective sense-making in the stories and storytelling of one organization. *Organization Studies, 16* (1), 107–131.

Brown, L. D. (1991). Bridging organizations and sustainable development. *Human Relations, 44*, 807–829.

Bruner, J. (1986). *Actual minds, possible worlds.* Cambridge: Harvard University Press.

Bryk, A., Lee, V., & Holland, P. (1993). *Catholic schools and the common good.* Cambridge: Harvard University Press.

Bushe, G. R. (1995). Advances in appreciative inquiry as an organizational development intervention. *Organization Development Journal, 13* (3), 14–22.

Bushe, G. R. (1998). Appreciative inquiry with teams. *Organization Development Journal, 16* (3), 41–50.

Bushe, G. R. (2001). *Clear leadership.* Palo Alto, CA: Davies-Black.

Bushe, G. R., & Coetzer, G. (1995). Appreciative inquiry as a team development intervention: A controlled experiment. *Journal of Applied Behavioral Science, 31* (1), 13–30.

Bushe, G. R., & Pitman, T. (1991). Appreciative process: A method for transformational change. *Organization Development Practitioner, 23* (3), 1–4.

Carter, S. L. (1996). *Integrity.* New York: Harper Trade.

Chandler, D. (1998). Appreciative inquiry as a means of engaging employees in the mission and strategies of an organization. Research submitted in partial fulfillment of the requirements for the degree of Master of Science in Organization Development, George L. Graziadio School of Business and Management, Pepperdine University.

Collins, J., & Porras, J. (1994). *Built to last.* New York: HarperCollins.

Cooperrider, D. L. (1999). Positive image, positive action. In S. Srivastva & D. L. Cooperrider (Eds.), *Appreciative management and leadership: The power of positive thought and action in organizations* (Rev. ed., pp. 91–125). Euclid, OH: Williams Custom.

Cooperrider, D. L., & Dutton, J. (Eds.). (1999). *No limits to cooperation: The organization dimensions of global change.* Newbury Park, CA: Sage.

Cooperrider, D. L., Sorensen, P. F., Whitney, D., & Yaeger, T. F. (2000). *Appreciative inquiry: Rethinking human organization toward a positive theory of change.* Champagne, IL: Stipes.

Cooperrider, D. L., & Srivastva, S. (1987). Appreciative inquiry in organizational life. In W. A. Pasmore & R. W. Woodman (Eds.), *Research in organization change and development* (Vol. 1, pp. 129–169). Greenwich, CT: JAI Press.

Cooperrider, D. L., & Whitney, D. (1999). Appreciative inquiry (monograph pamphlet). In P. Holman & T. Devine (Eds.), *Collaborating for change.* San Francisco: Berrett-Koehler.

Deal, T. E., & Kennedy, A. A. (1982). *Corporate cultures.* Reading, MA: Addison-Wesley.

Elliott, C. (1999). *Locating the energy for change: An introduction to appreciative inquiry.* Winnipeg, Manitoba, Canada: International Institute for Sustainable Development.

Frankl, V. (1978). *The unheard cry of meaning: Psychotherapy and humanism.* New York: Simon & Schuster.

Freire, P. (1994). *Pedagogy of hope: Reliving pedagogy of the oppressed* (R. R. Barr, Trans.). New York: Continuum.

French, W. L. (1969). Organization development objectives, assumptions, and strategies. *California Management Review, 12* (2), 23–24.

French, W., Bell, C. H., Jr., & Zawacki, R. (Eds.). (1994). *Organization development and transformation: Managing effective change.* Burr Ridge, IL: McGraw-Hill.

Gergen, K. J. (1994). *Realities and relationships: Soundings in social construction.* Cambridge: Harvard University Press.

Goleman, D. (1985). *Vital lies, simple truths: The psychology of self-deception.* New York: Touchstone Books.

Gottman, J. (1994). *Why marriages succeed or fail . . . and how you can make yours last.* New York: Fireside.

Haley, J. (1973). *Uncommon therapy.* New York: Touchstone Books.

Hammond, S., & Royal, C. (Eds.). (1998). *Lessons from the field: Applying appreciative inquiry.* Plano, TX: Practical Press.

Harvey, J. (1988). *The Abilene paradox.* Lexington, MA: Lexington Books.

Hillman, J. (1996). *The soul's code: In search of character and calling.* New York: Warner Books.

Hock, D. (1999). *Birth of the Chaordic age.* San Francisco: Berrett-Koehler.

Hodder, I. (1995). The interpretation of documents and material culture. In N. Denzen & Y. Lincoln (Eds.), *Handbook of qualitative research* (pp. 393–402). Thousand Oaks, CA: Sage.

Homans, G. (1950). *The human group.* New York: Harcourt Brace.

Isen, A., & Shalker, T. (1982). The influence of mood state on evaluation of positive, neutral, and negative stimuli. *Social Psychology Quarterly, 45,* 58–63.

Isen, A., Shalker, T., Clark, M., & Karp, L. (1978). Affect, accessibility of material in memory, and behavior: A cognitive loop? *Journal of Personality and Social Psychology, 36,* 1–12.

Janis, I. L. (1972). *Victims of groupthink.* Boston: Houghton Mifflin.

Johnson, P. C., & Cooperrider, D. L. (1991). Finding a path with heart: Global social change organizations and their challenge for the field of organization development. In R. W. Woodman & W. A. Pasmore (Eds.), *Research in organization change and development* (Vol. 5, pp. 223–280). Greenwich, CT: JAI Press.

Katzenbach, J. R., & Smith, D. K. (1993). *The wisdom of teams.* New York: Harper Business.

Khalsa, G. S., & Kaczmarski, K. M. (1996). *The United Religions Initiative summit conference summary, June 24–28.* San Francisco: United Religions Initiative. Copies may be requested from the URI at P.O. Box 29242, San Francisco, CA 94129, 415–561–2300.

Kotter, J. (1995). Leading change: Why transformation efforts fail. *Harvard Business Review, 73* (2), 59–67.

Levinson, H. (1972). *Organizational diagnosis.* Cambridge: Harvard University Press.

Lewin, K. (1951). *Field theory and social science.* New York: Harper & Row.

Ludema, J. D., Cooperrider, D. L., & Barrett, F. J. (2000). Appreciative inquiry: The power of the unconditional positive question. In P. Reason & H. Bradbury, (Eds.), *Handbook of action research* (pp. 189–199). Thousand Oaks, CA: Sage.

McGregor, D. (1960). *The human side of enterprise.* New York: McGraw-Hill.

Nisbett, R., & Ross, L. (1985). *Human inference: Strategies and shortcomings of social judgment.* New York: Prentice Hall.

Owen, H. (1991). *Riding the tiger: Doing business in a transforming world.* Potomac, MD: Abbott.

Pagès, M. (1999). The illusion and disillusion of appreciative management. In S. Srivastva & D. L. Cooperrider (Eds.), *Appreciative management and leadership: The power of positive thought and action in organizations* (Rev. ed., pp. 353–380). Euclid, OH: Williams Custom.

Perkins, A. L., Shaw, R. B., & Sutton, R. I. (1990). Human service teams. In J. R. Hackman (Ed.), *Groups that work (and those that don't)* (pp. 349–358). San Francisco: Jossey-Bass.

Phillips, N. (1995). Telling organizational tales: On the role of narrative fiction in the study of organizations. *Organization Studies, 16* (4), 125–149.

Quinn, R. E., & Cameron, K. S. (Eds.). (1988). *Paradox and transformation.* Cambridge, MA: Ballinger.

Rosenhan, D., Salvoey, P., & Hargis, K. (1981). The joys of helping: Focus of attention mediates the impact of positive affect on altruism. *Journal of Personality and Social Psychology, 40,* 899–905.

Rubenstein, S. (1996). Blessed are the brainstormers. *San Francisco Chronicle,* 26 June, p. 16A.

Ryan, F., Smither, J., Soven, M., Sullivan, W. M., & Van Buskirk, W. (1999). Appreciative inquiry: Using personal narratives for initiating school reform. *The Clearing House, 72* (3), 164.

Schein, E. H. (1973). Personal change through intepersonal relationships. In W. Bennis, D. Berlew, E. H. Schein, & F. Steele (Eds.), *Interpersonal Dynamics* (3d ed., pp. 237–267). Homewood, IL: Dorsey.

Schein, E. H. (1988). *Process consultation* (Vol. 1). Cambridge, MA: Addison-Wesley.

Shaw, R. B. (1990). Mental health treatment teams. In J. R. Hackman (Ed.), *Groups that work (and those that don't)* (pp. 330–348). San Francisco: Jossey-Bass.

Smith, K. K., & Berg, D. N. (1987). *Paradoxes of group life.* San Francisco: Jossey-Bass.

Srikantia, P., & Fry, R. (2000). Appreciative capacity building. *Global Social Innovations, 1* (3), 38–48.

Srivastva, S., & Barrett, F. J. (1988). The transforming nature of metaphors in group development: A study in group theory. *Human Relations, 41,* 31–64.

Srivastva, S., & Fry, R. (Eds.). (1992). *Executive and organizational continuity: Managing the paradoxes of stability and change.* San Francisco: Jossey-Bass.

Srivastva, S., Obert, S. L., & Neilsen, E. H. (1977). Organizational analysis through group processes: A theoretical perspective for organization development. In C. Cooper (Ed.), *Organizational development in the U.K. and the U.S.A.* (pp. 83–111). New York: Macmillan.

Tannenbaum, R., & Hanna, R. W. (1985). Holding on, letting go, and moving on: Understanding a neglected perspective on change. In R. Tannenbaum, N. Margulies, & F. Massarik (Eds.), *Human systems development* (pp. 95–121). San Francisco: Jossey-Bass.

Van Maanen, J., & Kunda, G. (1989). Real feelings: Emotional expression and culture. In L. L. Cummings & B. M. Shaw (Eds.), *Research in organizational behavior* (Vol. 11, pp. 43–104). Greenwich, CT: JAI Press.

Watzlawick, P., Weakland, J., & Fisch, R. (1974). *Change: Principles of problem formation and problem resolution.* New York: W. W. Norton.

Weick, K. (1993). The collapse of sense-making in organizations: The Man Gulch disaster. *Administrative Science Quarterly, 38,* 628–652.

Weisbord, M. R. (1987). *Productive workplaces.* San Francisco: Jossey-Bass.

Weisbord, M. R., & Janoff, S. (1995). *Future search: An action guide to finding common ground in organizations and communities.* San Francisco: Berrett-Koehler.

White, T. H. (1996). Working in interesting times. *Vital Speeches of the Day, 42* (15), 472–474.

Whitney, D., & Cooperrider, D. L. (1998). The appreciative inquiry summit: Overview and applications. *Employment Relations Today, 25* (2), 17–28.

Selected Bibliography

Compiled by Dawn Dole,
Loren R. Dyck, and Leslie Sekerka

Appreciative inquiry: An approach to organizational analysis and learning. (1996). Rosslyn, VA: Volunteers in Technical Assistance.

Banaga, G. (1998). An essay on appreciative inquiry: A spiritual path to organizational renewal. In S. Hammond & C. Royal (Eds.), *Lessons from the field: Applying appreciative inquiry* (pp. 258–269). Plano, TX: Practical Press.

Barrett, F. J. (1995). Creating appreciative learning cultures. *Organizational Dynamics, 24* (1), 36–49.

Barrett, F. J. (1998). Creativity in improvisation in jazz and organizations: Implications for organizational learning. *Organizational Science, 9,* 605–622.

Barrett, F. J., & Cooperrider, D. L. (1990). Generative metaphor intervention: A new approach for working with systems divided by conflict and caught in defensive perception. *Journal of Applied Behavioral Science, 26,* 219–239.

Barrett, F. J., & Peterson, R. (2000). Appreciative learning cultures: Developing competencies for global organizing. *Journal of Applied Behavioral Science, 31* (3), 352–372.

Barros, I., & Cooperrider, D. L. (2000). A story of nutrimental in Brazil: How wholeness, appreciation and inquiry bring out the best in human organization. *Organizational Development Journal, 18* (Special Issue), 22–29.

Bilimoria, D., Wilmot, T., & Cooperrider, D. L. (1996). Multi-organizational collaboration for global social change: Opportunities for organization development and change. In W. A. Pasmore & R. W. Woodman (Eds.), *Research in organization development and change* (Vol. 9, pp. 201–236). Greenwich, CT: JAI Press.

Blair, M. (1998). Lessons from using appreciative inquiry in a planning exercise. In S. Hammond & C. Royal (Eds.), *Lessons from the field: Applying appreciative inquiry* (pp. 184–213). Plano, TX: Practical Press.

Booy, D., & Sena, S. O. (1998). *Capacity building using the appreciative inquiry approach: The experience of World Vision Tanzania.* Arusha, Tanzania: World Vision Tanzania.

Bosch, L. (1998). Exit interviews with an appreciative eye. In S. Hammond & C. Royal (Eds.), *Lessons from the field: Applying appreciative inquiry* (pp. 228–241). Plano, TX: Practical Press.

Bowling, C., Ludema, J., & Wyss, E. (1997). *Vision twin cities appreciative inquiry report.* Cleveland: Case Western Reserve University, Department of Organizational Behavior.

Brittain, J. (1998). Do we really mean it? In S. Hammond & C. Royal (Eds.), *Lessons from the field: Applying appreciative inquiry* (pp. 214–227). Plano, TX: Practical Press.

Browne, B. (1998). Imagine Chicago. In S. Hammond & C. Royal (Eds.), *Lessons from the field: Applying appreciative inquiry* (pp. 76–89). Plano, TX: Practical Press.

Buckingham, S. T. (1998). *Leadership skills in public health nursing: An appreciative inquiry.* Unpublished master's thesis, Royal Roads University, Victoria, BC, Canada.

Bunker, B. B. (1990). Appreciating diversity and modifying organizational cultures: Men and women at work. In S. Srivastva & D. L. Cooperrider (Eds.), *Appreciative management and leadership: The power of positive thought and action in organizations* (pp. 126–149). San Francisco: Jossey-Bass.

Bunker, B. B., & Alban, B. T. (1997). *Large group interventions.* San Francisco: Jossey-Bass.

Bushe, G. R. (1995). Advances in appreciative inquiry as an organizational development intervention. *Organization Development Journal, 13* (3), 14–22.

Bushe, G. R. (1997). *Attending to others: Interviewing appreciatively.* Vancouver: Discovery and Design.

Bushe, G. R. (1998). Appreciative inquiry with teams. *Organization Development Journal, 16* (3), 41–50.

Bushe, G. R., & Coetzer, G. (1995). Appreciative inquiry as a team development intervention: A controlled experiment. *Journal of Applied Behavioral Science, 31* (1), 13–30.

Bushe, G. R., & Pitman, T. (1991). Appreciative process: A method for transformational change. *Organization Development Practitioner, 23* (3), 1–4.

Carnegie, K. L., Nielsen, H., & Glover, C. (2000). Stepping upsteam "naturally" for cleaner production through community environmental learning. *Journal of Cleaner Production, 8,* 391–396.

Carter, J. D., & Johnson, P. (1992). *Institutionalizing change through dialogue: The round table, an appreciative inquiry organizational intervention*. Cleveland: John D. Carter and Associates.

Chaffee, P. (1997). *Unafraid of the light: Appreciative inquiry and faith communities*. Unpublished manuscript, Interfaith Center at the Presidio, San Francisco.

Chin, A. (1998). Future visions. Unpublished papers of Abraham Maslow. *Journal of Organizational Change Management, 11* (1), 74–77.

Clemson, B. A., & Lowe, E. (1993). Which way to Rome? Choosing a path for change. *Engineering Management Journal, 5* (4), 26–40.

Columns, C. (2000). Appreciative inquiry and your career. *Journal of Environmental Health, 63* (1), 1.

Cooperrider, D. L. (1986). *Appreciative inquiry: Toward a methodology for understanding and enhancing organizational innovation*. Unpublished Ph.D. diss., Case Western Reserve University, Cleveland.

Cooperrider, D. L. (1990). Positive image, positive action: The affirmative basis of organizing. In S. Srivastva & D. L. Cooperrider (Eds.), *Appreciative management and leadership: The power of positive thought and action in organizations* (pp. 91–125). San Francisco: Jossey-Bass.

Cooperrider, D. L. (1995). Introduction to appreciative inquiry. In W. French & C. Bell (Eds.), *Organization development* (5th ed.). Englewood Cliffs, NJ: Prentice Hall.

Cooperrider, D. L. (1996). The "child" as agent of inquiry. *OD Practitioner: Journal of the Organization Development Network, 28* (1–2), 5–11.

Cooperrider, D. L. (1996). Resources for getting appreciative inquiry started: An example OD proposal. *Organization Development Practitioner, 28* (1–2), 23–33.

Cooperrider, D. L. (1998). Getting started. In S. Hammond & C. Royal (Eds.), *Lessons from the field: Applying appreciative inquiry* (pp. 144–157). Plano, TX: Practical Press.

Cooperrider, D. L., Barrett, F., & Srivastva, S. (1995). Social construction and appreciative inquiry: A journey into organizational theory. In D. Hosking, P. Dachler, & K. Gergen (Eds.), *Management and organization: Relational alternatives to individualism* (pp. 157–200). Aldershot, UK: Avebury Press.

Cooperrider, D. L., & Bilimoria, D. (1993). The challenge of global change for strategic management: Opportunities for chartering a new course. *Advances in Strategic Management, 9*, 99–141.

Cooperrider, D. L., & Dutton, J. (Eds.). (1999). *No limits to cooperation: The organization dimensions of global change*. Newbury Park, CA: Sage.

Cooperrider, D. L., & Khalsa, G. (1997). The organization dimensions of global environmental change. *Journal of Organization and Environment, 10*, 331–341.

Cooperrider, D. L., & Pasmore, W. A. (1991). The organization dimension of global change. *Human Relations, 44*, 763–787.

Cooperrider, D. L., & Pratt, C. (1996). *Appreciative inquiry: A constructive approach to organization development and change*. Unpublished paper, Case Western Reserve University, Cleveland.

Cooperrider, D. L., Sorensen, P. F., Whitney, D., & Yaeger, T. F. (2000). *Appreciative inquiry: Rethinking human organization toward a positive theory of change.* Champagne, IL: Stipes.

Cooperrider, D. L., & Srivastva, S. (1987). Appreciative inquiry in organizational life. In W. A. Pasmore & R. W. Woodman (Eds.), *Research in organization change and development* (Vol. 1, pp. 129–169). Greenwich, CT: JAI Press.

Cooperrider, D. L., & Srivastva, S. (1998). An invitation to organizational wisdom and executive courage. In S. Srivastva & D. L. Cooperrider (Eds.), *Organizational wisdom and executive courage* (pp. 1–22). San Francisco: New Lexington Press.

Cooperrider, D. L., & Thachenkery, T. (1995). Building the global civic culture: Making our lives count. In P. Sorenson, T. Head, N. Mathys, J. Preston, & D. L. Cooperrider (Eds.), *Global and international organization development* (pp. 282–306). Champaign, IL: Stipes.

Cooperrider, D. L., & Whitney, D. (1996). *Appreciative inquiry: A workshop* [A set of eight audiotapes presented by the Taos Institute]. Boulder, CO: Perpetual Motion Unlimited.

Cooperrider, D. L., & Whitney, D. (1998). When stories have wings: How "relational responsibility" opens new options for action. In S. McNamee & K. Gergen (Eds.), *Relational responsibility* (pp. 57–64). Thousand Oaks, CA: Sage.

Cooperrider, D. L., & Whitney, D. (1999). *Appreciative inquiry.* San Francisco: Berrett-Koehler.

Cooperrider, D. L., & Whitney, D. (1999). Appreciative inquiry (monograph pamphlet). In P. Holman & T. Devine (Eds.), *Collaborating for change.* San Francisco: Berrett-Koehler.

Cooperrider, D. L., & Whitney, D. (2001). A positive revolution in change. In R. Golembiewski (Ed.), *Handbook of organizational behavior* (2d ed., pp. 611–629). New York: Marcel Dekker.

Cummings, T. G. (1990). The role of executive appreciation in creating transorganizational alliances. In S. Srivastva & D. L. Cooperrider (Eds.), *Appreciative management and leadership: The power of positive thought and action in organizations.* San Francisco: Jossey-Bass.

Curran, M. (1991). Appreciative inquiry: A third wave approach to OD. *Vision/Action, 11*, December, 12–14.

Curran, M., & Work, G. (1998). Creating opportunities for learning. In S. Hammond & C. Royal (Eds.), *Lessons from the field: Applying appreciative inquiry* (pp. 242–257). Plano, TX: Practical Press.

Drogin, S. (1997). *An appreciative inquiry into spirituality and work.* Unpublished Ph.D. diss., Seattle University.

Elliott, C. (1999). *Locating the energy for change: An introduction to appreciative inquiry.* Winnipeg: International Institute for Sustainable Development.

EnCompass, I. (2000). A "can-do" process for a "can-do" community: Collaborating for change in housing and community development in Dubuque. *Julien's Journal.*

Foster, M. (1998). Imagine Dallas. In S. Hammond & C. Royal (Eds.), *Lessons from the field: Applying appreciative inquiry* (pp. 90–99). Plano, TX: Practical Press.

Frantz, T. G. (1998). Visioning the future of social systems: Evolutionary and discontinuous leap approaches. *Systems Research and Behavioural Science, 15*, 173–182.

French, W. L., & Bell, C. H. (1994). *Organization development: Behavioral science interventions for organization improvement* (5th ed.). Englewood Cliffs, NJ: Prentice Hall.

Frost, P. J., & Egri, C. P. (1990). Appreciating executive action. In S. Srivastva & D. L. Cooperrider (Eds.), *Appreciative management and leadership: The power of positive thought and action in organizations* (pp. 289–322). San Francisco: Jossey-Bass.

Fry, R. (2000). Unlimited cooperation. *Management Magazine*, February, pp. 46–47. Auckland: New Zealand Institute of Management.

Fuller, C. S., Griffin, T. J., & Ludema, J. D. (2000). Appreciative future search: Involving the whole system in positive organizational change. *Organizational Development Journal, 18* (2), 29–41.

Gergen, K. J. (1990). Affect and organization in postmodern society. In S. Srivastva & D. L. Cooperrider (Eds.), *Appreciative management and leadership: The power of positive thought and action in organizations* (pp. 153–174). San Francisco: Jossey-Bass.

Gergen, K. J. (1994). *Realities and relationships: Soundings in social construction*. Cambridge: Harvard University Press.

Gibbs, C., & Ackerly, S. (1997, June). *United Religions Initiative global summit summary report*. Paper presented at the United Religions Initiative Global Summit, San Francisco.

Golembiewski, B. (2000). Three perspectives on appreciative inquiry. *OD Practitioner: Journal of the Organization Development Network, 32* (1), 53–58.

Golembiewski, R. T. (1998). Appreciating appreciative inquiry: Diagnosis and perspectives on how to do better. In W. A. Pasmore & R. W. Woodman (Eds.), *Research in organization change and development* (Vol. 11, pp. 1–45). Greenwich, CT: JAI Press.

Golembiewski, R. T. (1999). Fine-tuning appreciative inquiry: Two ways of circumscribing the concept's value-added. *Organization Development Journal, 17* (3), 21–28.

Gotches, G., & Ludema, J. (1995). Appreciative inquiry and the future of OD. *Organization Development Journal, 13* (3), 5.

GTE. (1997). *GTE asks employees to start a grassroots movement to make GTE unbeatable in the marketplace*. Dallas, TX: GTE.

Hall, J. (1998). Strength-based youth development: The banana kelly experience. In S. Hammond & C. Royal (Eds.), *Lessons from the field: Applying appreciative inquiry* (pp. 112–123). Plano, TX: Practical Press.

Hammond, S. (1996). *The thin book of appreciative inquiry*. Plano, TX: Thin Book.

Hammond, S. (1998). *The thin book of appreciative inquiry* (2d ed.). Plano, TX: Thin Book.

Hammond, S. (1998). What is appreciative inquiry? *The Inner Edge, 1* (2), 26–27.

Hammond, S., & Royal, C. (Eds.). (1998). *Lessons from the field: Applying appreciative inquiry.* Plano, TX: Practical Press.

Harman, W. W. (1990). Shifting context for executive behavior: Signs of change and revaluation. In S. Srivastva & D. L. Cooperrider (Eds.), *Appreciative management and leadership: The power of positive thought and action in organizations* (pp. 37–54). San Francisco: Jossey-Bass.

Head, R. L. (1999). *Appreciative inquiry as a team development intervention for newly formed heterogeneous groups.* Unpublished Ph.D. diss., Benedictine University, Lisle, IL.

Head, R. L. (1999). Appreciative inquiry as a team-development intervention for newly formed heterogeneous groups. *OD Practitioner: Journal of the Organization Development Network, 32* (1), 59–66.

Head, R. L., & Young, M. M. (1998). Initiating culture change in higher education through appreciative inquiry. *Organization Development Journal, 16* (2), 65.

Head, T. C. (1997). *Why does appreciative inquiry work? Speculation and a call for empirical study.* Unpublished working paper, Tennessee State University, Nashville.

Head, T. C. (2000). Appreciative inquiry: Debunking the mythology behind resistance to change. *OD Practitioner: Journal of the Organization Development Network, 32* (1), 27–35.

Head, T. C., Sorensen, P., Preston, J., & Yaeger, T. (2000). Is appreciative inquiry the philosopher's stone? In D. L. Cooperrider, P. F. Sorensen, D. Whitney, & T. F. Yaeger (Eds.), *Appreciative inquiry: Rethinking human organization toward a positive theory of change* (pp. 217–232). Champagne, IL: Stipes.

Holman, P., Paulson, A., & Nichols, L. (1998). Creating a healthy Hilltop community. In S. Hammond & C. Royal (Eds.), *Lessons from the field: Applying appreciative inquiry* (pp. 62–75). Plano, TX: Practical Press.

Hopper, V. (1991). *An appreciative study of highest human values in a major health care organization.* Unpublished Ph.D. diss., Case Western Reserve University, Cleveland.

Hubbard, B. M. (1998). *Conscious evolution: Awakening the power of our social potential.* Novato, CA: New World Library.

Jaffe, D. T. (1998). Visions for the people: A brief look at the organizational visioning literature. *The Inner Edge, 1* (2), 30–31.

Johnson, P. C. (1992). *Organizing for global social change.* Unpublished Ph.D. diss., Case Western Reserve University, Cleveland.

Johnson, P. C., & Cooperrider, D. L. (1991). Finding a path with heart: Global social change organizations and their challenge for the field of organization development. In R. W. Woodman & W. A. Pasmore (Eds.), *Research in organization change and development* (Vol. 5, pp. 223–284). Greenwich, CT: JAI Press.

Johnson, S. P. (1998). *Straight to the heart: Cleveland leaders shaping the next millennium.* Unpublished Ph.D. diss., Case Western Reserve University, Cleveland.

Johnson, S. P., & Ludema, J. (Eds.). (1997). *Partnering to build and measure organizational capacity: Lessons from NGOs around the world.* Grand Rapids, MI: Christian Reformed World Relief Committee.

Jones, D. A. (1998). A field experiment in appreciative inquiry. *Organization Development Journal, 16* (4), 69–78.

Jones, D. A. (1999). *Appreciative inquiry: A field experiment focusing on turnover in the fast food industry.* Unpublished Ph.D. diss., Benedictine University, Lisle, IL.

Kaczmarski, K., & Cooperrider, D. L. (1997). Constructionist leadership in the global relational age. *Journal of Organization and Environment, 10,* 234–258.

Kaczmarski, K., & Cooperrider, D. L. (1998). The birth of a worldwide alliance: The story of the mountain forum. In D. L. Cooperrider & J. Dutton (Eds.), *No limits to cooperation: The organization dimensions of global change* (pp. 57–87). Thousand Oaks, CA: Sage.

Kaye, B., & Jacobson, B. (1999). True tales and tall tales: The power of organizational storytelling. *Training & Development, 53* (3), 45–50.

Kelm, J. (1998). Introducing the appreciative inquiry philosophy. In S. Hammond & C. Royal (Eds.), *Lessons from the field: Applying appreciative inquiry* (pp. 158–171). Plano, TX: Practical Press.

Khalsa, G. S. (2000). The pilgrimage toward global dialogue: A practical visionary approach. *Breakthrough News,* January–April, 8–10.

Khalsa, G. S., & Kaczmarski, K. M. (1996). *The United Religions Initiative summit conference summary, June 24–28.* San Francisco: United Religions Initiative.

Khalsa, G. S., & Kaczmarski, K. M. (1997). Chartering and appreciative future search. *Global Social Innovations: Journal of the GEM Initiative, 1* (2), 45–52.

Khalsa, G. S., & Steingard, D. S. (1999). The relational healing dimension of organizational development: Transformative stories and dialogue in life-cycle transitions. In R. W. Woodman & W. A. Pasmore (Eds.), *Research in organization change and development* (Vol. 12, pp. 269–318). Greenwich, CT: JAI Press.

Krantz, J. (1990). Comments on the preceding article commentary on the Barrett and Cooperrider article. Additional info: Generative metaphor intervention. *Journal of Applied Behavioral Science, 26,* 241–244.

Liebler, C. J. (1997). Getting comfortable with appreciative inquiry: Questions and answers. *Global Social Innovations: Journal of the GEM Initiative, 1* (2), 30–40.

Liebling, A., Price, D., & Elliott, C. (1999). Appreciative inquiry and relationships in prison. *Punishment & Society, 1* (1), 71.

Liebling, A., Price, D., & Elliott, C. (1999). Appreciative inquiry and relationships in prison. *Violence & Abuse Abstracts, 5* (4).

Livingston, J. (1999). An appreciative inquiry interview with Robert Golembiewski: The human and organizational dimensions of global change. *Organization Development Journal, 1* (17), 109.

Lord, J. G. (1995). *The philanthropic quest: A generative approach for professionals engaged in the development process*. Cleveland: Philanthropic Quest International.

Lord, J. G. (1998). *The practice of the quest: Evolving a new paradigm for philanthropy and social innovation—A casebook for advancement professionals grounded in the quest*. Cleveland: Philanthropic Quest International.

Ludema, J. D. (1996). *Narrative inquiry*. Unpublished Ph.D. diss., Case Western Reserve University, Cleveland.

Ludema, J. D., Cooperrider, D. L., & Barrett, F. J. (2000). Appreciative inquiry: The power of the unconditional positive question. In P. Reason & H. Bradbury, (Eds.), *Handbook of action research* (pp. 189–199). Thousand Oaks, CA: Sage.

Ludema, J. D., Wilmot, T. B., & Srivastva, S. (1997). Organizational hope: Reaffirming the constructive task of social and organizational inquiry. *Human Relations, 50*, 1015–1052.

Machan, E. (2000). The inter-religious friendship group: A visible force for peace. *Weatherhead: The Magazine of the Weatherhead School of Management, 10* (1), 18–19.

Mann, A. J. (1997). An appreciative inquiry model for building partnerships. *Global Social Innovations: Journal of the GEM Initiative, 1* (2), 41–44.

Mantel, M. J., & Ludema, J. D. (2000). From local conversations to global change: Experiencing the worldwide ripple effect of appreciative inquiry. *Organization Development Journal, 18* (2), 42–53.

Mellish, L. (1998). A case study at an Australian university. In S. Hammond & C. Royal (Eds.), *Lessons from the field: Applying appreciative inquiry* (pp. 48–59). Plano, TX: Practical Press.

Mohr, B. J., Smith, E., & Watkins, J. M. (2000). Appreciative inquiry and learning assessment. *OD Practitioner: Journal of the Organization Development Network, 32* (1), 36–52.

Murrell, K. (1998). An essay on a personal cross-cultural exile into appreciative inquiry. In S. Hammond & C. Royal (Eds.), *Lessons from the field: Applying appreciative inquiry* (pp. 270–279). Plano, TX: Practical Press.

Muscat, M. (1998). The federal quality consulting group: Using the vision story process to rebuild an organization. *The Inner Edge, 1* (2), 18–19.

Muscat, M. (1998). Imagine Chicago: Dreams and visions for a "second city" of the future. *The Inner Edge, 1* (2), 23–24.

Odell, M. (1998). Appreciative planning and action. In S. Hammond & C. Royal (Eds.), *Lessons from the field: Applying appreciative inquiry* (pp. 124–143). Plano, TX: Practical Press.

Pagès, M. (1990). The illusion and disillusion of appreciative management. In S. Srivastva & D. L. Cooperrider (Eds.), *Appreciative management and leadership: The power of positive thought and action in organizations* (Rev. ed., pp. 353–380). Euclid, OH: Williams Custom.

Pascarella, P. (1998). Building corporate castles in the air. *The Inner Edge, 1* (2), 5–8.

Pearson, C. S. (1998). Who is visioning? Who lives the vision? *The Inner Edge, 1* (2), 3–4.

Pepitone, J. S. (1995). *Future training: A roadmap for restructuring the training function.* Dallas, TX: Addvantage Learning Press.

Pesch, G. G., Galloway, W. B., & Campbell, D. E. (1998, July). *Appreciative inquiry: A mechanism for maximizing empowerment in social systems.* Paper presented at the 42nd Annual Academy of Management Conference, Atlanta, GA.

Peterson, R. (1993). *Designaid™: A multimedia tool for appreciative organization design.* Unpublished master's thesis, California Institute of Integral Studies, San Francisco.

Pinto, M., & Curran, M. (1998). The Laguna Beach education foundation: School power. In S. Hammond & C. Royal (Eds.), *Lessons from the field: Applying appreciative inquiry* (pp. 16–47). Plano, TX: Practical Press.

Pratt, C. S. (1996). *Constructing unitary reality: An appreciative inquiry.* Unpublished Ph.D. diss., Case Western Reserve University, Cleveland.

Quintanilla, G. L. (1999). *An appreciative inquiry evaluation of a science enrichment program for children and youth: Preliminary findings.* Unpublished master's thesis, San Diego State University.

Radford, A. (1998). Appreciative inquiry newsletter, February.

Radford, A. (1998). Appreciative inquiry newsletter, May.

Radford, A. (1998). Appreciative inquiry newsletter, August.

Radford, A. (1998). Appreciative inquiry newsletter, November.

Radford, A. (1999). Appreciative inquiry newsletter, May.

Rafferty, T. M. (1999). *Whose children are these? An appreciative inquiry.* Unpublished Ph.D. diss., Union Institute, Cincinnati.

Raimy, E. (1998). Precious moments. *Human Resource Executive, 12* (11), 1, 26–29.

Rainey, M. A. (1996). An appreciative inquiry into the factors of culture continuity during leadership transition. *Organization Development Practitioner, 28* (1–2), 34–41.

Robinson-Easley, C. A. (1998). *The role of appreciative inquiry in the fight to save our youth.* Unpublished Ph.D. diss., Benedictine University, Naperville, IL.

Royal, C. (1994). *The NTL diversity study: The use of appreciative inquiry to discover best experiences around diversity in a professional OD organization.* Alexandra, VA: NTL Institute for Applied Behavioral Science.

Royal, C. (1996). *Appreciative inquiry.* Occasional paper, The MacArthur Foundation, Chicago.

Royal, C. (1996). *Appreciative inquiry, community development and sustainability.* Occasional paper, The MacArthur Foundation, Chicago.

Royal, C. (1997). *The fractal initiative: Appreciative inquiry and rethinking social identities.* Unpublished Ph.D. diss., Fielding Institute, Santa Barbara, CA.

Royal, C. (1997). *What is appreciative inquiry?* Occasional paper, The MacArthur Foundation, Chicago.

Royal, C., & Hammond, S. (1998). A follow-up to the thin book: Frequently asked questions. In S. Hammond & C. Royal (Eds.), *Lessons from the field: Applying appreciative inquiry* (pp. 172–183). Plano, TX: Practical Press.

Ryan, F. J., Smither, J., Soven, M., Sullivan, W. M., & Van Buskirk, W. (1999). Appreciative inquiry: Using personal narratives for initiating school reform. *The Clearing House, 72* (3), 164.

Salter, C. (2000). We're trying to change world history. *Fast Company, 40*, 230.

Schiller, M. (1998). A dialogue about leadership and appreciative inquiry. *Organization Development Journal, 16* (4), 79.

Scott, C. F. (1997). *An appreciative exploration of the career and parenting experiences of dual-career mother and fathers.* Unpublished Ph.D. diss., Case Western Reserve University, Cleveland.

Sena, S. O., & Booy, D. (1997). Appreciative inquiry approach to community development: The World Vision Tanzania experience. *Global Social Innovations: Journal of the GEM Initiative, 1* (2), 7–12.

Sharkey, L., Sorensen, P., & Yaeger, T. (1998, June). *Integrating traditional and contemporary approaches to change: Culture, survey feedback and appreciative inquiry.* Paper presented at the Creating Healthy Organization Cultures Conference, Loyola University, Chicago.

Sorensen, P. F., & Yaeger, T. F. (1997). Exploring organizational possibilities: Appreciative inquiry. *Training Today*, 7–8.

Sorensen, P. F., & Yaeger, T. F. (1998). A universal approach to change: Appreciative inquiry. *Training Today*, 7–8.

Sorensen, P. F., Yaeger, T. F., & Nicoll, D. (2000). Appreciative inquiry 2000: Fad or important new focus for OD? *OD Practitioner: Journal of the Organization Development Network, 32* (1), 3–5.

Sperry, S. L. (1999). *A descriptive study of the impact of appreciative processes on self and organization-based self-esteem.* Unpublished Ph.D. diss., Pepperdine University, Malibu, CA.

Srikantia, P., & Fry, R. (2000). Appreciative capacity building. *Global Social Innovations, 1* (3), 38–48.

Srivastva, S., & Barrett, F. J. (1990). Appreciative organizing: Implications for executive functioning. In S. Srivastva & D. L. Cooperrider (Eds.), *Appreciative management and leadership: The power of positive thought and action in organizations* (pp. 381–400). San Francisco: Jossey-Bass.

Srivastva, S., Bilimoria, D., Cooperrider, D. L., & Fry, R. E. (1995). Management and organization learning for positive global change. *Management Learning, 26* (1), 37–54.

Srivastva, S., & Cooperrider, D. L. (Eds.). (1990). *Appreciative management and leadership: The power of positive thought and action in organizations.* San Francisco: Jossey-Bass.

Srivastva, S., & Cooperrider, D. L. (Eds.). (1998). *Organizational wisdom and executive courage.* San Francisco: New Lexington Press.

Srivastva, S., & Cooperrider, D. L. (Eds.). (1999). *Appreciative management and leadership: The power of positive thought and action in organizations* (rev. ed.). Euclid, OH: Williams Custom.

Stavros, J. M. (1998). *Capacity building: An appreciative approach. A relational process of building your organization's future.* Unpublished Ph.D. diss., Case Western Reserve University, Cleveland.

Stewart, A., & Royal, C. (1998). Imagine South Carolina. In S. Hammond & C. Royal (Eds.), *Lessons from the field: Applying appreciative inquiry* (pp. 100–111). Plano, TX: Practical Press.

Thachenkery, T. J. (1996). Affirmation as facilitation: A postmodernist paradigm in change management. *Organization Development Practitioner, 28* (1), 12–22.

Watkins, J. M., & Cooperrider, D. L. (1996). Organizational inquiry model for global social change organizations. *Organization Development Journal, 14* (4), 97–112.

Watkins, J. M., & Cooperrider, D. L. (2000). Appreciative inquiry: A transformative paradigm. *OD Practitioner: Journal of the Organization Development Network, 32* (1), 6–12.

Watkins, J. M., & Mohr, B. (2001). *Appreciative inquiry: Change at the speed of imagination.* San Francisco: Jossey-Bass/Pfeiffer.

Whalley, C. (1998). Using appreciative inquiry to overcome past OFSTED syndrome. *Management in Education, 12* (3), 6.

White, T. W. (1996). Working in interesting times. *Vital Speeches of the Day, 42* (15), 472–474.

Whitney, D. (1998). Let's change the subject and change our organization: An appreciative inquiry approach to organization change. *Career Development International, UK: Special Edition, 3* (7), 314–319.

Whitney, D., & Cooperrider, D. L. (1998). The appreciative inquiry summit: Overview and applications. *Employment Relations Today, 25* (2), 17–28.

Whitney, D., & Cooperrider, D. L. (2000). The appreciative inquiry summit: An emerging methodology for whole system positive change. *OD Practitioner: Journal of the Organization Development Network, 32* (1), 13–26.

Whitney, D., & Schau, C. (1998). Appreciative inquiry: An innovation process for organization change. *Employment Relations Today, 25* (1), 11–21.

Williams, R. F. (1996). Survey guided appreciative inquiry: A case study. *Organization Development Practitioner, 28* (1–2), 43–51.

Wilmot, T. B. (1996). Inquiry and innovation in the private voluntary sector. *Global Social Innovations: Journal of the GEM Initiative, 1* (1), 5–12.

Wilmot, T. B., & Ludema, J. D. (1995). Odyssey into organizational hope. In D. Marcic (Ed.), *Organizational behavior experiences and cases.* New York: West.

Wilson, T. (1995, June 13). Imagine shaping a better Chicago. *Chicago Tribune,* p. 2.

Wishart, C. G. (1998). *Toward a language of human abundance: The holistic human logic of sustainable development.* Unpublished Ph.D. diss., Case Western Reserve University, Cleveland.

Woodman, R. W., & Pasmore, W. A. (Eds.). (1987). *Research in organizational change and development: An annual series featuring advances in theory, methodology and research* (Vol. 1). Greenwich, CT: JAI Press.

Woodman, R. W., & Pasmore, W. A. (Eds.). (1998). *Research in organizational change and development: An annual series featuring advances in theory, methodology and research* (Vol. 11). Stamford, CT: JAI Press.

Wright, M. (1998). Scotland incorporated. *People Management, 4* (24), 25.

Yaeger, T. (1999). Responses from Russia: An appreciative inquiry interview with Konstantin Korotov, RODP. *Organization Development Journal, 17* (3), 85–91.

Yballe, L., & O'Connor, D. (1998). *Appreciative pedagogy: Constructing positive models for learning*. Unpublished paper, LeMoyne College, Syracuse, NY.

Zemke, R. (1999). Don't fix that company! *Training, 36* (6), 8–14.

Zolno, S. (1998). Crisis at home: Fostering agreement in an intentional community. *Vision Action Journal, 17* (3), 13–17.

NOTE

The editors are grateful to Loren R. Dyck and Leslie Sekerka, advanced doctoral students in the department of organizational behavior at Case Western Reserve University, and Dawn Dole, administrative officer for the Taos Institute, for compiling this current (as of March 2001) list of AI literature.

Index

About the Editors
and Contributors

Frank Barrett is associate professor of management and organizational behavior at the Naval Postgraduate School in Monterey, California. Dr. Barrett has written and lectured widely on organizational change, organizational learning, and appreciative inquiry. He has published articles in *The Journal of Applied Behavioral Science, Human Relations, Organization Science,* and *Organizational Dynamics*, as well as numerous book chapters. He coauthored "Generative Metaphor Intervention: A New Approach to Intergroup Conflict" with David L. Cooperrider, which won the award for best paper from the Academy of Management Organizational Change and Development division in 1988.

Gervase Bushe is a professor and Area Coordinator of the Management and Organization Studies Group in the Faculty of Business Administration at Simon Fraser University in Vancouver, British Columbia. He has been active as an OD Consultant since 1978, has published award winning articles on organizational change, is on the editorial boards of major research journals, and is listed in *Who's Who in Canadian Business*. His latest book is *Clear Leadership* (2001).

David L. Cooperrider is associate professor of organizational behavior at Case Western Reserve University, where he serves as chairman of the SIGMA (Social Innovations in Global Management) program. He is past president of the Academy of Management's division of organizational development and cofounder of the Taos Institute. He recently concluded a six-year grant, working with fifty-seven organizations in more than one-hundred countries in Africa, Asia, Europe, and North and South America in projects dealing with global issues of human health, environment sustainability, economic development, and organizational capacity building, all inspired by the AI methodologies for which he is best known.

Ronald Fry is associate professor of organizational behavior at Case Western Reserve University, where he is director of the Weatherhead School's executive MBA program. He has published and taught widely on team development, organization change, organization development, executive leadership, and appreciative inquiry. He was coinvestigator with David L. Cooperrider on the Global Excellence in Management (GEM) project, a U.S. AID–funded program using appreciative inquiry to benchmark and develop capacity-building approaches for global social change organizations. He directed the GEM Certificate Program, which has trained over one-hundred leaders of social change organizations from over thirty different countries in areas of appreciative leadership and organizing, partnering, and change agentry.

Maureen Garrison is currently the director of organization effectiveness, Verizon, and is responsible for implementing three strategic culture initiatives within network services. Garrison has over twenty-six years of experience in the telecommunications industry, with special emphasis in organizational effectiveness strategies targeting cultural and change management approaches. Garrison has an instrumental role in consulting with senior leadership on culture change initiatives that support the front-line employee. In 1997, she was part of a team whose work was recognized by the American Society of Training and Development (ASTD) with the Excellence in Practice award in the category of managing change.

Marsha George is a director of McLean & George Ltd., a process consultancy that specializes in long-term change initiatives. Marsha is also an associate of Ashridge Management College in England. Along with Adrian McLean, she has pioneered new approaches to cultural change in organizations and supported leaders and managers through fundamental changes at the organizational, group, and individual levels. Most recently, she has been using an appreciative inquiry approach to organizational and community-wide change.

Gurudev S. Khalsa is president of Trilight Services based in Boulder Colorado, offering heart-centered organizational, personal, and spiritual development consultation. His Ph.D. dissertation, "Organizing as Pilgrimage," is based on his work with the United Religions Initiative, writing about the spiritual dimensions and personal implications of transformational organizing. As a management consultant for over fifteen years, he has served the corporate world as well as the nonprofit sector.

James D. Ludema is an associate professor of organization development at Benedictine University. His research and consulting interests include appreciative inquiry, organizational redesign and whole system change, large-group interventions, the role of human hope in organization change, and organizational storytelling. Jim has lived and worked in Asia, Africa, and Latin America, and has served as consultant to a variety of organizations.

Adrian McLean is a director of McLean & George Ltd., a U.K.–based consultancy specializing in facilitating long-term organizational change. He is an associate of Ashridge Management College, Warwick University Business School, and Roffey Park Management College. Adrian specializes in supporting organizations through periods of cultural change, working with the leadership, senior management, and key personnel over a sustained period of time. He has lectured at Bath University for many years in organizational change and development and has many publications in the field of OD and cultural change.

Jean Moore is executive director of workforce development for Verizon. She is responsible for curriculum design, e-learning, and workforce performance. Jean has been a college professor and held a variety of positions within GTE. In addition, she is coowner of GTE's Culture Initiative, which won an Excellence in Practice award at the 1998 ASTD conference in San Francisco. In May 2000 Dr. Moore was a speaker at the ASTD conference in Dallas, Texas, representing GTE for its Excellence in Practice award for the GTE Leadership Development series.

Charleyse Pratt is a lecturer and workshop facilitator on topics of large system change, leader development, and community building utilizing appreciative inquiry methodology. She has more than twenty-five years of experience as a human resource professional and as an internal and external consultant in the private and public sectors. She is an adjunct faculty instructor at Case Western Reserve University.

Marjorie Schiller is an organizational consultant, teacher, writer, and speaker with international experience in the public and private sectors. She uses appreciative inquiry to support attracting, retaining, and satisfying people who work in diverse organizations. Marge lives in Hingham, Massachusetts.

Jane Seiling is an OD consultant, author, and speaker, and founder of the Business Performance Group, Lima, Ohio. She is also an associate of the Taos Institute. Seiling's book, *The Membership Organization: Achieving Top Performance Through the New Workplace Community,* was the 1998 Society for Human Resource Management Book of the Year. Her most recent book is *The Meaning and Role of Organizational Advocacy: Responsibility and Accountability* (Quorum Books, Spring 2001).

Amanda Trosten-Bloom is a principal with Clearview Consultants in Golden, Colorado, and an organizational consultant focusing on the co-construction of appreciative organizations. One of the first consultants to use appreciative inquiry for whole-system culture change in business settings, she has facilitated appreciatively based strategic planning, enhancement of customer service, business process improvement, and team building. Along with Diana Whitney, she is coauthor of "Appreciative Inquiry: A Path to Positive Change," and "Creating Power-Full Organizations Using Appreciative Inquiry."

William Van Buskirk is associate professor of management at La Salle University in Philadelphia. He has published articles in *Human Relations, The Handbook of Organization Development, The Journal of Organizational Change Management, The Journal of Management Education,* and *Public Administration Quarterly.* Bill's interests include organizational cultures, interorganizational partnerships, and urban educational reform. He is a senior research fellow at the National Center for Educational Alliances.

Diana Whitney is president of the Corporation for Positive Change in Cleveland, Ohio, and cofounder of the Taos Institute, Taos, New Mexico. She is an international speaker and appreciative inquiry consultant. She supports clients in the design and facilitation of resource-based, participatory processes for strategic planning, organization culture change, and organization design. Her work with David L. Cooperrider has been instrumental in introducing many to the concepts of appreciative inquiry in organizational and community work.